Uncertainty and Expectations
in Economics

PROFESSOR G.L.S. SHACKLE

Uncertainty and Expectations in Economics

ESSAYS IN HONOUR OF
G. L. S. SHACKLE

EDITED BY
C. F. CARTER and J. L. FORD

Augustus M. Kelley · Publishers
New Jersey 1972

© in this collection Basil Blackwell, 1972

All Rights Reserved. No part of this publication may be reproduced, stored in a retrieval system, or transmitted, in any form or by any means, electronic, mechanical, photocopying, recording or otherwise, without the prior permission of Basil Blackwell & Mott Limited.

Published in the United States by
Augustus M. Kelley · Publishers
Clifton, New Jersey 07012

SBN 0 678 06277 3

Library of Congress Catalog Card No: 72–184239

Printed in Great Britain

Contents

Frontispiece

Introduction — C. F. Carter and J. L. Ford ... vii

An Optimality Criterion for Decision-making under Ignorance — Kenneth J. Arrow and Leonid Hurwicz ... 1

Expectations, Uncertainty and Investments in Human Beings — Mary Jean Bowman ... 12

On Degrees Shackle: or, the Making of Business Decisions — C. F. Carter ... 30

On the Theory of Bargaining — A. Coddington ... 43

Acceptable Risk — Ansell Egerton ... 58

Expectations, Uncertainty, and the Term Structure of Interest Rates — J. L. Ford and J. C. Dodds ... 74

Uncertainty and Dynamic Axioms — Sir Roy Harrod ... 122

Liquidity, Uncertainty, and the Accumulation of Information — Jack Hirshleifer ... 136

Uncertainty and Probability in International Economics — Harry G. Johnson ... 148

Decision-taking and the Theory of Games — B. S. Keirstead ... 160

The Treatment of Expectations in Econometrics — L. R. Klein ... 175

Information and Profit *D. M. Lamberton*	191
Potential Surprise in the Context of Inquiry *Isaac Levi*	213
Uncertainty and Crisis Behaviour: An Illustration of Conflict and Peace Research *Michael Nicholson*	237
Risk as a Dimension in Measuring Level of Service *Carl S. Shoup*	266
The Political Economy of the Environment: Problems of Method *Paul Streeten*	276
G. L. S. Shackle: Bibliographical Data	291

Introduction

George Shackle was born in 1903, and educated at the Perse School, Cambridge, and the London School of Economics, where he obtained his first degree in 1931 and a Ph.D. in 1937. Oxford awarded him the degree of D.Phil. in 1940. Before the Second World War, he worked for the Oxford University Institute of Statistics and for the University of St. Andrews. Then, in 1939, began eleven years of Government service, including periods in the Prime Minister's Statistical Branch (Mr. Churchill's personal source of information for the guidance of the war economy) and in the Economic Section of the Cabinet Office. In 1950 George Shackle became Reader in Economic Theory at the University of Leeds, and in 1951 the Brunner Professor of Economic Science at Liverpool, where he was to remain until his retirement as Professor Emeritus in 1969. He is a Fellow of the British Academy, and has been Visiting Professor at Columbia and at Pittsburgh.

So much for the public record. To his friends George Shackle is a very special sort of person. He is so invariably kind, courteous, and generous in his appreciation of others. He is always ready to enter into discussion and to clarify a subject by his exceptional gifts of precise argument; not since Marshall has an economist had so splendid a command of language. Above all, he is an initiator of original ideas, whose full effect on the corpus of economic theory is still to come. Generations of scholars will find in his writings a stimulus to fresh thought.

The quality we know so well was apparent in Shackle's first book, *Expectation, Investment and Income* (Oxford University Press, 1938: 2nd edition, 1968). Hugh Townshend, reviewing it for the *Economic Journal*, wrote 'If it is, as I think, not too much to say that the book makes some advance at almost every point it touches (even on the analysis of such a familiar concept as the "multiplier"), this is due to the author's avoidance, practically throughout, of anything approaching the slipshod either in terminology or in reasoning. It is an unusual characteristic of the book that its most original parts are also the best parts.' The title of this work reminds us already of Shackle's special interest in *expectations*, in which he was building on an essential part of Keynes's ideas, but at the same time searching for a better theoretical expression than even the *Treatise on Probability* had provided. In 1949 this theory was ready, in his greatest and most original work, *Expectation in Economics* (Cambridge University Press: 2nd edition, 1952). This was an attempt to provide, in the form of precise axioms and theoretical constructs, a means of dealing with the problems of uncertainty in decisions which are crucial and unique: that is which, by their very taking, so alter the universe that one can never go back and face the same decision again.

The problem, which Shackle attacked with the concepts of 'potential surprise' and 'focus-outcomes', had not of course been wholly neglected before. The idea of 'surprise' as being something different from 'unbelief', and as being applicable to a single event, is to be found in the 1880s in John Venn's *The Logic of Chance*. The limits to the applicability of frequency-ratio probability are clearly set out in Keynes's *Treatise on Probability* and in Jeffreys's *Theory of Probability*. Nevertheless, statistical or frequency-ratio probability continued, and still continues, to be used or implied in discussions of economic situations to which this concept is inappropriate. This would not matter so much if the wrong path led to the right results; it was therefore of crucial importance that Shackle should be able to demonstrate the consequences of the application of his theory.

His efforts to do so, in *Expectation in Economics*, were not entirely successful. In the succeeding years, however, in a great period of creativity, he developed both the theory and its consequences not only in articles, but in book after book: in his contribution to *Uncertainty and Business Decisions* in 1954, in *Uncertainty in Economics* (a volume of collected essays) in 1955, in *Time in Economics* in 1958, and in *Decision, Order and Time in Human Affairs* in 1960. In the same period, in wholly characteristic experiments with his own matchless powers of exposition, he wrote *Mathematics by the Fireside* (1952) to introduce advanced mathematical ideas to young children: and *Economics for Pleasure* (1959), a book for the general reader which he is invited (in the Preface) to peruse 'for his own sinister pleasure'.

The interest in problems associated with *time* was further developed in *A Scheme of Economic Theory* (1965), which classifies economic theories according to the way in which time enters into them. The reviewer for the *Economic Journal*, Professor H. D. Dickinson, wrote of this book:

Like all Professor Shackle's work, this book is full of brilliant and stimulating aperçus. Also, like his other work, it associates things that are usually not thought of together. Professor Shackle's is one of the boldest and most original minds active today in economic thought.

Similarly, Sir Roy Harrod, reviewing *The Years of High Theory* (1967)—a study of economic thought in the period 1926–1939—said

The book is one of great originality ... [Shackle] probes deeply into the essential nature of an economic theory and its relation to the facts of life. He shows the need for mathematical economics and discusses its scope; but he shows the need also for the play of the imagination in framing named concepts that can give us hints and guidance about how to handle the vast heterogeneous mass of economic phenomena.... His style is full of life and imagery....

Such opinions explain why his friends, in gratitude, offer to him this volume. It is a particularly happy feature of George Shackle's work in recent years that it shows a broadening of interest, from the central subjects of Time and Expectations on which he has done so much, towards other areas of economic thought: and this without any lessening of originality, rigour and clarity. We all look forward to the further contributions which he will make, in the golden years miscalled 'retirement'.

C. F. CARTER
J. L. FORD

An Optimality Criterion for Decision-making under Ignorance

KENNETH J. ARROW and
LEONID HURWICZ*

Harvard University and University of Minnesota

1. INTRODUCTION

It is intended here to offer a possible characterization of the concept of complete ignorance. Like other formulations, the problem is taken to be that of choice of an action from a given set when the consequences of any action are functions of an unknown state of nature. However, the properties regarded as defining an optimal choice are designed to reflect completely the idea that there is no *a priori* information available which gives any state of nature a distinguished position. Most importantly, the optimality criterion differs from those in the now more standard subjective probability framework by not presupposing a fixed list of states of nature. As we note shortly, the arguments and conclusions are much closer to Shackle's [1949] than to those of Ramsey [1931], de Finetti [1937], and Savage [1954].

The axiom systems of these last authors imply the existence of subjective probabilities as weights to be assigned to the different

---

* The basic result of this paper was established by Hurwicz and circulated in a hectographed form, "Optimality Criteria for Decision-Making Under Ignorance," Cowles Commission Discussion Paper: Statistics, No. 370, 11 December 1951. The proof was considerably simplified by Arrow and circulated in mimeographed form, "Hurwicz's Optimality Criterion for Decision-Making Under Ignorance," Technical Report No. 6, Office of Naval Research Contract N6onr-25133 (NR-047-004), Stanford University, 1 February 1953, on which the text of the present paper is largely based. Neither report has been published previously.

possible states of nature. These authors thus provide a foundation for the centuries-old use of probability as a guide to action. The concept of complete ignorance can be expressed in this subjective probability framework only by the assignment of equal probabilities to all the states of nature, which is the principle of indifference or insufficient reason implicit in the earliest combinatorial probability calculations of Pascal and Fermat and explicit in Jacob Bernoulli, Bayes, and Laplace. But it may be questioned whether the ignorance expressed by this concept is complete enough. A state of nature is a complete description of the world. But how we describe the world is a matter of language, not of fact. Any description can be made finer by introducing more elements to be described; hence, any state of nature can be expressed as a union of more elementary states of nature. Suppose, for example, there are two coins, but coin two is flipped only if coin one shows tails. There are then three states of nature. But if the betting was solely on the outcome of coin one, one would be loth to base a decision on the assumption that the three states of nature were equally probable, even if there was no *a priori* knowledge about the possible biases in the two coins.

Shackle's [1949] formulation permits a different outlook. In this case, complete ignorance is to be interpreted as meaning that all states of nature have zero potential surprise. Then dividing a state of nature into two would have no effect on the action chosen if the reward to an action is the same under either substate. Indeed, more specifically, the standardized focus-gain and focus-loss become simply the maximum and minimum payoff to a given action, and the final decision among possible actions is made on the basis of the gambler indifference map, which, in this case of complete ignorance, simply orders these pairs.* In the present paper, we demonstrate that a plausible set of desirable properties for a rational criterion of choice under complete ignorance in fact leads to this special case of Shackle's theory.

The properties here are essentially drawn from a set developed by Chernoff [1954].† However, though Chernoff presents the crucial

---

* It has been noted elsewhere that the statistical decision theory of Neyman and Pearson and especially the minimax theory of Wald can be interpreted as special cases of Shackle's theory; see Arrow [1951, sections 3.2.4, 4.2.4.]

† Hurwicz's original manuscript (see footnote p. 1) drew upon a series of hectographed reports. See H. Chernoff, "Remarks on a Rational Selection of a Decision Function," Cowles Commission Discussion Papers: Statistics, Nos. 326, 326A, 346, and 346A, January 1949, and April 1950.

condition referred to below as Property C in section 4 (optimality of an action is unaffected by deletion of repetitious states), he does not in the final published version make use of it.

Milnor [1954] presented some ten desirable properties for decision-making under ignorance; they are shown to be inconsistent as a whole, and he investigated the implications of various subsets. The conclusion of one of his results (Lemma 3) is implied by that of our theorem below, but the assumptions differ somewhat. Most importantly, he assumes that the choice is a continuous function of the payoffs, an assumption which we avoid.*

2. NOTATION AND BASIC CONCEPTS

In accordance with the von Neumann—Morgenstern utility theorem, the consequences of an action under any particular state of nature can be represented by a real number. An action may be regarded as defined by its consequences under each alternative state of nature. Formally, an *action a* is a real-valued function over some set Ω of states of nature. The letter a will stand for the function, while $a(\omega)$ is the value taken on by the function for a given $\omega \in \Omega$.

A *decision problem A* is a set of actions, all of which have the same domain, denoted by $\Omega(A)$. Note that different decision problems may correspond not merely to different sets of available actions but also to different sets of possible states of nature. All of the studies mentioned in Section 1, other than that of Chernoff, consider only a fixed set of possible states of nature.

The problem of decision-making under ignorance is to assign to a decision problem A a subset $\hat{A}$, known as the *optimal set* for A. It is not assumed that every decision problem has an optimal set. We consider a fixed class $\tilde{P}$ of decision problems, each of which is supposed to have a non-null optimal set. If $a_1, a_2 \in A$, and either $a_1, a_2 \in \hat{A}$ or $a_1, a_2 \in A - \hat{A}$, we will say that a_1 and a_2 are *optimally equivalent* with respect to A, symbolized by

$$a_1 \; \tilde{o} \; a_2 \; [A].$$

The relation of optimal equivalence with respect to a fixed set A is clearly transitive, symmetric, and reflexive, and therefore properly an equivalence relation. If $a_1, a_2 \in A$ and $a_1 \in \hat{A}$, we shall say that a_1 is

* Milnor drew upon an earlier unpublished paper by Hurwicz, among others.

revealed preferred or *indifferent** to a_2 with respect to A, and symbolize it by

$$a_1(\geqq)a_2[A].$$

Similarly, if $a_1\ a_2 \in A$, $a_1 \in \hat{A}$, and $a_2 \in A - \hat{A}$, a_1 is said to be *revealed preferred* to a_2 with respect to A; the relation is symbolized by

$$a_1(>)a_2[A].$$

In particular, we will be concerned with decision problems containing just the actions a_1, a_2 (which are assumed to have the same domain) and denoted by (a_1, a_2). Define

$$a_1 \tilde{o} a_2 \text{ if } a_1 \tilde{o} a_2\ [(a_1, a_2)],$$

$$a_1(\geqq)a_2 \text{ if } a_1(\geqq)a_2\ [(a_1, a_2)],$$

$$a_1(>)a_2 \text{ if } a_1(>)a_2\ [(a_1, a_2)].$$

Two decision problems A_1 and A_2 are said to be *isomorphic* if there exists a one–one mapping f of A_1 onto A_2 and a one–one mapping g of $\Omega(A_1)$ onto $\Omega(A_2)$ such that $f(a)\ o\ g = a$ for all a in A_1.† In effect, two decision problems are isomorphic if they can be obtained from each other by relabeling actions and states of nature.

If A_1 and A_2 are two decision problems, we shall say that A_2 is *derived from* A_1 *by deletion of repetitious states* if (1) $\Omega(A_2) \subset \Omega(A_1)$; (2) there is a one–one mapping f of A_1 onto A_2 such that $f(a)$ coincides with a on $\Omega(A_2)$; (3) for each ω in $\Omega(A_1) - \Omega(A_2)$, there is an ω' in $\Omega(A_2)$ such that $a(\omega) = a(\omega')$ for all a in A_1. In symbols,

$$A_1 \to A_2.$$

3. ASSUMPTIONS ON THE CLASS OF DECISION PROBLEMS

The class $\tilde{P}$ of decision problems which have non-null optimal sets will be assumed to satisfy certain assumptions.

---

* This is closely related to the concept of revealed preference introduced in consumers' demand theory by Samuelson [1947], pp. 151–2.

† The symbol $h_1 o h_2$ denotes the *composition* of the functions h_1 and h_2, i.e., h_1 is a function whose domain includes the range of h_2, and, if x is any value in the domain of h_2, the function $h_1 o h_2$ is also defined for x and takes on the value $h_1[h_2(x)]$. Thus, in the above case if the function f maps the action a into the action a', and the function g maps the state of nature ω into the state of nature ω', then $a'(\omega') = a(\omega)$, for all actions a and states of nature ω.

Assumption 1: If A is a decision problem with a finite number of actions, for each of which $\min_\omega a(\omega)$ and $\max_\omega a(\omega)$ exist, then $A \in \tilde{P}$.

Assumption 2: If $A_1 \to A_2$ and $A_1 \in \tilde{P}$, then $A_2 \in \tilde{P}$.

Assumption 3: If $a \in A$, where $A \in \tilde{P}$, then $\min_\omega a(\omega)$ and $\max_\omega a(\omega)$ exist.

Assumption 1 may be disputable if it is held that with every set of actions the set of probability distributions over those actions (the mixed strategies) must also be regarded as available. Assumption 3 is restrictive; however, it is automatically satisfied when $\Omega(A)$ is finite. A relaxation of this assumption is undoubtedly possible if some additional continuity properties are postulated for the optimality criterion.

4. PROPERTIES OF THE OPTIMALITY CRITERION

By the *optimality criterion* is meant the rule defining $\hat{A}$ for every A in P. Certain properties of this criterion will be postulated, and the form of the criterion then deduced.

Property A: If $A_1 \subset A_2$ and $A_1 \cap \hat{A}_2$ is non-null, then $\hat{A}_1 = A_1 \cap \hat{A}_2$.

I.e., if an action is deemed optimal in a certain set of alternatives and if subsequently the range of alternative actions available is contracted but the optimal action is still available, then the optimal action for the larger problem is still optimal.*

Property B: If A_1 is isomorphic to A_2 and a is optimal in A_1, then $f(a)$ is optimal in A_2.

I.e., relabeling actions and states of nature is of no fundamental importance.†

Property C: If $A_1 \to A_2$, then $f(a)$ is optimal in A_2 if and only if a is optimal in A_1.

If $a(\omega) = a(\omega')$ for all a in A_1, then, in effect, for that problem ω and ω' are the same state of nature, and deleting one of them from consideration should lead to no change in the optimal set.‡

Property D: (1) If a is optimal in A, $a' \in A$, and $a'(\omega) \geqq a(\omega)$ for all ω, then a' is optimal in A.

---

* Property A is closely related to several of Chernoff's [1954] requirements, postulates 4, 5, and 6, though stronger than these even taken together.

† Property B is Chernoff's [1954] postulate 3.

‡ Property C is Chernoff's [1954] postulate 9.

(2) If a is not optimal in A, $a' \in A$, and $a'(\omega) \leq a(\omega)$ for all ω, then a' is not optimal in A.

5. SOME LEMMAS

Lemma 1: (1) If $a_1 \tilde{o} a_2$, then $a_1 \tilde{o} a_2 [A]$ for all A for which $a_1, a_2 \in A$.
(2) If $a_1 (\geq) a_2 [A]$ for some A, then $a_1 (\geq) a_2$.
(3) If $a_1 (>) a_2 [A]$ for some A, then $a_1 (>) a_2$.

Proof: (1) If a_1, a_2 are not optimally equivalent with respect to A, suppose $a_1 \in \hat{A}$, $a_2 \in A - \hat{A}$. Since (a_1, a_2) intersects A, the optimal set for (a_1, a_2) consists of the one element a_1, by Property A, contradicting the hypothesis. (2) and (3) follow by similar applications of Property A.

Lemma 2: Suppose a_1 and a_2 have the same domain, $a_1(\omega_1) = a_2(\omega_2)$, $a_1(\omega_2) = a_2(\omega_1)$, $a_1(\omega) = a_2(\omega)$ for all $\omega \neq \omega_1, \omega_2$. Then $a_1 \tilde{o} a_2$.

Proof: Let g be defined by $g(\omega_1) = \omega_2, g(\omega_2) = \omega_1, g(\omega) = \omega$ for $\omega \neq \omega_1, \omega_2$. Let $b_i = a_i \circ g (i = 1, 2)$, and define a function f by $f(a_i) = b_i (i = 1, 2)$. It is easy to verify that (a_1, a_2) and (b_1, b_2) are isomorphic. Hence, if a_1 is optimal in (a_1, a_2), then b_1 is optimal in (b_1, b_2). But $b_2 = a_1, b_1 = a_2$, so that (a_1, a_2) and (b_1, b_2) are the same decision problem. That is, if a_1 is optimal in (a_1, a_2), then so is a_2. We can also interchange a_1 and a_2 in this statement, so that $a_1 \tilde{o} a_2$.

Lemma 3: Suppose m, M are real numbers with $m \leq M$, and a_1, a_2 take on the values m, M and no others. Then $a_1 \tilde{o} a_2$ if a_1 and a_2 have the same domain.

Proof: If $m = M$, then $a_1 = a_2$, and the result is trivial. Suppose $m < M$. Let Ω, the domain of a_1 and a_2, be broken up into four subsets:

$$\Omega_1 = \{\omega | a_1(\omega) = a_2(\omega) = m\},$$
$$\Omega_2 = \{\omega | a_1(\omega) = a_2(\omega) = M\},$$
$$\Omega_3 = \{\omega | a_1(\omega) = m, a_2(\omega) = M\},$$
$$\Omega_4 = \{\omega | a_1(\omega) = M, a_2(\omega) = m\}.$$

First suppose that Ω_3 and Ω_4 are both non-null. Let $\omega_3 \in \Omega_3$, $\omega_4 \in \Omega_4$. Let Ω', be formed from Ω by deleting all elements of Ω_3 and Ω_4 except ω_3 and ω_4, and define f by letting $f(a_i)$ coincide with a_i over Ω' and be undefined elsewhere. Since $a_i(\omega) = a_i(\omega_3)$ for $\omega \in \Omega_3 - (\omega_3)$, $a_i(\omega) = a_i(\omega_4)$ for $\omega \in \Omega_4 - (\omega_4)$,

(1) $$(a_1, a_2) \rightarrow (f(a_1), f(a_2)).$$

By construction $f(a_1)$ coincides with $f(a_2)$ for all $\omega \in \Omega'$ other than ω_3, ω_4; $f(a_1)(\omega_3) = m = f(a_2)(\omega_4)$, $f(a_1)(\omega_4) = M = f(a_2)(\omega_3)$. By Lemma 2, $f(a_1)\tilde{o}f(a_2)$. Since the optimal set for $(f(a_1), f(a_2))$ is non-null, both $f(a_1)$ and $f(a_2)$ must be optimal in $(f(a_1), f(a_2))$. By Property C, a_1 and a_2 are both optimal in (a_1, a_2) and therefore $a_1 \tilde{o} a_2$.

Now suppose Ω_4 is null, Ω_3 non-null. Since a_1 and a_2 must both take on both values, m and M, neither Ω_1 nor Ω_2 can be null. Let ω_j be any element of Ω_j ($j = 1, 2, 3$). Let $f_1(a_i)$ coincide with a_i for $\omega = \omega_j$ ($i = 1, 2; j = 1, 2, 3$), and be undefined elsewhere. Since $a_i(\omega) = a_i(\omega_j)$ for $\omega \in \Omega_j - (\omega_j)$ for each i and j,

(2) $$(a_1, a_2) \rightarrow (f_1(a_1), f_1(a_2)).$$

Define a_3 as follows: $a_3(\omega_1) = M$, $a_3(\omega_2) = m$, $a_3(\omega_3) = M$. Then $f_1(a_2)(\omega_1) = a_2(\omega_1) = m = a_3(\omega_2)$; $f_1(a_2)(\omega_2) = a_2(\omega_2) = M = a_3(\omega_1)$; $f_1(a_2)(\omega_3) = a_2(\omega_3) = M = a_3(\omega_3)$. From Lemma 2,

(3) $$f_1(a_2) \tilde{o} a_3.$$

Let A be the decision problem with elements $f_1(a_1), f_1(a_2), a_3$. Note that, since $a_1(\omega_1) = m = a_1(\omega_3)$,

(4) $$f_1(a_1)(\omega_1) = f_1(a_1)(\omega_3), \; a_3(\omega_1) = a_3(\omega_3).$$

Let f_2 map the actions $f_1(a_1)$ and a_3 into actions having the same values for ω_1 and ω_2 and undefined for ω_3. Then, by (4),

(5) $$(f_1(a_1), a_3) \rightarrow (f_2 \circ f_1(a_1), f_2(a_3)).$$

In the last decision problem, the first action has the values m and M for ω_1 and ω_2, respectively, while the second action has the values M and m for ω_1 and ω_2, respectively. By Lemma 2, $f_2 \circ f_1(a_1) \tilde{o} f_2(a_3)$, and hence both must be optimal in $(f_2 \circ f_1(a_1), f_2(a_3))$. By Property C and (5), $f_1(a_1)$ and a_3 are both optimal in $(f_1(a_1), a_3)$ and hence $f_1(a_1) \tilde{o} a_3$. In conjunction with (3), it follows easily that all the elements of A are optimal, and therefore $f_1(a_1) \tilde{o} f_1(a_2)$, by Property A. From (2) and Property C, $a_1 \tilde{o} a_2$, which was to be proven.

The case where Ω_3, is null but Ω_4 is non-null follows by merely interchanging a_1 and a_2. The case where Ω_3 and Ω_4 are both null is trivial, since then $a_1 = a_2$.

Lemma 4: For any given action a, let a' be an action with the same domain, where $a'(\omega_0) = \min_\omega a(\omega)$, $a'(\omega) = \max_\omega a(\omega)$ for $\omega \neq \omega_0$. Then $a \tilde{o} a'$.

Proof: Let ω_1 be any state of nature for which a attains its minimum, ω_2 a state of nature for which a attains its maximum. Define a_1 as follows:

$a_1(\omega_2) = \max_\omega a(\omega) = M$(say), $a_1(\omega) = \min_\omega a(\omega) = m$

(say) for $\omega \neq \omega_2$. Define a_2 as follows:

$a_2(\omega_1) = m$, $a_2(\omega) = M$ for $\omega \neq \omega_1$. Let A be the decision problem with the four elements a, a', a_1, a_2. Suppose a is not optimal in A; since $a_1(\omega) \leq a(\omega)$ for all ω, a_1 is not optimal by Property D (2). But $a_2 \tilde{o} a_1$ by Lemma 3, and therefore $a_2 \tilde{o} a_1$ [A] by Lemma 1, so that a_2 is not optimal in A. By the same argument, a' is not optimal in A, so that $\hat{A}$ is null, which is impossible. Therefore, a is optimal in A. Since $a_2(\omega) \geq a(\omega)$ for all ω, a_2 is optimal by Property D (1). Since $a' \tilde{o} a_2$ [A], a' is optimal in A. By Property A, the optimal set for (a, a') consists of both those elements, so that $a \tilde{o} a'$.

6. CHARACTERIZATION OF THE OPTIMALITY CRITERION

Theorem: Under Assumptions 1–3, a necessary and sufficient condition that an optimality criterion possess Properties A–D is that there exist a weak ordering $\geq$ in the space of ordered pairs of real numbers (m, M) with $m \leq M$ possessing the following properties: (1) if $m_1 \geq m_2$, $M_1 \geq m_{,2}$ then $(m_1, M_1) \geq (m_2, M_2)$; (2) for any $A \in \tilde{P}$, $\hat{A} = \{a \mid (\min_\omega a(\omega), \max_\omega a(\omega)) \geq (\min_\omega a'(\omega), \max_\omega a'(\omega))$ for all $a' \in A$.

Proof: To prove necessity, we assume the existence of an optimality criterion satisfying Properties A–D. We first define the ordering over the half-space of ordered pairs of real numbers (m, M). Let ω' and ω'' be any two given states of nature; let $b(m, M)$ be the action defined by $b(m, M)(\omega') = m$, $b(m, M)(\omega'') = M$. (The function $b(m, M)$ maps each ordered pair into an action defined for two states of nature.) We will say

$(m_1, M_1) \geq (m_2, M_2)$ if and only if $b(m_1, M_1)(\geq)b(m_2, M_2)$.

It should be noted that varying ω' and ω'' changes the decision problem $(b(m_1, M_1), b(m_2, M_2))$ into another decision problem isomorphic to the first. The relation $\geq$ is therefore, by Property B, independent of the choice of ω', ω''.

It must first be shown that the relation $\geq$ is in fact an ordering. Suppose $(m_1, M_1) \geq (m_2, M_2)$ and $(m_2, M_2) \geq (m_3, M_3)$. Let A be the decision problem with elements $b(m_1, M_1)$, $b(m_2, M_2)$, $b(m_3, M_3)$. There is at least one optimal action. Suppose $b(m_3, M_3)$ is the only optimal action; then $b(m_3, M_3)(>)b(m_2, M_2)$ $[A]$. By Lemma 1, $b(m_3, M_3)(>)b(m_2, M_2)$, which contradicts the hypothesis that $(m_2, M_2) \geq (m_3, M_3)$. Suppose now that $b(m_2, M_2) \in \hat{A}$ but not $b(m_1, M_1)$. This also leads to a contradiction since $(m_1, M_1) \geq (m_2, M_2)$. Hence, we must conclude that $b(m_1, M_1) \in \hat{A}$, so that $b(m_1, M_1)(\geq) b(m_3, M_3)$ $[A]$, and therefore $b(m_1, M_1)(\geq)b(m_3, M_3)$, or, by definition, $(m_1, M_1) \geq (m_3, M_3)$.

The relation $\geq$ is therefore transitive. Since any decision problem $(b(m_1, M_1), b(m_2, M_2))$ has at least one optimal element, either $(m_1, M_1) \geq (m_2, M_2)$ or $(m_2, M_2) \geq (m_1, M_1)$, so that the relation $\geq$ is a weak ordering.

Suppose now $m_1 \geq m_2$, $M_1 \geq M_2$. If $(m_2, M_2) > (m_1, M_1)$, then $b(m_2, M_2)$ is the only optimal action in $(b(m_1, M_1), b(m_2, M_2))$. But $b(m_1, M_1)(\omega) \geq b(m_2, M_2)(\omega)$ for both values of ω, so that $b(m_1, M_1)$ is also optimal, a contradiction. Hence, $(m_1, M_1) \geq (m_2, M_2)$, which is conclusion (1) of the necessity part of the theorem.

Suppose $a \in \hat{A}$. Then $a(\geq)a'$ $[A]$ for all $a' \in A$, and therefore $a(\geq)a'$ for all $a' \in A$. For some fixed ω', define

$$a_1(\omega') = \min_\omega a(\omega), \; a_1(\omega) = \max_\omega a(\omega) \text{ for } \omega \neq \omega';$$
$$a_2(\omega') = \min_\omega a'(\omega), \; a_2(\omega) = \max_\omega a'(\omega) \text{ for } \omega \neq \omega'.$$

By Lemma 4,

(1) $$a_1 \tilde{o} a, \; a_2 \tilde{o} a'.$$

Let A_1 be the decision problem with elements a, a', a_1, a_2. If a is not optimal in A_1, then neither is a_1 by (1). Hence, either a_2 or a' is optimal in A_1, and therefore both are by (1). Since $a'(>)a$ $[A_1]$, $a'(>)a$, which is impossible since $a(\geq)a'$. Hence $a \in \hat{A}_1$; by (1) $a_1 \in \hat{A}_1$, so that $a_1(\geq)a_2$ $[A_1]$ and $a_1(\geq)a_2$.

Let ω'' be any element of Ω other than ω'. For $\omega \neq \omega'$, ω'', $a_i(\omega) = a_i(\omega'')$ $(i = 1, 2)$. Let $f(a_i)$ coincide with a_i for $\omega = \omega'$, ω'' and be undefined elsewhere. Then

$$(a_1, a_2) \to (f(a_1), f(a_2)).$$

By Property C, $f(a_1)(\geqq)f(a_2)$. But $f(a_1) = b(\min_\omega a(\omega), \max_\omega a(\omega))$, $f(a_2) = b(\min_\omega a'(\omega), \max_\omega a'(\omega))$. Therefore,

(2) if $a\in\hat{A}$, $(\min_\omega a(\omega), \max_\omega a(\omega)) \geqq$
   $\geqq (\min_\omega a'(\omega), \max_\omega a'(\omega))$ for all $a'\in A$.

Suppose now that $a\in A - \hat{A}$. Let a' be any element of $\hat{A}$, so that $a'(>)a$. By a repetition of the preceding argument, with the symbols $(\geqq)$ and $\geqq$ replaced by $(>)$ and $>$, respectively, and a and a' interchanged, it can be concluded that

(3) if $a\in A - \hat{A}$, $(\min_\omega a'(\omega), \max_\omega a'(\omega)) >$
   $> (\min_\omega a(\omega), \max_\omega a(\omega))$ for some $a'\in A$.

(2) and (3) together are equivalent to part (2) of the conclusion of the necessity part of the theorem. The sufficiency part of the theorem is very easily verified.

Remark. The dominance property D is very weak; it is not excluded, for example, that one action may strictly dominate another, $a(\omega) > a'(\omega)$ for all ω, and yet a' may be optimal; it is only required that a must also be optimal in that case. There would be no difficulty in introducing an additional condition that an action strictly dominated by another not be optimal; in that case property (1) of the Theorem would be supplemented by the condition that if $m_1 > m_2$, $M_1 > M_2$, then $(m_1, M_1) > (m_2, M_2)$, where $>$ is the strict preference relation generated by the weak ordering $\geqq$. It would not, however, be possible to require that an action semi-strictly dominated by another (i.e., an action a' for which there exists a such that $a(\omega) \geqq a'(\omega)$ for all ω, $a(\omega) > a'(\omega)$ for at least one value of ω is not optimal. For clearly one action might semi-strictly dominate another and yet both have the same maximum and minimum payoffs.

REFERENCES

K. J. Arrow, 1951 Alternative approaches to the theory of choice in risk-taking situations. *Econometrica* 19: 404–437. Reprinted in K. J. Arrow 1971 *Essays in the Theory of Risk-Bearing*. Chicago: Markham, chapter 1.

H. Chernoff, 1954 Rational selection of decision functions. *Econometrica* 22: 422–443.

B. De Finetti, 1937 La prévision: ses lois logiques, ses sources subjectives. *Annales de l'Institut Henri Poincaré* 71–68. Translated by H. E. Kyburg in H. E. Kyburg, Jr., and H. E. Smookler (eds.) 1964 *Studies in Subjective Probability*. New York: Wiley, pp. 95–158.

J. Milnor, 1954 Games against nature. In R. M. Thrall, C. H. Coombs, and R. L. Davis (eds.) 1954 *Decision Processes*. New York and London: Wiley and Chapman & Hall, chapter IV.

F. P. Ramsey, 1931 Truth and probability. In F. P. Ramsey 1931 *The Foundations of Mathematics and Other Logical Essays*. London: K. Paul, Trench, Trubner, and Company, pp. 156–198.

P. A. Samuelson, 1947 *Foundations of Economic Analysis*. Cambridge, Mass.: Harvard University Press.

L. J. Savage, 1954 *The Foundations of Statistics*. New York: Wiley.

G. L. S. Shackle, 1949 *Expectation in Economics*. Cambridge, U.K.: Cambridge University Press.

Expectations, Uncertainty and Investments in Human Beings

MARY JEAN BOWMAN

University of Chicago

Investments in human beings will always be shrouded in some uncertainty, whether the decision-maker be an individual, a firm, or a national collectivity. Non-divisibility and non-seriability may reach an extreme in decisions of individuals to make major commitments to investments in themselves, on the one hand, in decisions of comparable relative magnitude by national states on the other. Yet there are also decisions with respect to investments in human beings that carry lesser degrees of uncertainty.

This paper will focus entirely on investment decisions of the individual. No fine line is drawn on the risk–uncertainty continuum, but I shall bypass discussions of human investment decisions in which expectations are treated as if certain and in disregard of attitudes toward risk.*

---

* Among the hard choices were: (1) Concentration centrally on decisions, to the virtual exclusion of any sort of market analysis (which meant exclusion not only of the dynamics of adjustments in labor markets, but also of the non-marketability of risk and substitutions for such marketability in capital markets for funds for investments in human beings); (2) the exclusion of decisions of businessmen to invest in their employees; (3) exclusion of the economics of information and applications of Bayesian inference to human investment decisions, except as this comes in very incidentally; and (4) most regretfully, in the end I opted to eliminate a systematic theoretical discussion of sequential decisions, expectations of expectations, and the clarification of expectations under uncertainty simply because it would have made this paper far too long. An analysis touching upon these questions in a human-investment context is included in Chapter II of M. J. Bowman, Hideo Ikeda, and Yasumasa Tomoda, *Schooling and the Future*, which went to press in the fall of 1971.

The discussion will be divided into two main parts. Section I explores a few aspects of theories of choice under risk and uncertainty in their applications to human investment decisions. In Section II discussion shifts more completely over to crucial educational decisions in a dynamic, imaginative, and uncertain world—the world in which Professor Shackle's work has bloomed.

I. ATTITUDES TOWARD RISK AND INVESTMENTS IN EDUCATION

Attitudes toward risk could enter into the specification of a decision model for choice under risk and uncertainty in one or more ways: (a) in the translation of each outcome or prospect into its concomitant subjective face value; (b) in effects of risk attitudes on assessments of probabilities or on the degrees of disbelief—introducing unconscious biases into perceptions of "the strength of the claim [of an hypothesis] to be treated as if it were true"—or (c) through the decision rules by which expectations are translated into action. Rarely, however, is the second of these explicitly considered, and I shall forego further comment about it here. The first and third will be taken up as appropriate in the ensuing discussions first of risk aversion and then of what I will call the "attractive longer chance."

Risk Aversion: Theories and Evidence

Most theories of choice under risk and uncertainty treat expected outcomes or prospects as monetary, at least in the first instance. Attitudes toward risk are then introduced as biased transformations of expected monetary returns (the nominal expectations) into their subjective equivalents. Risk aversion is associated with diminishing marginal utility of income. Regardless of the uncertainty variable in the model, the effect is to give small marginal-utility weights to a dollar in the range of anticipated high nominal incomes and large ones to a dollar in the range of anticipated low nominal returns.

As is well known, in conventional probability models risk aversion will reduce the certainty-equivalent value below that of the mathematical expectation, and the higher the variance of the expectations the greater will be this downward adjustment. The decision rule is simple: behavior will be determined by rational comparisons among the certainty equivalents associated with alternative lines of action. If it is assumed further that the individual's perceived nominal expectation structure matches distributions of empirically estimated net present values of earning streams, then very high objectively estimated rates of return (well above the criterion external discount rate) might be interpreted as indicative of pervasive risk aversion in the making of educational decisions. Such results have sometimes been found and have been so interpreted. But is even this conditional inference justified? Surely, in the context of decisions with respect to investments in education it is intuitively plausible to argue that the conservative action alternative is to ensure against low future incomes by attending college rather than to enter the labor market upon finishing secondary school. What, if anything, in that case has gone wrong? At least four possibilities deserve mention.

(a) Serious imperfections in capital markets would tend to constrain investments in education and so to peg high internal rates of return. This has been a favorite hypothesis in contemporary rate-of-return studies of investments in human beings. It has a special appeal because it pushes the uncertainties outside of the decision model proper into the capital markets, leaving the quasi-certain world of the theory of individual human-investment decisions intact. There is neither risk aversion nor its opposite, but just external distortions of the decision parameters.

(b) The difficulty might be in the decision rule, with its simple application of certainty equivalence. Perhaps a minimax, strongly risk-avertive choice would in long-term perspective point to taking the college option despite the fact that an immediate known outlay is entailed and the future remains less than certain. Observed high internal rates of return to college education might then suggest (other things equal) that at the margin the decision-makers who opt not to attend college are by no means clear risk-averters, and may indeed be quite the opposite.

(c) A third consideration highlights another feature of decision making with respect to an individual's schooling that is often neglected. "The" decision-maker is not identified unambiguously in the real world: is it the child, his parents, a teacher? This could be a complex game.

(d) The analysis has shifted too readily from mental experiments with decisions entailing only a single (and timeless) Yes–No eventuality in the outcome (so favored in much of the literature about choice under risk and uncertainty) to investments that are expected to yield their returns over a considerable time span into the future. The shift was made by introducing "present values" to sum up an expected income path, but without questioning how this might come about. It is evident that the "expectation elements" in investments in human beings must constitute entire paths of returns projected by the imagination into the future. Each expectation element is initially multi-dimensional in that it is made up of components that are distinguished by the timing of their expected appearance. A critical step in any investment decision will be the translation of these components into a summary evaluation, or "face value" from the viewpoint perspective. But this means that we must allow for anticipatory "state preferences" in utility evaluations of income at one versus another stage of the life cycle. There are consequent effects of the time shapes of expectation elements on their rankings that cannot be covered by conventional discounting procedures at a single discount rate. The utility transforms of income-path expectation elements require consideration of the whole path; neither a nominal present value computed at a single discount rate nor a nominal internal rate of return can provide the basis for that utility transform. If near incomes carry high loadings of utility, without consideration of risk aversion the result still will be a tendency for college education to have high internal rates of return.

This last point brings us closer to Professor Shackle's theories, despite the fact that the "state preference" idea has been developed in its formal variants as part of more conventional probabilistic treatments of choice under risk and uncertainty. Though Professor Shackle does not normally use the term risk aversion, so far as I am aware, it is of considerable interest to ask how far attitudes toward risk enter into his model, and in what ways.

As I interpret Professor Shackle, the greater the degree of risk aversion the closer must the ascendancy contours on the unfavorable side of his desirability scale crowd up against the neutral position. If outcomes are treated as nominally monetary, these ascendancy contours will incorporate effects of diminishing marginal utility of income on the subjective "face values" of hypothesized outcomes— that is, on their "desiredness." But this means also that strong risk aversion would bring both the primary focus loss and the standardized focus loss close to the neutral position on the desiredness scale.

It should be noted immediately, however, that risk aversion could be introduced into Professor Shackle's model in this fashion only insofar as we identified it with diminishing marginal utility of income; if the outcomes are mainly or largely of a non-monetary sort in the first place, the whole concept of risk as I have used it up to this point would seem to melt away. It survived in the more conventional probability models only by a transmutation that virtually identified it with diminishing marginal utility of income; this was done tautologically by the identification of certainty equivalents as the automatic determinants of behavior. Professor Shackle does not make such an identification, and his theory is capable, therefore, of treating risk attitudes independently of the determinants of face values of expectation elements, or of the views of the decision-maker concerning either probabilities or implausibilities.

This brings us to a second step. Risk aversion comes again into Professor Shackle's model with his gambler-indifference maps. Presumably with a strong risk aversion the indifference curves will rise steeply when the standardized focus loss is plotted on the horizontal axis, the standardized focus gain on the vertical axis. Given the prior processes of determination of focus outcomes, I am not quite sure of this, however, and I hope clarification may come from Professor Shackle in the future.

More important, his model brings out clearly the value of considering asymmetries both in utility functions of incomes and in attitudes toward possibilities of loss on the one hand, of gains on the other. It invites but does not require anticipatory utility structures such as those of Friedman and Savage (1948) and then of Markowitz (1952), even though discarding the probability calculus.

The Attractive Longer Chance

Popular as assertions about the high returns to investments in education may be, the facts are not as uniform as the belief. It would appear, for example, that *ex post* internal rates of return to private investments in upper-secondary education in Japan and to university education in Columbia are decidedly below the returns that could be obtained monetarily on other investments. And while there has been some favorable change recently, ten years ago Negro men in the United States were barely recovering their foregone earnings while in college—if that; the puzzle was not that some dropped out but that so many persisted in school so long. In other words, objectively estimated *ex post* private (let alone social) rates of return to education do not always turn out to be high. Exceptionally strong tastes for education as a consumer good seem to be an unlikely explanation in most cases. Setting such tastes aside, what structures of expectations and risk attitudes might we assume to induce investments in education beyond what the realized monetary returns would suggest to be "economically rational?"

Every example that has suggested itself to me of a situation in which this might occur entails an interpretation of subjective evaluations of very high monetary outcomes that are exaggerated because of their association with something that could be interpreted as a "state preference" factor or, a different but closely related matter,* relevant non-monetary components of outcomes that are associated with the high income prospect. If, further, there is also a marked positive skewness in the distribution of expectations in probabilistic terms, or if returns below the neutral point on Professor Shackle's desiredness scale carry extremely high potential surprise, any exaggeration in the anticipatory appeal of high-return outcomes is the more likely to dominate the decision in favor of the investment. Professor Ozga's interpretation of Markowitz's increasing marginal utility of anticipated income to the right of the individual's present or normal situation may fit the case of the American Negro a decade or more ago, even though the initial model was concerned with lotteries, where losses are anticipated but cannot be large and there is an outside chance of a big gain. In Ozga's words:†

Small increases in income which do not lead to any changes in the individual's status may not give him as much satisfaction as to make him accept a fair gamble for them; and large increases, which help him to jump to a higher socio-economic group may give him so much more of it that he may be prepared to gamble for them even on conditions which are not quite fair to him.

When a youth feels that he really has little to lose and little hope of gain, he may feel that he has at least a chance in life with more

* A "state preference" entails a state of the world such that the utility of a given outcome will be different from what it would be in some other state of the world. Examples that have been cited in the literature are ice cream on a hot versus a cold day, or the value of insurance to a married man with dependants, as opposed to a bachelor.
† S. A. Ozga (1965) p. 196.

education, but virtually none without it. A welfare state may contribute to such a decision by providing partial financial support, thus reducing the magnitude of the immediate private investment in further schooling, while at the same time putting a floor under incomes regardless of education and thus reducing the anticipated most likely or non-surprising differentials of college over non-college earnings. The idea that anticipatory utilities or subjective "face values" may rise in disproportion to the increase in nominal monetary values of outcomes in their upper ranges seems especially plausible with respect to investments in human beings, if only because the income anticipations will be related to the individual in a peculiarly personal way, as in some part a confirmation of his worth. But more than that is involved. If, in the individual's expectation elements, the present values of anticipatory non-monetary occupational satisfactions rise parallel to present values of the income anticipations themselves—and they may be in part the condition of the latter—the total or consolidated value must be greater than the subjective present value of the anticipated income alone, without the non-monetary occupational context.

It seems much more natural to move into this type of analysis from Professor Shackle's model than from a probability model with state-preference adornments. At the very heart of this matter is the emphasis placed by Shackle on power to draw and focus the individual's attention, and even to stimulate imagination, yet within the bounds of plausibility in hypotheses concerning the future. The conventional calculus of probability, despite all its elegance and power in many applications, lacks precisely those elements that to Shackle are so important—and that may be no less important to youth at the decision points in their careers. Furthermore, Shackle's model, especially in its later formulations, applies very explicitly and directly to non-continuous and non-monetary, multi-dimensional expectational elements. It is in this latter respect, but not in the handling of uncertainty variables, that Shackle's approach and probability theories incorporating state preference begin to come partially together.

II. INVESTMENTS IN EDUCATION AND BOUNDED UNCERTAINTY

The preceding section wove back and forth to a certain extent between probability theories and some aspects of Professor Shackle's model, but starting with an emphasis on the former. In the remaining pages of this essay that emphasis will be reversed, but again with such weaving back and forth as may seem most appropriate to the question at issue and the particular decision situations visualized.

Uncertainties, Preferences, and Decision Frontiers

That occupations are intervening variables between schooling and income is a commonplace. But so are the facts that income variance within occupations is considerable, that a large proportion of young people are vague about their occupational destinations, and that among those who may be quite specific in articulating occupational anticipations those anticipations may nevertheless turn out to be unreliable predictors of subsequent events.

To emphasize the fact that schooling decisions may be oriented to occupations not only as intervening variables but also for their more direct non-monetary appeal is of course implicitly to underline the multiplicity of factors in anticipated outcomes of an action that may affect its "desiredness."* Let us take this in our stride, however, and assume that we can arrive at subjective rankings of desiredness and further, just for convenience and elegance in the representation of the model, that we can apply a Jevonsian operation to convert the utility rankings of anticipations into cardinal utility variables. What, if anything, might this mean for treatment of the uncertainty variable?

We cannot even begin to answer this last question until we take explicit note of another feature of human investment decisions, a feature that in fact characterizes virtually all major business (not gambling) decisions as well: Each choice among alternative lines of action in the present affects future events in part through its effects

---

* Each "expectation element," in Shackle's terminology, may itself constitute a mix of many dimensions, and possible mixes could be almost unlimited, but each mix is *ipso facto* incompatible with any other mix. This mutual exclusiveness is definitionally necessary in the specification of outcomes or "expectation elements."

on the options open to the individual for choices at some future decision point; expectations of future expectations are conditioned not only by prospects for relevant future *states of the world*, but by present and future actions that are in some degree at least under the control of the individual. Furthermore, in most cases, and even when a particular occupation is envisaged in anticipation of the future, young people are less than certain about what their occupational preferences will turn out to be some years hence. That uncertainty stems in part from a conscious lack of present knowledge about the characteristics of particular occupations—a lack that, it is anticipated, will be at least partially reduced with the accumulation of information over time. It stems also, in part, from an awareness of lack of present knowledge about the full spectrum of possibly appealing occupations some of which will become visible only as the date of entry into the world of work comes nearer, or even only over the first years of work experience and investments in learning at work. But at the decision viewpoint there may be uncertainty also about one's own future occupational preferences and, more profoundly, one's self. It seems that we may be faced not only with questions as to when or whether to use additive probability or non-probabilistic uncertainty variables, but also with what to count among the relevant outcomes or "expectation elements," given that uncertainty has intruded itself inescapably into the occupational ends as well as into judgments concerning probabilities or plausibilities.* These two problems are interconnected.

The *residual hypotheses* of Professor Shackle's theory come to the rescue here. "Residual hypotheses" are clearly distinguished from hypotheses that have been considered and discarded (implicitly or explicitly) because their realization carries too great a degree of potential surprise. Residual hypotheses are outcomes that have not been thought of in particularized terms, or possibly imagined at all. To the decision-maker the possibility that the future event will turn

* The following quotation from G. L. S. Shackle (*Decision, Order and Time*, p. iii) is peculiarly pertinent to decisions about human investments, to which it applies in a double sense:

> How important a part in life is played by non-divisible experiments? They are unavoidable, for no experiment can be repeated which by its nature necessarily destroys a condition essential to it; and no divisible experiment can be built up of trials or performances which cannot be repeated. Such *self-destructive experiments* are exemplified by every deed which will leave human knowledge and human memory of experience different from what it is; and what deed will not?

out to be in this presently unspecified residual category may easily carry zero potential surprise, even though at the same time the individual anticipates with zero potential surprise that he will be surprised at the occurrence of any particular future event in the residual. The fact that at the college decision point large proportions of young people remain uncertain about not only future states of the world outside of themselves but also what their future occupational preferences may be, and thus what later decisions they would make for any given anticipated state of the world, falls clearly into place once we admit the category of residual hypotheses as an integral part of the model of decision-making under uncertainty. The residual hypotheses as a whole (though not any particular unanticipated element that comes later to separate out from it) will then fall within the *inner range* of zero potential surprise—along with specific occupational anticipations, if any, that carry zero potential surprise in themselves. But what determines this inner range, and the face values of expectation elements over which it extends?

Whether or not at any given age and stage in his education a youth has a clear set of specific career preferences within the bounds of "realistic" imaginings, with a redefinition of occupations in terms of sets of relevant characteristics individuals could (and do) exclude many objective possibilities from consideration. In other words, in a decision situation in which ultimate prospects are determined not only by anticipations of future states of the world but also of intervening future options and action choices of the individual, he will eliminate some possible anticipated outcomes *by choice*. Professor Shackle does not to my knowledge explicitly discuss such *elimination of anticipations by choice*, but I would take it to be fully consistent with his model. Moreover, elimination by choice helps us out on an aspect of the Shackle model that rests otherwise on little more than an arbitrary theoretical aesthetics. It strengthens the basis for the assumption that to the left, outside of the inner range, degrees of disbelief will rise monotonically with degrees of undesiredness in anticipation. On the positive side, elimination by choice will hardly enter in, but the multi-dimensionality of occupational and economic success may nevertheless lend some support to the assumption of monotonic relationships between the present utility of an expectation element and the degrees of disbelief that it will carry. It does this, paradoxically perhaps, because it piles up multiplicative probabilities against the realization of all possible favorable features together within a single anticipated outcome. The potential surprise curve has now become a *decision frontier* in that it has been purged of expectation elements that might carry low potential surprise as objectively available options, but that carry maximal potential surprise in terms of anticipated future preferences.

A Caveat or Two on Non-Surprise and Betters' Odds

The insights that can be contributed by Professor Shackle's model to the study of human investment decisions under uncertainty are impressive, and I shall come back to this theme. It is indeed precisely because of the value I see in the potential surprise approach that I am concerned about what seem to me to be some confusing if not erroneous responses Professor Shackle has given to commentators who have been uncomfortable about treating all outcomes that carry zero potential surprise as always on the same footing. The illustrations are directly relevant to human investment decisions.

The first comes from Professor Shackle's report of an interchange with C. F. Carter.* Professor Carter had hypothesized that he had two daughters, Mary and Lucy, both of whom were fairly bright, but Lucy was definitely the brighter. He would not be surprised at all if both passed the eleven-plus examination, but he had more confidence in the case of Lucy than of Mary. He then asked Professor Shackle: "Am I right in thinking that, for you, this difference in degree of assurance can only be accommodated by attaching non-zero potential surprise to Mary's passing?" Professor Shackle's response was that the two cases would be distinguished by the differences between them in degrees of disbelief in failure on the examination. He goes on to say: "Now if we insisted (surely against reason) on speaking in terms of chances or odds, it would of course be true that to give Lucy a smaller number of 'chances' of not passing (a lower probability of not passing) than Mary would be the same thing as to give Lucy a larger number of chances (a higher probability) of passing than Mary." Why Professor Shackle should consider such a calculation of chances to be "surely against reason" I do not understand, since it would seem to be a situation well suited to use of Bayesian inference, with plenty of relevant cumulative evidence of performance on earlier tests or examinations to predict grade likelihoods and

* G. L. S. Shackle (1961) pp. 102–3.

hence the likelihood of exceeding a pass level for either of the girls. It is curious that in this interchange there is no reference whatsoever to any *decision* to which the structure of expectations is presumed to be relevant. In brief, it would appear here that there has been confusion between a *crisis event* (the probability of which could be approximated very well by Bayesian inference) and a *crucial decision*, which would be a very different matter.

The second illustration refers to what might be termed for short "Shackle's numbers paradox." In pushing his opposition to use of probability variables, Shackle has argued as follows:*

> To sum the degrees of possibility assigned to various rival hypotheses is to fall back on the idea that it is the *number of rivals* which gives a hypothesis its status, rather than its own particular character. An outstandingly well-qualified candidate for some post is not less likely to be appointed merely because a score, rather than half a dozen, second-rate applicants also present themselves. If we do not know what qualities are required, we cannot say which of a number of candidates *is* well qualified, but which ever man has, in fact, the requisite attributes, he has not them in less degree because of the presence of other men who do not possess them at all. . . . It is precisely this idea, that *a small share of a total*, and a share which varies with the size of that total, can suitably indicate the status of *perfect possibility*, that I cannot agree with. If an outcome is looked on as perfectly possible, it is looked on as such regardless of what else is also looked on as perfectly, or in any other degree, possible.

This is where either I misinterpret Professor Shackle or his argument evades the point. Surely to state that the individual has no competitors who can match him in quality is to *exclude* any numbers effect. It is difficult for me to accept intuitively the suggestion that, let us say, John will not see his prospects for getting a good job in civil engineering as dependent in part, at least, on how many young men *at his ability level* (*or better*) will be competing with him. John might consider it perfectly possible that he would get such a job even if the number of equally qualified seekers for such a post were doubled, but he might assess his *chances* of getting it quite differently nonetheless, until at some point he will begin to view the prospect of success in this respect with something greater than zero potential surprise. The point is not trivial for the understanding of human-investment and career decisions.

In more general terms, perhaps the paradox at least could be quite

* G. L. S. Shackle (1961) p. 92.

easily resolved if Professor Shackle is willing to consolidate an infinity of possible hypothetical outcomes into sets falling within specified ranges on the desiredness scale; either degrees of potential surprise or probabilities could then be defined for each of these sets as a whole, depending on other features of the decision situation; the number of fine distinctions made within such a set would in either case be irrelevant. It is entirely possible, furthermore, that a very great diversity of specified outcomes carrying zero potential surprise could be clustered very close together on an anticipatory desiredness scale. The flatness or peakedness of an expectation structure taken against anticipatory utility units is not the same thing as the flatness or peakedness in terms of either diversities in kinds of nominal outcomes or even in terms of the spread over a nominal dollar scale—whatever the probability or potential surprise structure. This is quite independent of the argument that additive probabilities are inappropriate in analysis of decisions under true uncertainty, which I am not challenging. In this connection it is interesting to look at the *residual hypothesis* again. That hypothesis could be merged in a grouping or set such as I just suggested if, but only if, the likelihood in sum of the occurrence of some (any) of the unspecified outcomes could be assessed without prior specification of all the possibilities. This, of course, is not the way in which Professor Shackle thought of it.

Flexibility, the Inner Range, and the Shaping of Potential Surprise

Thirty years ago, starting from a probability orientation to analysis of business behavior, Albert Hart rationalized selections of production techniques less than the most efficient for any given level of output by showing that such seeming "inefficiency" could be the result of a strategy that would maximize the mean value of expected profits from a range of output prospects.* As Ozga has pointed out, Hart showed in this model that "adjustment to a sure-prospect equivalent of profits may not be consistent with the firm adjusting itself to a sure-prospect equivalent of output."†

The very fact that this theoretical construct was built up in terms of certainty equivalents means that the behavioral logic could easily

* A. G. Hart (1940).
† S. A. Ozga (1965) p. 131.

be adapted to a human investment model in which, instead of Hart's probabilities of probabilities, we assumed the virtual *certainty of change* in states of the world over the years ahead. This, indeed, is the simple homespun logic of educational choices that are believed to provide men with a high capacity to adapt and to learn over their future working years, rather than with a particular skill that might maximize income at a particular target date. If the anticipated changes in future states of the world and their anticipated implications for life earning paths associated with one education as against another were highly predictable, then (with proper utility transforms) the individual's decision problem could be solved unambiguously by any self-respecting IBM machine. The solution might or might not require some substantial trade-off between the advantages of specialization and those of more general training, but the solution would be a determinate one in either case. It would also be "empty" in the sense in which Professor Shackle has applied that adjective. The greater the demand among employers for men with the sheer capacity to adapt in the face of change, and the greater the anticipated future scope for adaptive entrepreneurial activity, the greater would be the emphasis on acquisition of flexibility in the computer's solution.

The real tensions in the choices between general and special training, tensions that accompany "creativity" (in Shackle's sense) in decision-making, come not because of expectations of change *per se*, but because of the uncertainties in which those expectations are shrouded. When we look at decisions in such a truly dynamic perspective, the significance of the "inner range" in the potential surprise model, together with the steepness or flatness of the potential surprise curve to each side of that range, takes on particular interest for human investment decisions. *Ipso facto*, the choice of an alternative that would increase a man's adaptability would almost necessarily raise the potential surprise curve over the lower ranges in desiredness of outcomes. Under favorable circumstances it might lower the potential surprise at higher levels (to the right) in desiredness, in which case the individual would have no real problem; the choice of flexibility would win the day on all counts. But where some trade-off in anticipation is entailed, the raising of potential surprise in the lower ranges would go along with raising it in the upper ranges as well; this implies a definite narrowing of the utility or "desiredness" spread in the range of outcomes carrying little or no potential surprise. That narrowing would be accompanied, however paradoxically, by an actual increase in the diversity of particular occupational outcomes included among the individual's anticipations.

Focused Outcomes, Aspirations, and Cautions

The ascendancy contours which Professor Shackle draws as functions of his "desiredness" and "potential surprise" variables constitute a formalization for his decision model of the power of an hypothesized outcome to attract and hold the attention of the decision maker, whether from a positive or a negative slant. The two points of tangency of these contours with the potential surprise curve give us the "primary focus gain" and "primary focus loss" that are at the heart of his analysis of how human minds work under uncertainty. And it is in Professor Shackle's view of the human mind that we must look for an interpretation of the meanings of those focus outcomes, whether the crucial decisions are in business or in educational and career choices.

The place of imagination in this approach goes well beyond the mere idea of subjective experience in the present as an anticipation of possible future outcomes. It is what makes decisions "non-empty" and in some measure "creative." Some years ago Professor Shackle put it this way:*

... a policy for action in the face of ignorance has two distinct rational objectives: one is to allow a man's hopes to rise to the height of his imagination, the other is to give him a feeling of "limited liability" in case the worst should happen.

More recently, Shackle wrote in somewhat the same vein of "treating *uncertainty as a release of imagination*, as a positive *resource*, neutral in itself, which the human spirit can bend to its purpose of anticipatory experience."† The soarings of imagination are not unbounded, however. It is the role of the "potential surprise" variable to constrain the individual's imagination—a "device of the organism for self preservation"‡ against the crash that could follow on wildly unbounded dreams of glory or the utter despair that could incapacitate a man for action in the face of "nightmare possibilities."

The affinity between the concept of focus gain as it emerges in

* G. L. S. Shackle (1955) p. 37.
† G. L. S. Shackle (1961) p. 105.
‡ G. L. S. Shackle (1955) p. 21.

Professor Shackle's work and the notion of "aspirations" in the sociological literature is impressive. So is the implicit relationship between the idea of *focus gains* and that of *goals*, which are essentially focused aspirations tempered by assessment of realistic potentials. It does not matter whether the goals are those of a businessman when he is making strategic decisions with major significance for the future or those of a young man whose perceptions of his purposes and possibilities are coming progressively more sharply into focus. But this is precisely why Shackle's model provides by far the best clue, in my judgment, to the factors that explain educational decisions and their sequential adjustments up to progressively narrowed and specified expectations with the increasing imminence of entry to the labor market. That model is complementary with, not a substitute for, econometric studies of supply responses to changes in the demands for men with one qualification or another.

In sum, if we are to understand the decision-making process and the ways in which one decision follows another, both over calendar time and (a quite different matter) as projected from the decision viewpoint into the future, it is ultimately impossible to avoid facing up to the complex relationships between expectations and goals—including the biases that may slant men's perceptions of the believable or the relatively likely. A tempered optimistic bias in goals (approximated by "focus gains") together with a quiet awareness of possible unfavorable outcomes (focus loss?) may be the best description of how people approach the real decisions of life—including their educational and career decisions, but not those alone. Damped optimistic bias is then functional, in the focus gains, and so is damped pessimistic bias, in the focus losses. This creates problems for applications of decision theory in the quasi-certain mold to critical human investment; it creates problems also for the notion of *standardized* focus gains or losses. To take exception to the standardizing of focus gains and losses is to deprive the model of a theoretically determinate solution, and it sets the gamblers' indifference map afloat. But it leaves the potential surprise and ascendancy concepts relatively unscathed. This, in fact, may be quite enough to generate fresh and testable hypotheses concerning determinants of changes in the tenor and scale of human investment decisions. Such hypotheses must necessarily include determinants of expectations seen as selective and as developmental with the accumulation of experience.

Ruth Mack underlined this necessity indirectly in her comments, characteristically full of insight, on Professor Radner's paper for the session on "New Ideas in Pure Theory" at the meetings of the American Economic Association in 1969.* Remarking that though Radner revised conventional assumptions about sure information, he still left out important ways in which "natural man is in essence, both as consumer and producer, a fundamentally different animal from economic man," she listed five such characteristics. Three of them were: "(a) his perception is not catholic but selective and pre-organized; (b) he is characterized by a developmental and indeed a partially selective level of aspiration; (c) his value schemes are likewise developmental." These three, in her words, "provide the foothold of learning."

Ultimately, Professor Shackle brings us to the creation of history. It does not matter that future history remains unknown. Indeed, "In a moment when the future is being created (by the act of choice of the individual, and those of many other individuals), it makes no sense to ask whether this or that figment concerning that future is true or false."† It does make sense, however, both to view the making of human investment decisions in terms of bounded uncertainties and to re-examine those investments as preparation for the making of other decisions that in turn create the future.

REFERENCES

K. J. Arrow and G. Debreu, 'Existence of an Equilibrium for a Competitive Economy,' *Econometrica*, 22: 265–90. July 1954.

Milton Friedman and L. J. Savage, 'The Expected-Utility Hypothesis and the Measurability of Utility,' *Journal of Political Economy*, 60: 463–74. Dec. 1952.

Albert Gailord Hart, *Anticipations, Uncertainty, and Dynamic Planning*, Chicago, 1940 (2nd ed., published by Augustus M. Kelley, 1951.)

Jack Hirshleifer, 'Investment Decision under Uncertainty; Choice-theoretic Approaches', *Quarterly Journal of Economics*, 79: 509–36, Nov. 1965.

* Ruth Mack (1970) pp. 461–2.
† G. L. S. Shackle (1952) p. 5.

Jack Hirshleifer, 'Investment Decision under Uncertainty: Applications of the State-preference Approach,' *Quarterly Journal of Economics*, 80: 252–77, May 1966.

Ruth P. Mack, Comment on Roy Radner, 'Problems in the Theory of Markets under Uncertainty', *American Economic Review, Papers and Proceedings*, May 1970, pp. 461–2.

H. Markowitz, 'The Utility of Wealth.' *Journal of Political Economy*, 60: 151–8, April 1952.

S. A. Ozga, *Expectations in Economic Theory*, Chicago, Aldine Publishing Co., 1965.

G. L. S. Shackle, *Decision, Order and Time*, Cambridge, Cambridge University Press, 1961.

G. L. S. Shackle, *Expectation in Economics* (2nd ed.), Cambridge, Cambridge University Press, 1952.

G. L. S. Shackle, *Uncertainty in Economics*, Cambridge, Cambridge University Press, 1955.

On Degrees Shackle: or, the Making of Business Decisions

C. F. CARTER

University of Lancaster

The first edition of *Expectation in Economics* was published in 1949. This book, and Professor Shackle's subsequent works, attracted a great deal of attention, in Britain and Europe at least, and a considerable literature grew up round the theory of expectations. But the theory has not been further developed, to any significant extent; it is not at most universities part of the *corpus* of economics which is taught to undergraduate students; it has not been fully tested against the reality of economic behaviour. What has gone wrong?

Professor Shackle's main interest is in a decision which is unique, in the sense that it relates to a particular organisation at a particular point of time, with a pattern of assets or available factors, of technology and of market opportunities which is most unlikely to be replicated anywhere else in the economic system: and in a decision which is crucial, in the sense that, once it is carried out, the pattern is altered, and one can never go back to repeat the 'experiment' and make the decision anew. His criticism of the use of the concept of probability, in such circumstances, is conclusive. Actuarial or statistical probability has no application to an experiment which is non-divisible and non-seriable; and it makes no sense to apply the arithmetical processes which belong to actuarial probability to a purely subjective estimate of probability:

When the question is: What will be the outcome of this non-divisible non-seriable experiment? the decision-maker can make no use of objective, actuarial probability. He is reduced to using *subjective* probability, which has no claims to be knowledge, which cannot offer objective support to such constructions as the mathematical expectation, cannot validly or meaningfully be used to arrive at a *weighted average* outcome, save when this phrase has a purely formal meaning and indicates no more than that an arithmetical procedure of multiplications and additions of the resulting products has been performed. For now we are brought face to face with the core of the matter: When the experiment is a non-divisible one, the hypotheses regarding its outcome are cut-throat *rivals*, denying and excluding each other. What, then, is the sense of *averaging* them?*

The case is, in fact, rather stronger than this. What we are after is to discover how decisions are made; there is only a limited interest in discussing how they *might* be made, if one knows that they are not so made in practice. It is conceivable that people think of the chance of an uncertain event in the terms appropriate to probability: we are all of us familiar with statements of statistical probability:

Smokers of 25 or more cigarettes per day have a one in ten chance of dying in the decade of age 45 to 54

—and it is natural enough to carry over the same manner of speech to describe our feelings about an outcome which does not belong to a statistical series—

I am trying out a new process, and I think there is a fifty–fifty chance that it will come off.

What is not at all plausible, however, is that the mind subconsciously performs the operation of forming a mathematical expectation. It is not simply that, as Professor Shackle points out, the arithmetical operation (applied to exclusive alternatives) is doubtful in logic. The point is that no ordinary business man makes such a calculation consciously (the exception being a few who have learnt a 'statistical' theory of decision-making, and consciously apply it): and it stretches credulity too far to suppose that the human mind is so constructed that the mental arithmetic required is done automatically, without the decision-maker being aware of anything except the outcome.

What we have to do, then, is to find a theory which can be related to the way in which people talk and think about uncertainty, and which contains operations which they can be observed to perform, or

* *Decision, Order and Time in Human Affairs*, Cambridge, Cambridge University Press, 1961, p. 60.

whose existence can be deduced indirectly by observation or experiment. Considered in these terms, Professor Shackle's theory has three elements—

(a) The statements (often vague) which people make about the 'chance', 'likelihood' or 'probability' of an outcome can be related to the surprise which they would feel at the occurrence or non-occurrence of that outcome.

(b) The anticipated pleasure of each desirable outcome is related to the degree of potential surprise which it carries, so as to produce, for each outcome, an intensity of enjoyment-in-anticipation: and similarly for the distress-in-anticipation of each undesirable outcome.

(c) Attention is focussed on the greatest enjoyment and the greatest distress: and alternative plans of action are compared by looking at their focus-gains and focus-losses, the decision-maker being supposed to have psychological characteristics expressible as an indifference map, by means of which it is possible to say whether one combination of focus-gain and focus-loss is better than, worse than or equivalent to another.

As I now see it, the theory has two weaknesses: (a) is wrong, and (b) involves an unobserved and implausible process. It then follows that an alternative to (c) must be found.

My difficulty with (a) is that the concept of 'surprise' cannot, in fact, be related to the way in which people are observed to think about uncertainty. I have made the point before, and Professor Shackle has parried it with his invariable generosity of appreciation, combined with his equally invariable unwillingness to concede an inch of his own views. The difficulty relates to the central set of outcomes which carry zero potential surprise, and it is explored on pp. 87–9 of *Decision, Order and Time*. I contend that, unless the word 'surprise' is to be given a special meaning, outcomes which carry zero potential surprise can have attached to them different (subjective) probabilities: and that consequently the Shackle theory fails to use all the available information about the mental state of the decision-maker.

Suppose that I am told, two days before a General Election, that the Conservatives are judged by an opinion poll to be likely to get 44% of the votes cast, and the Labour party 43%, the rest being Liberals, supporters of other parties, or undecided. I weigh this evidence with any ideas I may have about the bias of opinion polls, last minute changes of allegiance, and so on, and I conclude that the

Conservatives are rather more likely to win than Labour. A Conservative win would be unsurprising. Nevertheless, I would say that a Labour victory also carries zero potential surprise, because I have heeded Cromwell's plea, 'In the bowels of Christ, think it possible you may be mistaken'; and the margin between the Labour Party and victory is less than my subjective assessment of the amount by which I may be wrong. In other words, if a subjectively less probable event has associated with it a high degree of doubt about the correctness of the estimate of probability, the prospect of the occurrence of that event may occasion no surprise.

Professor Shackle, having decided that a Conservative win is more likely, would find it necessary to stretch his imagination to encompass a Labour victory; it would involve 'a snag or an unrealism or an incongruity'. In short, he would be surprised. This seems to me to give a special meaning to the word 'surprise'. Readers of Agatha Christie's novels will remember that Miss Marple had the characteristic of being quite unsurprised at evidence of villainy in apparently highly respectable persons. Her experience of life had shown her that estimates of goodness based on outward appearance are subject to a wide margin of error. In fact, in general, experience decreases surprise. Young brash tycoons, straight from the Business School, make calculations and act on them as though they were certain: older and wiser business men, experienced in the fallibility of evidence and of human judgement, are unsurprised at very wide departures from a calculated outcome, and this may affect the decisions they take.

In other words, outcomes may be unsurprising (in an ordinary, everyday use of that word) because of *second-degree uncertainty*—our lack of confidence in our first-degree judgements of probability. Professor Shackle is using the word 'surprise' in a sense which ignores second-degree uncertainty. My state of belief about the outcome of the election really takes a form like this:

  Conservative vote   41–48%
  Labour vote   40–46%

—and *both* outcomes are unsurprising because the ranges represent a high degree of belief and *overlap*. However, the ranges are different: to describe both outcomes as having zero potential surprise throws away some of the information, which is surely likely to be used in practice.

My second difficulty relates to the formation of focus-outcomes.

What Shackle invites us to believe is that, in reviewing the possible results of a course of action, a decision-maker may find that he focusses his attention on a good, and not excessively surprising, gain, as affording more enjoyment-in-anticipation than either a small unsurprising gain, or a vast but exceedingly surprising gain. This is reasonable enough. However, the theory assumes a mental procedure by which the value of each favourable outcome is combined with its associated potential surprise, and the set of outcomes is then reviewed to arrive at a single focus-gain; that each decision-maker has a personal *ascendancy function*, on which a maximum can be identified. This seems to me to be altogether too precise. The existence of a subconscious process of forming the function and identifying its maximum is no more plausible than the subconscious calculation of a mathematical expectation. Furthermore, it seems to me illegitimate to proceed from the assertion (which is firmly based on observation) that the human mind *simplifies* problems in order to solve them to the assertion that it simplifies this particular problem to a consideration of *two* outcomes, and not one, or three, or four. The latter assertion is *not* based on observation; and it yields results which are contrary to observed behaviour, as can be seen from the chapter on 'Assets to be held for speculative gain' in *Expectation in Economics* (2nd edition, p. 90).

My previous efforts to set out an alternative theory (in *Uncertainty and Business Decisions*, 2nd edition, Liverpool University Press, 1957) were too vague. Let me, therefore, try again—though it is necessary to avoid creating a spurious precision for the sake of getting a tidy theory.

Let us take as the object of interest a business man who has to decide between a number of alternative investments (whether in plant, machinery and buildings, or in financial assets). Each investment has a number (and probably a very large number) of possible outcomes; and an 'outcome' may itself be a set of numbers, representing (for instance) the profit to be expected in the first, second, third, and later years after making the investment. The latter point is worth remembering, because there is no uniquely correct method of summing up the consequences of an investment as a single number.

Introspection suggests that the order in which the problem is simplified is different from that proposed by Professor Shackle. Each set of outcomes is the consequence of a particular set of *surrounding circumstances*; for instance, the rate of inflation, the size of the

The Making of Business Decisions

national income, the trade balance, the technical difficulty of bringing a new process into operation, the availability of high management skill, the price of a commodity. The first step towards making a decision is the heroic one of ignoring nearly all the possible combinations of surrounding circumstances. Some may be ignored because they contain one or more elements regarded as impossible (or occasioning maximum potential surprise)—for instance, a Liberal victory in the next General Election. Others may be ignored because they contain one or more elements which are too difficult or unpleasant to contemplate. An example is the occurrence of worldwide nuclear war during the next five years: this is certainly not impossible, but it is ignored in almost all business decisions. Other combinations of surrounding circumstances will be ignored because they are considered to be below a threshold of possibility (that is to say, barely possible combinations of events will be treated as impossible): or below a threshold of relevance to the particular decision (that is to say, distantly relevant events will be treated as irrelevant): or worthy of rejection on these two grounds taken together.

Attention is focussed, then, on a limited set of possible surrounding circumstances—limited in two ways; first by a restriction of the number of different factors taken into account, and second by a restriction of the number of alternatives or 'values' for each factor. For instance, in making a Stock Exchange investment today I might look at the implications of the present rate of inflation of the general price level, a faster rate and a slower rate—say, 7%, 12% and 4% per annum; I would not solemnly examine all the possibilities, by one per cent intervals, from minus 10% to plus 40%.

I shall describe the members of the remaining set as having attached to them *degrees of uncertainty*. I use this phrase to get away from the implications of the word 'surprise', discussed above, and also to avoid the tendency to think of the probability of events as a partition of the number One between all the possible alternatives. In the course of simplifying the problem, we may have thrown into the discard bin a large number of alternatives, and this introduces a certain ambiguity about what is meant by the subjective probability of those that remain.

Now, of course, the probability of the *exact* occurrence of an event or circumstance is often negligible. If I say 'I think prices will go up 10% next year' I would nevertheless be very surprised if a chosen index of prices went up by *exactly* 10%, when the index is calculated so as to show tenths or hundredths of a point. In fact, a statement that a given circumstance is 'likely' or 'unlikely' usually carries with it an assumption about a *range* of circumstances which will be accepted as equivalent to the one described. The set of circumstances on which attention is focussed must be thought of as defined, where appropriate, in terms of ranges of alternatives or values: so that a statement of the possibility that prices will rise by 10% really means that the rise will be between (say) 9% and 11%. In common speech, these ranges are often left undefined, and this is a source of misunderstanding (for a speaker may have in mind a narrower or a wider range than his hearers). The lack of definition confuses judgements of uncertainty. One person, saying that 'very likely prices will rise by 10%', means that he thinks it likely that the rise will lie between 8% and 12%: while another, saying that 'it is not very likely that prices will rise by 10%' means that he regards it as likely that the price will lie in some range other than 9.5% to 10.5%. The two apparently contradictory statements therefore contain no *necessary* contradiction.

In what follows, however, I ignore this vagueness of our habits of speech. I suppose a decision-maker to have in mind a set of imagined future circumstances, members of the set being defined where necessary by *ranges* in which they may fall. Some members of the set may take the form of *related groups* of circumstances: for instance. 'Conservative victory—no more nationalisation—no curb on dividends' is a related group, and can be treated as though it were a single happening.

Now a *ranking* of the uncertainty of these potential or imagined surrounding circumstances can be observed to be made. In everyday speech, we are constantly ranking things in rough 'uncertainty classes': 'I think that is almost certain', or 'very likely', or 'quite likely', or 'quite possible', or 'possible', or 'just possible'. If these were the only conceivable classes, we could give them numbers from 6 down to 1, and rate Certainty at 7 and Impossibility at 0, so that we would have an ordinal scale from 0 to 7. But it is evidently possible to do better than this, because it will often happen that, given two circumstances A and B rated as (say) 'possible', we shall be able to say that A is more possible than B; in other words, the ordinal scale can have finer subdivisions. But these cannot be indefinitely fine, because it is important to remember second-degree uncertainty—

our lack of assurance about whether our first-degree estimate is right. Consequently I do not think that it makes sense to assume an ability to answer precisely the question 'Is the uncertainty of C closer to that of A or to that of B?' If there were precise answers to such questions, then it would be possible to develop a *cardinal* measure of uncertainty. It might appear that one could have a cardinal measure anyway, because one could find out (in principle, at least) how a person would be prepared to bet on different occurrences. However, the imprecision of judgements of uncertainty implies that the bets would not necessarily be consistent: so it will be best to assume that what we have available is a personal ordinal ranking—like the temperature scale which one could derive by feeling a series of objects, hot, lukewarm, and cool, with one's hands.

Following the gracious habit of the physicists in immortalising their pioneers, I propose that the ranking of uncertainty should be expressed on a scale of degrees Shackle (degrees S). Among the imagined future occurrences which the decision-maker has in mind, some will be alternatives (a Conservative *or* a Labour victory); others can occur together (a Conservative victory *and* old Bert cracking that technical problem). So he has, in effect, a list showing sets of circumstances which *can* occur together; and to each member of each set, he can assign an uncertainty (that is, he can answer questions about the possibility or likelihood of the occurrence). The list has already been drastically simplified, by leaving out a large number of things which could be said to have some possibility and some relevance. It can now be simplified further, by observing that some sets contain several members which have low rankings in degrees Shackle—that is, sets which require the *simultaneous* occurrence of a number of not very likely events.

For instance, suppose that three types of circumstance, A, B and C, can occur simultaneously and are considered relevant, and each can occur in two ways—A_1 and A_2, B_1 and B_2, C_1 and C_2. On a scale of degrees Shackle, with impossibility set at 0 and certainty at 10, let these have uncertainties as follows:

A_1	5	B_1	7	C_1	4
A_2	2	B_2	1	C_2	2

Eliminate $(A_2\ B_2\ C_1)$, $(A_2\ B_2\ C_2)$, $(A_2\ B_1\ C_2)$, and $(A_1\ B_2\ C_2)$ as requiring the simultaneous occurrence of two or more not-very-likely events. Suppose that the decision-maker is considering three alternative lines of action, P, Q, and R—this may already be a simplification of a much larger list of *possible* actions. To simplify the problem, I suppose that the outcomes can be measured by a single money measure. (The possible complications are that the outcomes might require a mutli-dimensional measure, and that the relevant scale might be, not of money, but of utility.) Then the decision-maker has before him a *decision array* of this kind—

Happenings	Ranks of happenings	Outcomes (£000) of—		
		P	Q	R
$A_1 \ B_1 \ C_1$	5, 7, 4	7	10	−3
$A_1 \ B_1 \ C_2$	5, 7, 2	8	−6	−2
$A_1 \ B_2 \ C_1$	5, 1, 4	3	5	8
$A_2 \ B_1 \ C_1$	2, 7, 4	−2	3	−3

In this array, P is unfavourably affected by A_2, and Q by C_2 while R is very favourably affected by B_2. But R produces losses except in a combination of circumstances which looks less probable than the other three. If, therefore, P, Q and R are strictly *alternatives*, R will be rejected; but, if this is not so, perhaps the decision-maker will undertake a little of course R as a 'hedge' against the occurrence of B_2.

Let us now look at P and Q, considered as strictly alternative. Q is better on three lines, but shows a large loss if C_2 turns up. If the maximum tolerable loss is 5, then clearly P must be chosen: the decision-maker will be heard to say 'I'd like to try Q, but I daren't risk it'. Suppose, however, that a much larger loss could be tolerated. It is not, I think, plausible to postulate a subconscious process by which a function is formed out of three rankings and an outcome. What the business man does, when he has got the alternatives down to two (or at any rate, to a small number) between which it is difficult to decide, is to simplify the problem further.

In the particular case taken, Q is superior for three of the sets of happenings, including the one with the highest rankings; so that a decision-maker who is prepared to risk the loss of 6 if C_2 turns up will choose Q. Suppose, however, that the sets of happenings had been reduced to two, with the outcomes shown:

	P	Q
$A_1\ B_1\ C_1$	5, 7, 4	7 −4
$A_1\ B_1\ C_2$	5, 7, 4	−7 4

Here the decision-maker is unable to discern any difference in uncertainty of the circumstances he takes into account, and the outcomes are symmetrical. It is reasonable to suppose that in a case like this the choice will depend on the gambling characteristics of the decision-maker: the man who 'plays safe' will choose Q, while the gambler (provided always that he can risk a loss of 7) will choose P.

The discussion of a particular constructed array is naturally not convincing; the reader may like to try his hand at inserting other numbers, and considering how he would then reach a decision. It is, of course, a condition of the problem that decision-makers have to reach decisions. Often this has to be done in a hurry; but if an event, say (A_1, A_2), is not too far into the future, it may be worth while to wait for it to occur—thus simplifying the problem by replacing an uncertainty by a certainty. This is why (as Shackle has pointed out) decisions may be delayed during the period before some moment of clarification (e.g. a general election).

I believe, however, that the process I have described—which, instead of assuming the existence of a mental process which forms an ascendancy function, relates outcomes to rankings of uncertainties of *selected* relevant events, and then proposes a process of successive simplification (by the discarding of alternatives) until the problem becomes soluble—is much nearer to what really happens than Shackle's original theory. On the day of writing this, I have, as Director of a company, formally endorsed a committee decision about the company's next-generation computer. Watching this decision through its various stages, I note that it has emerged from a state of confusion (due to the great complexity and uncertainty of the issues) by a process of successive simplification. Ignoring some less-likely combinations reduced the possibilities to two ('stay with Honeywell or change to IBM'). Then some relevant future circumstances about which one had no means of guessing were ignored; for if A is relevant, but all its alternatives $A_1, A_2, A_3 \ldots$ are indistinguishably rated as 'perfectly possible', then one may as well leave A out of account. The end-result was that a single remaining circumstance decided the issue. It may turn out not to be the most important factor after all; there is a danger in business decisions that some item which has been discarded will prove to be extremely important.

One cannot be certain, of course, that the process of successive simplification will yield a clear result. It seems to me, however, that this possibility of an irreducible state of indecision is a realistic one. Decisions of great moment have been made by tossing a penny. More typically, the indecision is resolved by a committee vote, the members of the committee making up their own minds by using minor or irrelevant issues. The managing director wants the new factory to be at X because he likes the golf there; one director wants it at Y because he likes to be near London; another prefers Y on the principle that anything proposed by the managing director is likely to be wrong. It is the job of a good manager to devise more subtle ways of assessing the *relevant* issues, in order to avoid the casual making of important decisions.

The theory I have adumbrated above requires, of course, development at the length of a book, rather than a chapter; what I have given is no more than the approach which, I believe, is adopted by decision-makers in many or most practical situations. As set down here, this is a development of what is described as the 'Carter–Egerton' theory in the second edition of *Uncertainty and Business Decisions* (p. 148). In my earlier statement, however, I left rather too much to be decided by the toss of a coin; a greater experience of business decisions leads me to suppose that a stage-by-stage simplification of the issues will very frequently enable the decision-maker to attain a point at which a result 'falls out'. The formal structure of the theory runs like this:

(a) There are alternative courses of action $P, Q, R. \ldots$ The set of such courses is simplified to bring it within the scope of the decision-makers mind, by omitting actions which he finds abhorrent or extraordinary, or by omitting actions which are similar to others on the list, or by dividing the decision into sub-decisions. (For instance, a complex decision may be reducible to a chain of choices of the type 'Do P or not-P').

(b) The outcomes of the courses of action depend on a set of surrounding circumstances about which the decision-maker can have expectations. This set is drastically reduced by—

(i) ignoring circumstances which are thought unlikely;

(ii) ignoring groups of circumstances which could occur together, if several are thought not very likely;

(iii) ignoring possibilities which are difficult or unpleasant to contemplate;

(iv) ignoring circumstances of low relevance to the decision;

(v) ignoring groups of circumstances which could occur together, if some are of low relevance and others not very likely;

(vi) ignoring minor variations in the 'values' of circumstances (i.e. taking into account only gross differences);

(vii) ignoring alternative occurrences if they are indistinguishably at the same rank of uncertainty.

(c) If this reduction still leaves the decision too complex, further circumstances which, occurring together, have a lesser likelihood or relevance will be ignored.

(d) The nature of the ultimate choice will depend on—

(i) the vulnerability of the decision-maker to loss: this may cause him to reject courses of action which, in certain circumstances would ruin him;

(ii) the possibility of 'hedging' by taking more than one course of action;

(iii) in certain cases, the reaction of the decision-maker to a gambling situation.

I would attach considerable importance to the following practical consequences:

(1) One way of deciding things is to wait for some of the uncertainties to resolve themselves: and the tendency to put off difficult decisions can frequently be noted. However, the resolved uncertainties may be replaced by others, so a waiting policy does not always work.

(2) A very large and complex decision, involving anticipation of many circumstances over a long period in the future, requires a heroic degree of simplification. This creates a tension in the mind of the decision-maker (who knows that he is ignoring so many conceivably relevant possibilities): in an extreme case, a very big decision may be indefinitely delayed. The history of the Channel Tunnel scheme provides an example of very long delay, and repeated attempts at reassessment.

(3) The final 'deciding circumstance' may be relatively unimportant; it becomes crucial simply because it emerges at the end of the chain of stages of simplification.

(4) Ignoring a surrounding circumstance does not necessarily imply that it is considered unimportant; it may simply mean that all the

alternatives appear perfectly possible. One reason for this may be lack of confidence in the correctness of a judgement of possibility: and this lack of confidence is more likely to grow with increasing experience than to diminish. Therefore immature decision-makers may try to take into account more factors than mature ones: but this does not mean that they are more often right.

(5) The pressure to reach a conclusion may lead to error, because significant issues have been ignored. This means, paradoxically, that decision-makers who are considered 'good' because they make sensible decisions at an appropriate time are nevertheless almost bound, on occasion, to make wrong decisions: because if they tried to take into account all the matters which would enable them to reach a right decision, they would become so confused that the decision would never be made.

(6) Highly satisfactory outcomes may have to be eliminated because a chance remains (arising from the set of circumstances retained in consideration) of an insupportable loss.

(7) 'Hedging', or spreading of risks, emerges as a natural solution to some classes of difficult decision: whereas in Professor Shackle's theory it is difficult to explain.

While I believe that the approach described can represent an advance in realism and power, as compared with the original Shackle theory, it nevertheless begins from his notable work in shaking established patterns of thought. Therefore, though I am sure Professor Shackle will not accept the correctness of all my contentions, I hope that he will allow me to dedicate this piece to him, in gratitude and appreciation.

On the Theory of Bargaining

A. CODDINGTON

Queen Mary College, University of London

In the context of economics, bargaining may be thought of as the process of communication by means of which the terms of an exchange are established, or fail to be established. It follows immediately from this that if one assumes that economic actors have complete information regarding the circumstances of contemplated trading, and perfect foresight regarding the behaviour of other actors, any process of communication is quite unnecessary; at best it could fulfil some sort of ritual function. Similarly, if the market situation is such that the potential traders have no leeway for agreement on one or another of a range of terms, the question of bargaining does not arise. In that branch of price theory which has been most refined, and articulated with greatest rigour—the theory of perfect competition—any possibility of bargaining is excluded for both these reasons: the market leaves no scope for it; and it would be pointless to postulate communication processes when the actors are assumed to know everything that they need to know.

At the opposite extreme of market forms from perfect competition is the situation of bilateral monopoly. The construction of a theory of price in this situation would seem to demand that attention be paid to the process of bargaining—if such there be—by which a price is established. The phenomenon of isolated exchange occurring in the situation of bilateral monopoly is the paradigm case of bargaining, although scope for such an activity exists in the wider class of market forms which we could call bilateral oligopoly. There could, of course, be bargaining on one side of the market—e.g. between duopolists or between duopsonists—but this is a rather different case, for the duopolists do not trade with each other, nor do the duopsonists: they can therefore continue to trade whether terms are mutually agreed or not. But in the paradigm case of bilateral monopoly, trading can occur only if mutually acceptable terms of trade can be established.

It is clear, then, that in a situation of bilateral monopoly there is, in general, a range of potential agreements which are jointly preferred to the status quo: that is to say, there is *scope* for bargaining; to the extent that complete information or perfect foresight is lacking there is also a *function* for bargaining. Whether bargaining processes actually occur depends partly on institutional arrangements: for example, if there is a practice whereby the seller sets a price and the buyer merely decides how much to buy at that price, the scope for bargaining disappears as long as the traders accept this practice.* And whether the theory of price determination under bilateral monopoly focusses on the bargaining processes which do occur depends on the remainder of the theoretical framework. It is clear that if perfect foresight is assumed, the framework leaves no room for such well-known bargaining tactics as bluffing and brinkmanship; and it is obvious that a framework in which complete information is assumed will necessarily fail to focus on bargaining as a process in which information (and possibly misinformation) is exchanged. This is amply substantiated by the literature on bilateral monopoly, where attempts to construct a theory within the framework of complete information lead to a focus on the structure of a situation, to the exclusion of the processes which may occur within that structure.† In fact, the situation is not quite so clear-cut as that. If we distinguish between a (formal) model and the (informal) discussion which attempts to interpret and justify the assumptions of the model, then it may be said that models of bilateral monopoly have neglected the process of arriving at the terms of exchange although this neglect may be blurred by the appearance—in an inessential way—of ideas about a process of bargaining in the discussion of the model.

These considerations become even more important when we come

* A. L. Bowley, "On Bilateral Monopoly", *Economic Journal*, 38, 1928, pp. 651–59.

† F. Y. Edgeworth, *Mathematical Psychics*, C. Kegan Paul, 1881. A. L. Bowley, *op. cit.* W. J. Fellner, *Competition Among the Few*, Knopf, 1949. L. Foldes, "A Determinate Model of Bilateral Monopoly", *Economica*, 122, 1964, pp. 117–31.

to consider bargaining itself as the process of communication by means of which the terms of an exchange are established in the class of situations of which bilateral monopoly provides the paradigm. In the literature on bargaining, one finds that nearly all existing theories omit to incorporate such processes in the underlying model, and mention them only in the discussion where the model is being interpreted and animated. This is true even in cases where the author may make claims to the contrary.* Of course, there are methodological precedents for this neglect of process: it has been possible to devise static theories depending only on the structure of markets as a first approximation, and then go on to tackle the dynamic behaviour in terms of adjustment processes. For this gambit to work, the static solution must be independent of the path by which it is approached, otherwise structure and processes cannot be separated. Of course, such a separation of theory-formation into stages is an enormous advantage where it works; although my own reading of the literature suggests that it does not work for bargaining processes. This need not imply that it was not worth trying.

The situation as regards a theory of the bargaining process is this: the economic structure of the situation in which the bargaining occurs does not appear sufficient to single out, by the application of the usual micro-economic reasoning, a particular agreement as the outcome of the process. This indeterminacy invites various interpretations: either one can conclude that the explanation of the process is beyond the scope of economics and must be handed over to some other discipline; or one can conclude that the economic theory is merely insufficiently developed, so that its extension and refinement should remove the indeterminacy; or one could even conclude that it is the situation rather than the theory which is somehow inherently indeterminate—that a correct theory of the process is *a priori* impossible.

Another possibility is that the outcome is not really indeterminate even within the traditional framework. For example, in the theories of Foldes and Bishop,† the introduction of considerations involving time preference is claimed to remove the indeterminacy. The postulated decision-making procedures on which these theories rest are

* E.g. J. Pen, "A General Theory of Bargaining", *American Economic Review*, 42, 1952, pp. 24–42.
† Foldes, *op. cit.* R. L. Bishop, "A Zeuthen–Hicks Theory of Bargaining", *Econometrica*, 32, 1964, pp. 410–17.

far from satisfactory: they do not make sense as individual utility-maximizing behaviour. Furthermore, the time-preference aspect of the situation, which is supposed to motivate the bargainers, turns out to be irrelevant, since the decision-rules postulated on the basis of such time-preference lead to an immediate agreement. What we have, then, is really a theory of no-bargaining! Much the same comments as these apply, but with even more force, to the attempts to produce a determinate theory without even postulating a further notion such as time-preference.* This is achieved by making strong assumptions concerning the decision process. These assumptions also are highly unsatisfactory as a theory of individual decision-making, but I will not enter into a discussion of them here,† since it should already be clear that I regard such theories as essentially missing the point.

The chief deficiency of all such theories is that they fail to face up to the *strategic* aspect of the bargaining situation. Why should one bargainer accept any agreement immediately if he thinks that by being intransigent, for example, he could do better? How one bargainer behaves will depend not only on the immediate circumstances but also on how he expects the other to behave, or to respond to his own behaviour; and this dependence is reciprocal. It is this strong and immediate inter-dependence which prevents the situation from being easily subsumed under the calculus of utility-maximization.

The theory which had addressed itself to the strategic aspects of decision-making is the theory of games, and, in the light of what has just been said, it might be thought that this is the appropriate framework in which to construct a theory of bargaining. It turns out, however, that game-theoretic reasoning alone has led only to a reformulation of Edgeworth's conclusion that the outcome is indeterminate within the bounds set by the contract zone.‡ This indeterminacy stems from game theory's exclusive concern with the strategic aspect of the situation—the inextricable interdependence of the actors' choices.

* F. Zeuthen, *Problems of Monopoly and Economic Welfare*, Routledge & Sons, 1930. J. F. Nash, "The Bargaining Problem", *Econometrica*, 18, 1950, pp. 155–62; "Two-person Co-operative Games", *Econometrica*, 21, 1953, pp. 128–40.

† See, however, J. G. Cross, *The Economics of Bargaining*, Basic Books, 1969, ch. II.

‡ J. von Neumann and O. Morgenstern, *Theory of Games and Economic Behaviour*, J. Wiley & Sons, 1964.

Posing the problem in game-theoretic terms, although it does not seem to get us very far, at least allows the question of parametrisation to be raised in a framework in which it has not already been prejudged—lack of parametrisation being the very essence of a game.

What follows from the study of either Edgeworth or game theory is that the indeterminacy of the bargaining process is to be removed by parametrisation of the situation over and above that involved in its economic structure. Parametrisation may be weaker or stronger depending on the assumptions involved: the limiting case of weak parametrisation being the theory of games. The theories referred to previously succeed in removing the indeterminacy of the situation, but only at the expense of introducing parametrisation which is far too strong: which does not even leave room for the essential elements of decisions based on expectations in the face of uncertainty. The problem is, therefore, to find a parametrisation which is strong enough to remove the indeterminacy but not so strong as to exclude the essential components of the situation.

What I am suggesting is that a theory of the bargaining process is to be seen as a theory of decision-making based on expectations in the face of uncertainty. And the existence of uncertainty—in the sense of the absence of perfect foresight—means that expectations will not in general be realised. Since what we are concerned with is a *process*, the bargainers have an opportunity not only to learn about their original expectations, but to formulate and act on the basis of new ones, these in turn being the object of learning and reformulation. A model of the bargaining process explicitly incorporating such features was first devised by John G. Cross.* I do not intend to expound the detailed assumptions of this or similar models,† but rather to discuss their general mode of working and the issues which arise in attempts to interpret them.

Before proceeding to the discussion of this class of models, we must make a distinction between two different types of interdependence. First, there is interdependence which is recognised by the actors, and of which they take account in their decision-making. Second, there is interdependence which arises from the workings of

---

* J. G. Cross, "A Theory of the Bargaining Process", *American Economic Review*, 55, 1965, pp. 67–94.

† See my *Theories of the Bargaining Process*, George Allen & Unwin, 1968, chs. III, VI.

the model, but which is unrecognised by the actors, and therefore not taken into account in their decision-making. It is worth pointing out that, in the theory of games, this distinction does not arise since all the inter-dependence which is present is assumed to be recognised by the actors. The essential characteristic of the class of model under discussion, however, is that the interdependence which is recognised by the actor is less than that which is actually present. The limiting case of this, and the case with which we will be primarily concerned, is where each actor makes decisions in the (false) belief that the other actor makes decisions independently of his own. Such beliefs are rendered false by the inclusion of an adaptive expectations process in the model. The result, then, is that decisions made in the belief of independence, but on the basis of expectations subject to adjustment in the light of experience, lead to a form of inter-dependence unrecognised by the actors themselves.

This scenario has the implication that the bargainers are deluded to a certain extent: that their expectations do not take full account of what is happening. It may be, though, that delusion of some type is an essential component of the process—that without it, there would be immediate agreement rather than bargaining.

Let us now turn to a discussion of the general workings of a bargaining process involving adaptive expectations and an independence assumption of the type just described.

Suppose we start by considering one of the bargainers (bargainer 1). He will come to the bargaining process with certain initial expectations regarding bargainer 2's behaviour. These expectations may well turn out to be mistaken. Bargainer 1 also brings with him a set of preferences among the possible outcomes—where an outcome is thought of as a particular bargain at a particular point in time. Although he may prefer agreements which are, at the time of agreement, more favourable to him, he will also prefer agreements which are arrived at sooner to those arrived at later. He therefore chooses his own plan, both from the point of view of the bargain to which he expects it to lead, and from the point of view of the time at which he expects the agreement to take place. Therefore, with an initial set of expectations about the form of bargainer 2's behaviour, bargainer 1 may weigh up his own alternative possibilities and choose a plan which leads, from his own point of view, to the best outcome attainable in the (conjectured) circumstances. He then puts this initial plan into action and makes his initial demand.

All this applies equally well to bargainer 2. He also has initial expectations regarding bargainer 1's behaviour and in the light of these he has also chosen his initial bargaining plan. The crucial point, however, is that as soon as the bargaining begins, each bargainer is in a position to test his initial expectations regarding the other's behaviour.

Suppose 1 makes his demand in the light of his initial expectations and then 2 makes his demand. Bargainer 1 is then in a position to see exactly whether bargainer 2's behaviour is in accord with his initial expectations. If this is not so, then 1 must revise his expectations about 2's behaviour, and in so doing he must revise his own plan. If it transpired that 1's expectations were fulfilled, then, of course, he

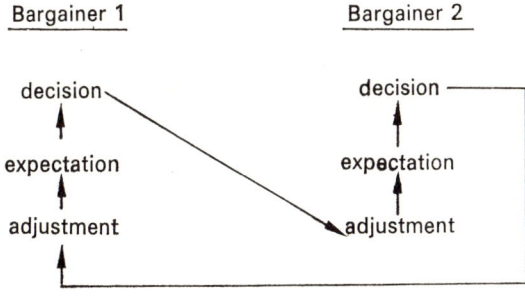

Figure 1

would continue to put into action his initial plan. But if his expectations have been revised, his second demand is made in accordance with the revised plan.

Now, this second demand of bargainer 1 (which could be the same as his first) enables 2 to test his initial expectations and revise them if necessary. If 2's expectations are revised, this leads to a revised plan in the light of which his second demand is made. If his expectations are fulfilled, his second demand is made in the light of his initial plan. And so it goes on.

This process is represented schematically in figure 1. Starting at some arbitrary point in the proceedings we may trace the repercussions of a single decision round one cycle as follows:

(a) In the light of his current expectations, 1 chooses a plan and announces his current demands in accordance with this plan.

(b) This demand is noted by bargainer 2 who uses it to test his

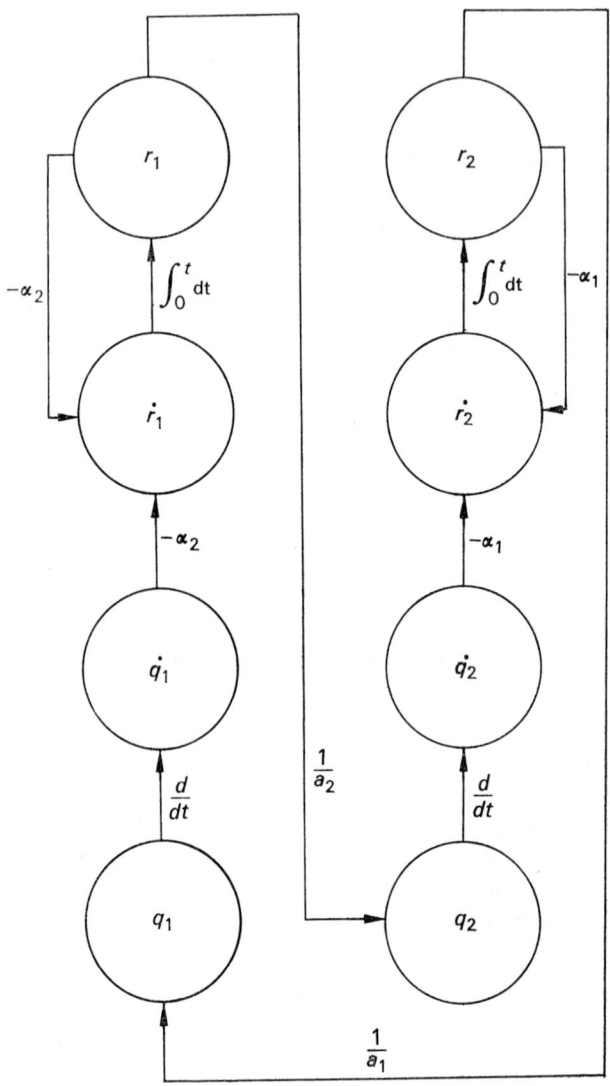

Figure 2

expectations about 1's behaviour. If his expectations are revised, he makes his current demand in the light of a revised plan. Otherwise he makes it in the light of his previously adopted current plan.

(c) 2's demand is noted by 1 and used to test his (1's) expectations regarding 2's behaviour. If his expectations are revised he makes his next demand in the light of his current plan. The dynamics of the model then consist simply of a repetition of these cycles until such time (if any) as agreement is reached.

It can be seen then that the model can be divided into three parts: a theory of decision-making; a theory of expectations and a theory of the adjustment of expectations.

In order to see more clearly the structure of the model, we may employ the kind of diagrammatic representation used in control theory. At the same time, this may shed some light on the kind of structure to be expected of models within the decision/expectation/adjustment framework.* The theory is represented in figure 2. Here the variables are shown enclosed in circles and the relations between the variables are shown along the arrows connecting the circles. The determination of each variable can be understood by considering all the arrows which end on that variable. The variable at the beginning of each arrow is acted upon by the operator along the arrow and the resulting expressions, when summed, may be put equal to the variable at the end of the arrows. In this way the equations of the model may be generated.

The formalisation which is represented by figure 2 can be roughly outlined as follows. Suppose there are a pair of variables q_1, q_2 representing the demands of the two bargainers at any point in time; a fixed amount, M, such that disagreement between the bargainers occurs if $q_1 + q_2 > M$; a pair of linear utility functions representing the preferences of the two bargainers among the possible agreements; a pair of discount rates, a_1 and a_2; a pair of "learning rates" α_1, α_2, which express how sensitively each bargainer revises his expectations in response to the discovery of errors in them; a second pair of variables, r_1, r_2 where, for example, r_2 is 1's expectation of 2's concession rate (i.e. his expectation of $\dot{q}_2$).

It is immediately apparent from the figure that the theory exhibits an overall closed-loop structure: each of the eight variables experiences feedback. A change in any one variable therefore has an

---

* See my *Theories of the Bargaining Process*, ch. III, for a more detailed discussion, especially in relation to Cross's model.

effect on all other variables and eventually on itself. There is no one-way causation in the model as a whole.

As well as the overall loop there are two sub-loops, each one corresponding to the feedback by means of which each bargainer's expectations are adjusted. The arrows corresponding to decision-making, within this scheme, are those connecting r_1 to q_2 and r_2 to q_1. The remaining arrows represent identities.

Let us turn now away from the general workings of this type of model, to look more closely at the reasoning which underlies the decision-making. In order to entertain expectations of 2's behaviour, 1 attributes some sort of decision-rule to 2. On the basis of this attribution he can then arrive at a decision-rule of his own, which could turn out to be the same or different from the one he has attributed to 2. Decision-rules can be referred to as "self-generating" in the first case, and "self-replacing" in the second. The former can be illustrated by the situation in the theory of zero-sum games. If player 1 attributes the maximin rule to player 2, this leads, according to game-theoretic reasoning, to player 1 adopting the maximin rule too. We could say that this rule is self-generating. This example is purely illustrative, for bargaining cannot be seen as a zero-sum game: the bargainers have a mutual interest in reaching *some* agreement even though their interests are opposed regarding *what* agreement they reach.

As an example of a self-replacing rule we may consider the case where 1 attributes to 2 the rule "make concessions as time elapses irrespective of what 1 does" (which is in fact the rule that is attributed in the context of the independence assumption). This leads 1 to adopt a rule which involves him in making, at each moment, a demand which depends on his expectations of 2's future course of demands, these expectations having been influenced because of the adjustment process, by 2's behaviour up to that moment. This generated rule is quite different from the one originally attributed to 2: it certainly fails to satisfy the independence assumption. It is in this sense that we say that the original rule was self-replacing.

In the theory of bargaining processes no self-generating decision rule has yet come to light—the theory has been involved exclusively with decision rules which are self-replacing. Whether this *must* be so is not at present clear.

There is a crucial difference between the logic involved in self-generating and self-replacing decision-rules. There is a finality about self-generating rules which is absent in self-replacing ones. A self-generating rule has the property of reinforcing its own plausibility once it has been hit upon. Suppose decision-rule G is self-generating. Then 1 knows that if 2 adopts G, then he too should adopt it; and this very fact of 1 arriving at rule G lends plausibility to the assumption that 2, who after all is in exactly the same situation as 1, may have arrived at this conclusion. Of course, this "plausibility" has no rigorous basis, but bargainers faced with uncertainty cannot be choosers. Suppose, now, that R is a self-replacing decision-rule. If 1 attributes it to 2, this leads 1 to adopt some other rule, R', say. But then 1 may ask himself whether 2, being in the same situation as himself, has not arrived at rule R' also. If this is so, then of course rule R' is no good for 1 after all, for R' is a rule based on the assumption that 1 follows rule R. The question now arises as to whether rule R' is also a self-replacing rule, for if 1 pursues this line of thought, it leads him to seek a new rule based on the assumption that 2 is following rule R'. If R' is self-replacing, then pursuit of this reasoning leads 1 to the adoption of yet another rule, R''. If self-replacing always generate other self-replacing rules, then there is no limit to the level to which the reasoning can be taken.

The first stage of such a process may be illustrated as follows. Suppose 1 assumes that 2 will simply make concessions as time lapses, and that he himself (1) will be intransigent and maintain his current demand. This leads 1 to make a demand which depends on the rate at which he expects 2 to concede. This demand will change as 1 learns about 2's actual concession behaviour (thus violating his own intentions of intransigence). But if 1 faces the possibility that 2 has arrived at the same understanding of the situation, his problem becomes much harder. It is to find a decision rule based on the assumption that 2 is choosing a demand which is influenced by 1's actual concession behaviour. 1 can no longer use his previous intransigence gambit, for his problem is now to choose the best time-path of demands, allowing for the influence which it will have on 2's sequence of demands. What appears to be happening is that as the reasoning is pursued to the higher level, the direct strategic interdependence which was avoided by the original parametrisation starts to re-emerge.

All the models of the bargaining process with which I am acquainted involve self-replacing decision-rules. They are also of a symmetrical form, in the sense that each bargainer attributes the same rule (R, say) to the other, and each then adopts the same rule as the other (R', say) although it should be noticed that this is not the same rule that he assumes the other is following. Both bargainers are therefore deluded. A possibility which has not been seriously explored* is that of an asymmetrical model, in which only one bargainer is deluded.

There is therefore something uncomfortably open-ended about self-replacing rules: they do not give rise to any assumptions which, once hit upon, would be self-reinforcing. All this, of course, involves a rather abstract veiwpoint. If we take a more concrete view of things, we could appeal to the quite well-established fact that people do bargain. Therefore, they do make decisions in bargaining situations, and are evidently not reduced to puzzled indecision by the possibilities for endless regresses of reasoning. We could appeal, as Herbert Simon does,† to the limited intelligence available for decision-making processes in real organisms, and suppose that each bargainer follows the reasoning up to such a level as he is capable of. This leaves wide open the question of what, in some idealised sense, would constitute 'rational' conduct in a bargaining situation: it avoids the question of whether the concept of individual rationality breaks down, or becomes inapplicable in this context.

Another possibility which has not been examined is where both bargainers are deluded but follow different rules from one another, e.g. 1 adopts R' on the assumption that 2 follows R, and 2 adopts S' on the assumption that 1 follows S (which is different from R).

What seems to be established, then, is not that there is a determinate theory of the bargaining process, but rather that there are various precarious determinacies, each based on a particular parametrisation of the process. These precarious determinacies are to be contrasted with the rigid determinacies of the static models which, as was argued, achieve their results by assuming away the very conditions—lack of information, or the existence of uncertain expectations—which create the need for a bargaining process.

What conclusion can be drawn from our discussion? The situation seems to me to be this. What we have been doing is attempting to subsume a certain kind of behaviour (bargaining) under the categories

---

* Except briefly and unsatisfactorily in my *Theories of the Bargaining Process*, pp. 64–67.

† H. A. Simon, "A Behavioural Model of Rational Choice", *Quarterly Journal of Economics*, 69, 1955, pp. 99–118.

of micro-economics. Of course, in a vacuous sense, any behaviour can be fitted into the standard framework of micro-economics. We may say that at each moment in time, each individual does the best he can in the circumstances as he sees them, and this must work for some suitable interpretation of the "circumstances" of the individual and what constitutes his "advantage" in choosing between alternative courses of action. But to impose this framework is illuminating only to the extent that we can give some substance to the notion of advantage by means of which the "best" course of action is selected, and some plausible account of the way the individual conceives of his circumstances at each moment. The situation is therefore that we do have a conceptual framework into which bargaining processes can be fitted; but it is one which, in this context, is lacking in descriptive capacity and explanatory power. Of course, bargaining processes may also be described and discussed using "everyday" language, rather than the concepts of micro-economics, and it is less than immediately evident what advantage is gained by the adoption of this more specialised set of categories. It may be that some illumination or clarification is produced but that this is so must be established; there is no guarantee that it will.

The foregoing considerations may therefore be seen as comments on the integration of bargaining behaviour into a pre-existing theoretical framework. There are alternative lines of development which have not been considered here: the systematisation of ideas about bargaining arising within everyday language: and such importing *en bloc* into micro-economics of new concepts as, for example, Siegel and Fouraker's* introduction of the notion of "levels of aspiration" into discussions of the bargaining process.

The study of actual bargaining processes may be suggestive but it cannot be decisive in the choice of a conceptualisation of the process. Conceptualisations are not true or false: they are fruitful or sterile; illuminating or pointless. One would not, for example, attempt to test the statement that all human actions have a motive. The idea of an action seems to involve some notion of motive on the part of the performer, although it does appear to make sense to talk of "spontaneous actions" or "reflex actions". But do such things properly constitute human action as we already understand it, or are they better seen as mere bodily movements or as some distinct category

* S. Siegel and L. E. Fouraker, *Bargaining and Group Decision-Making*, McGraw Hill, 1960.

of events ("behaviour" rather than "action")? The conclusion we come to will also depend crucially on whether we allow the possibility of "unconscious motives" for human action: motives which, although unknown to the actor, nevertheless have some explanatory value for his actions and some kind of existence, however shadowy. It is clear that such issues will not be settled by the observation of human action. Neither, however, can they be easily resolved by definitional fiat: for what we wish to know is the relationship between concepts which are already in use—the connections between already-understood (although possibly imprecise) terms, not between terms which (although possibly clearer) are created by stipulative definitions. This latter process does not constitute clarification of our own thought processes; rather it involves the substitution of new and neater problems. Conceptual problems are solved neither by empirical nor definitional means; they are solved by arguments about concepts.

It should be clear by now that I do not think that progress in bargaining theory is precluded by the lack of relevant data, or that severe empirical testing of the existing theories is long overdue.* It is in any case not entirely clear what sort of statements about bargaining would count as "empirical". Most of our discussion has related to such unobservable items as bargainers' expectations, decision-rules etc. Are we to take what a bargainer, on questioning, *claims*, he is doing as a datum? Or are our theories to be given an "as if" interpretation? Are the results of gaming experiments† to be treated as data? Or can we conclude, from the highly artificial nature of such exercises, that descriptions of the resulting behaviour have arguably as much theoretical content as the theories themselves?

In considering candidates for the status of "empirical statement" in this context, we may distinguish between the following items:

(i) A description in "everyday" language and from a third-person viewpoint of what a bargainer did in a particular situation.

(ii) The same as (i), together with an explanation, also in "everyday" terms, and also from a third-person viewpoint.

(iii) A description of the same process as in (i) but from the bargainer's own point of view (i.e. from the first-person viewpoint).

(iv) The same as (iii), together with an account of the mental

* See my *Theories of the Bargaining Process*, Preface.
† For example, those carried out by Siegel and Fouraker, *op. cit.*

processes—the reasoning—underlying the behaviour according to the bargainer himself.

(v) An account of a *stereotyped* bargaining process (embodying those features typified by statements of type (i)) from a third-person point of view.

(vi) The same as (v), together with the explanation.

(vii) The same as (v), but from the bargainer's point of view.

(viii) The same as (vii), but with an account of the bargainer's reasoning.

(ix) The application of economic logic to the explanation in (vi) i.e. its translation out of everyday language into the (possibly more precise) language of micro-economics.

It is this final item that describes the subject matter of the bargaining theory I have been discussing. This theory is concerned with the application of economic logic to a stereotyped process; it gives an essentially third-person account: one which does not stand or fall according to whether the actors involved use, or even understand, the economic categories. The theory is not concerned, therefore, with reproducing the mental processes of the actors; it is concerned rather with providing an account, in the language of micro-economics, of decision processes which would generate a stereotyped form of bargaining behaviour. The exercise does not stop there, however, since the subsequent refinements of the economic logic may enable us to make distinctions which were not possible (or at any rate, were far from clear or obvious) in the everyday account. Does this mean that we have gained some new insight into the process, that we have a firmer grasp on what the process involves? Or does it mean that the formalisation has become over-refined, that we are introducing spurious precision into our picture of the process? These are the sort of questions that immediately start to arise. And again, they are conceptual questions.

Acceptable Risk

ANSELL EGERTON

J. Henry Schroder Wagg & Co. Limited

Senior business executives, boards of directors and similar bodies are sometimes concerned with decisions involving large sums of money simply because the sums are large. Thus an industrial group might have a standing rule that all decisions involving the expenditure of more than £5m. have to be referred to the group board. However, most business men in positions of responsibility spend most of their decision-making time concerned with problems which are difficult to resolve not because the sums are large, but because the answer produced by the arithmetic is not a sufficient guide for action. Uncertainty still remains. Judgement has to be exercised. A risk exists that the decision taken will not produce the hoped-for outcome.

It is not totally unfair to suggest that a good deal of traditional economic theory regards decisions where uncertainty is a factor as being exceptional; and treats as much more typical situations where the outcome of decisions is known for certain and the real problem lies in the mechanics of drawing the marginal cost, marginal revenue and other curves—and finding the answer by an inspection of where the various inter-sections lie. By contrast Professor Shackle, in his view of the economic world, sees uncertainty not as an exceptional factor to be invoked only in a minority of extreme cases, but as something all-pervasive throughout the world of business decisions. Professor Shackle's view is a much closer reflection of what happens in the real world. Almost any decision which is not routine can involve uncertainty. Routine decisions are taken at a fairly low level in the business hierarchy. Entrepreneurs, partners, directors, and others with "top" responsibility spend most of their time dealing with non-routine matters—matters that is where uncertainty might even be regarded as the most common element.

It is natural that when decision-making under uncertainty is regarded in a theoretical framework, much of the discussion is conducted in terms of less and more. Whatever particular meanings are given to words it is assumed that if, in a crude sense, the likelihood of two ventures being successful is equal, the one which, if successful, will produce the larger profit will be preferred. Similarly it tends to be argued that if two ventures are expected to yield the same profit if successful then the less risky one, or the one where the likelihood of success is the greater, will be chosen. This is a perfectly logical approach assuming that in relation to these projects "other things are equal".

This contribution to the symposium is concerned with the impact of these other things on uncertainty-decisions. This paper is not written in any way as a criticism of Professor Shackle's theory. Rather, to try to use wording that Shackle himself would find acceptable, it tries to suggest the various considerations which may affect, for example, the shape of the gambler-indifference map. In more everyday terms, it tries to explore among other things the point that two business men may take exactly the same view of the relative likelihood of success of two propositions, and about the possibility or risk of failure—yet one man may still decide to choose one venture for preference, and the other man select the other.

The easiest way to express this point shortly is to say that business men are concerned in their decision-taking not merely with the less and more elements in an uncertain situation, but also with the quality of the uncertainty. More shortly still, there is an element of acceptability as well as quantity in decisions involving whether to take a risk. Indeed, business men frequently say that such and such a risk (or such and such a proposition in a situation involving uncertainty) is or is not acceptable. Moreover, two people who take the same relative view of two propositions, and who are similar in all respects except the standpoint from which they look at these propositions, may take different decisions because for one of them, one risk is the more acceptable, and for the other business man the other risk is more acceptable.

As so often in this field, it is convenient to begin by going back to Shackle. One of his most basic points right from the start has been that, when faced with the need to take a decision in the face of uncertainty, the business man reduces this uncertainty, not to the equivalent of one certain value, but to a pair of possible results (a focus loss and a focus gain) which, when viewed together, produce a focus outcome—that project with the highest focus outcome being preferred.

The fact that forward estimates are seldom reduced to a single figure can be seen easily enough from the great range of forecasts which are produced not as single figures but as ranges of possible outcomes. Shackle's point is, however, much more than this. He is not saying simply that people have to look at a range of possible results between two outside figures merely because it is impossible mathematically to be more precise: he is saying that business men in fact look at these two "outside" possibilities and weigh one against the other, or, in some sense, hold the two in combination in their mind's eye when determining the attractiveness of a business proposition. That this kind of approach is adopted fairly frequently can perhaps be seen from the way in which phrases such as "downside risk" and "upside potential" have crept into business jargon. From industrialists to stockbrokers it is perfectly normal to hear business men discussing some possible project say, for example, "there is not much downside risk and there is a lot of upside potential".

However, while it seems clear that this approach is at least common—if not even general—it does not necessarily follow that the same importance is attached, in Shackle's terminology, to the focus loss and the focus gain. In particular, it is often likely to be the case that business men, in considering decisions, pay much more attention to the focus loss than the focus gain of the project under consideration. Thus it is said, for example, that a number of major corporations will not adopt investment plans unless the people who put up a particular plan to the board of directors are confident that it will yield at least a minimum return. The minimum is much more important than the maximum. A smaller minimum return (larger focus loss) cannot be made acceptable by virtue of a larger maximum forecast (focus gain).

If this line of thought is pursued, and it is our view that the focus loss attached to a possible project can often be regarded as much more important than the focus gain, a number of possible conclusions emerge. One is that in certain circumstances the preferred venture among a number of business propositions available may be not the one with the most attractive focus outcome (combination of gain and loss) but the one with the most attractive or least unattractive focus loss.

Another possibility is that if firms lay down some sort of criterion of eligibility for new projects, which criterion is defined in terms of focus loss or its equivalent, then may it not be that these firms may wish to undertake all those projects which are eligible? Thus if a board of directors lays down that divisional heads must not bring forward for consideration projects expected to yield less than a 15% return, why should the directors not decide to adopt all those projects which incorporate a minimum forecast of something (anything) above 15%?

There are at least two major and inter-related questions here. One is whether, if a business man is faced with more than one eligible project, he will choose to concentrate on only the most eligible, or whether he will spread his resources in some proportion or another among at least some of the various eligible projects available to him. The second is the question on what scale will he invest, whether his investment is concentrated on the most eligible project or spread more widely.

Both questions are, in fact, related to scale; and the preliminary answer appears to lie in the fact that while a combination of a certain possible gain and a certain possible loss may be attractive, the combination of twice that gain associated with twice that loss may be unattractive. (In a sense the same factors are involved when a punter decides how much to bet on a horse. The fact that the odds available on a particular horse in a particular race decide him to bet on that horse does not imply that he is indifferent to the size of his stake. On the contrary, he will be well aware how much he is prepared to bet.) The prime factor here is that which, in old fashioned terminology, used to be called the diminishing marginal utility of money. If a man starts off with £100, the utility he loses by moving from £100 to £80 might be the same as the utility he gains from moving from £100 to £130. However, if this were so, it would not necessarily follow (and it certainly cannot be necessarily argued on the basis of proportions) that the loss of utility involved in a move from £100 to £60 would be equal to the gain in utility derived from a move from £100 to £160.

Another consideration is probably involved also. It will frequently be true, as Shackle has always argued, that a business man will concentrate on one loss and one gain. It may not necessarily follow, however, that he completely disregards any other outcome. Indeed, it may often be that in looking at an investment decision, the decision-making process may involve two stages. In the first, the business man may look just at the focus outcome and within this framework decide whether or not to go forward with a possible venture. As a second stage he may ask the question "on what scale?"; and here he may be concerned, not merely with the focus outcome—but may also ask the question, what would happen if everything went wrong, short of an Act of God.

These kind of considerations probably explain how the decision "how much" to put into a particular venture is reached; and why, when an entrepreneur is faced with a number of eligible propositions, he does not choose to concentrate only on the most eligible, but will frequently spread his investment among a number of them (from here also the argument can be extended to link up with the "safety first" principles which were elaborated some years ago now by A. D. Roy).

In practice, of course, other limitations also impose themselves on the question of scale. They may well be present even in situations where complete certainty exists. They are, however, certainly more powerful where uncertainty is present. The first is that at any time the resources available to an entrepreneur, a partnership or a company are limited. If the resources that a business wants to use are larger than those it already owns, it has to borrow. The business itself may define those ventures as eligible which are confidently expected to earn a minimum margin over the cost of money. It does not necessarily follow, however, that the lender is prepared to accept the calculations made by the would-be borrower—or at least that he does not accept them totally. Indeed, to some extent it may be impossible for him to do so, because they are not his calculations and because (typically) the lender will be an expert in finance but by no means necessarily in the branch of industry for which the money is wanted to be borrowed. Thus being as it were at one remove, the lender's evaluation of the profit possibilities is likely to be more cautious than that of the business man himself who wants to borrow: hence in turn a business's ability to borrow to finance a project is likely to be exhausted before the point at which the business itself regards the potential loss as outweighing the potential gain.

This element in the situation has another dimension too. In the last resort most businesses are concerned with return on capital—and return on equity capital at that. The more that borrowings increase in relation to equity capital (the owned funds of the owners of the business), the more the outcome of the business becomes "geared up" relative to the equity base. In other words, while in looking at an investment decision in isolation, it seems as if what is relevant is, for example, the relation between the minimum expected profit (or focus loss) to the cost of money, the ultimate consideration may be this minimum expectation related to the equity capital base. Here again, this consideration will impose a limit—and this limit is likely to occur before that which would have been imposed if only the direct focus loss–cost of money relationship were being considered.

Some might say that this argument has simply been stating that the supply of capital in respect of a venture with an uncertain outcome is not infinitely elastic. This is true. Moreover, putting it this way may incidentally add as a reminder that what in a broad sense might be called the elasticity of supply of other factors as well is not infinite. To some extent this inelasticity may be imposed from the outside. Factors of production may be unavailable; they may be available only after a time lag; they may be available only in limited quantities; or they may be available in increased quantities only at rising prices. Other inelasticities may arise, as it were, inside the business, or in relation to the venture itself as a decision is contemplated to consider an increase in scale. Operation on a larger scale than before may, of itself, produce fresh uncertainties. It can possibly involve the need to change the corporate structure of a firm—from single ownership to a partnership; from partnership to a private company; or from private to public company. This kind of consideration, and the uncertain consequences which may be thought possibly to lie in such a change, may again be sufficient at the margin to bring about a decision not to expand even though the direct arithmetic would itself have led to a decision to increase the scale.

One of the main features likely to be in the minds of business men when faced with this type of uncertainty is that, if the decision turns out to be wrong, it may be difficult to reverse. The question of reversibility is extremely important. It is relevant not merely to what might be described as general considerations like changing the corporate structure of a firm. It can also be relevant to a whole range of more technical considerations. These may perhaps be described by suggesting that the more specific to one particular venture is the physical investment required for that venture, the more satisfied the business will have to be that the venture is likely to be successful.

To put this another way, a business man, when considering the finance required to support an uncertain venture, will be concerned with the liquidity of that venture—or, more precisely, with the extent to which the capital which would be employed in that venture could still be regarded as part of his liquid capital. To look at this yet another way: a business may decide to undertake a particular project; that project may even be successful; even so, the business may wish to abandon that project because, in the time that has elapsed since the decision to start the project was taken, a new possibility offering an even more attractive focus outcome may have presented itself. (Similarly there will always be the possibility of a change in circumstances of a kind to cause a revision in expectations, which makes a venture which initially and correctly appeared attractive, now seem likely to lead to a loss, or at least to an unacceptable level of profit, if persevered with.)

It may be worth also emphasising at this point that to a large extent the chief uncertainties and changes in uncertainty with which a business is faced are likely to be little related to factors under the control of the business itself. It would be quite wrong to imply that important business uncertainty must be a reflection of the incompetence, lack of knowledge, or other failure on the part of an enterprise.

The real uncertainties are external. They come partly on the technical side and arise through the process of innovation. Businesses cannot be expected necessarily to be the sole or even the chief innovators in their own line of business, Moreover innovations which affect the expectation of a firm may well be those which have arisen in another industry in which they are not technically expert, but whose development may influence the pattern of demand facing the firm. Partly too the most important uncertainties and the most significant changes in expectations are brought about by political decisions. These are, as it were, simply imposed on a business. All it can do is try to be continually in a posture that will enable it to react as quickly as possible to these political changes and their impact—few specific political decisions being precisely foreseeable, but it being well enough known that a continual stream of these decisions, possibly with an impact on the firm, is much more likely than not to occur.

On the one hand this inevitable situation reinforces the need mentioned earlier for business to be concerned with the reversibility and liquidity of capital employed. On the other hand, since these factors can well impose a cost—and businesses simply cannot afford to ignore profit opportunities because they involve an element of illiquidity—they also mean that in certain circumstances entrepreneurs will have to guess what a political change is going to be and what it will mean to a decision of theirs, taking the risk that, if they guess wrong, a loss may follow.

This leads back to a point raised directly with Shackle some years ago, by C. F. Carter. Carter was looking at Shackle's concept of potential surprise and raised the question whether it was sufficient to use a concept that was essentially a negative one; and wondered whether some positive concept might not also be needed. Thus, Carter suggested, might it not be possible that the occurrence of two mutually exclusive events might both be associated with zero potential surprise—but that nevertheless one event might be regarded as positively more likely than the other? Shackle, for his part, never seemed to be quite clear about whether this was a real difference of opinion or just a difference in the use of words.

Whichever it is, an important point does seem to be involved here. Thus, to take a concrete example, a British business man might well have stated that he would not be in the least surprised whether or not Britain joined the Common Market, but that personally he thought Britain would (or would not). This statement does seem to mean something—and also it is a statement that could imply a possible decision, e.g. that if the business man had to take a decision (and could not postpone it) and that the result of the decision he took would be affected by British entry or not, that he would choose a decision from which the profit would be maximised if Britain did join (or did not).

This problem of the relationship between zero potential surprise and positive likelihood can be put forward in another way. It could be argued that it would not be sufficiently attractive for a business man to undertake a venture if the circumstances associated with the success of that venture were merely—even if totally—unsurprising. May he not possitively have to believe that the circumstances are likely to happen—or, leaving the circumstances out of it, may he not want to feel some positive association between the focus outcome and a positive decision to go ahead with the venture?

It certainly seems to be true that business men do look at projects, do say that they look very exciting, but then turn them down because they are not sufficiently sure, in a positive sense, that they are likely to come off. It may not be putting the matter too strongly to say that an entrepreneur could regard a certain outcome as being totally unsurprising, because he was completely ignorant about the surrounding circumstances—and hence because, in a sense, no outcome would surprise him. Clearly, this is no basis for a positive investment decision. In some respect or another the business has to be positively satisfied that an acceptable return, or better, is likely to be achieved.

Presumably a lack of enough confidence could be associated with a number of different kinds of factors. One, as mentioned already, might be an insufficient feeling that the situation surrounding the venture was likely to be favourable to its success. Another might be a lack of positive confidence that a new piece of technology would work; or that an entrepreneur felt insufficiently at home with the technology, cost structure and so on, in a new field of business. Again, an entrepreneur might not be confident enough about the business capabilities of possible new colleagues—even though he would not be in the least surprised if they turned out to be perfectly competent.

However, a board of directors might turn down a piece of business even though they were satisfied that it was likely to yield an acceptable return, even taking the associated elements of uncertainty into account, for quite another type of reason. Business men do say something like this: "this looks a very attractive proposition, but it really is not our kind of business". All kinds of restrictions of a totally non-mathematical kind do cause arithmetically attractive propositions to be declined.

These restrictions are sometimes self-imposed. For example, the publisher of a serious newspaper may just not be interested in publishing a popular paper and hence reject the opportunity of buying one, even though he had the cash resources available, and even though he was confident that, at the purhcase price, he would be likely to make a larger profit than the margin which he was already making on the serious paper—and which he found acceptable. Perhaps, more often than is realised, businesses which regard themselves as aiming to maximise their profits normally in every other respect do deliberately restrict the areas in which they look for new profit opportunities because they deliberately regard themselves as being involved in a particular industry, in a particular geographical area, or otherwise as working within a defined framework. As already mentioned, however, this limitation, where it exists, is self-imposed. The opposite of this limitation applies, for example, in the case of what nowadays tends to be called a conglomerate.

Other limitations, however, are imposed on businesses by nature of the kind of undertaking that they are. Restrictions may be legal or they may simply be unwritten—and be regarded as nonetheless binding for that. One example of legal restrictions applies in most countries in the case of trustees. Normally—though special exemptions can perhaps be arranged—trustees are limited in the range and type of security in which they are entitled to invest the moneys which they hold in trust. Thus, however attractive a proposition put to a trustee and however confident he may be personally that an investment in that project would be thoroughly profitable and sensible, yet as a trustee, he cannot make that investment with the trust funds in his care if it falls outside the permitted limits.

Again, banks are one class of institution which in some countries by custom, in others by law, are restricted in the ways in which their money is invested or lent. A crucial factor, so far as banks are concerned, is that to a large extent the funds they have at their disposal are deposits. Deposits are placed with banks for safe keeping and it is clearly not the function of an institution which has funds placed with it for safety to place them at risk.

Looking at both trustees and banks, it is perhaps convenient to view their investment position in Shackle's terminology. Whatever may be the focus gain attached to any project put before a trustee or a bank, it is extremely doubtful whether that project could be entertained if the focus loss was, in fact, a loss rather than a smaller positive return. More than this, trusts and banks may be two classes of business where it is not sufficient to look simply at the focus loss, but where the prudent man has to go further and ask what is the worse that could happen if everything went wrong short of the kind of Act of God which, if it were taken into consideration, would inhibit any positive business decision.

It is, of course, possible to argue that institutions like banks and trust companies are in a special situation and that they—or other specified institutions—may in fact be in business to avoid risk. On this basis it could be said not merely that they were disqualified from looking at any investment proposition which had a positive focus loss, but that their situation, as compared to the ordinary run of businesses, is so peculiar that it is not really possible to construct for them "gambler indifference maps" at all. Whether it is concluded at the extremity of the argument either that these peculiar kinds of businesses should be excluded from any discussion of situations involving uncertainty and risk because recognisable gambler indifference maps cannot be drawn for them, or whether it is concluded that while peculiar "gambler indifference maps" can be constructed, many kinds of venture would be ineligible to have their focus outcomes plotted on the maps, does not seem to matter (and, indeed, to push the argument to either extremity really does seem at least dangerously close to absurdity). The general point being made remains. This is that whatever the arithmetical attractions; whatever the degree of confidence in the likelihood of success; and however much the venture may seem to offer a higher focus outcome than its competitors, it may still be turned down by a board of directors on the ground that "it is not our kind of business". This is, in the last resort, a basic reason why various kinds of business tend to be done by particular kinds of firms.

Moreover, the point may be worth emphasising, because it is sometimes neglected in the theoretical work that has been done in this field, that the decisions which are open for a business man or a board of directors to take are confined by their outside responsibilities, obligations, or stated objectives. Few business men in fact are free, unless they are operating purely on their own account, to choose unfettered the ventures which they will support, purely on the basis of the focus outcome of the venture in front of them and regardless on the one hand of the characteristics of the venture and on the other hand of their legal, written, moral or unwritten obligation to depositors, debenture holders, shareholders—or other classes of people or interest, not forgetting employees and consumers.

This point touches on one which has frequently come up in a different way in the context of reports on the banking and financial system, the capital market, and the supply of funds for smaller businesses. It is perfectly possible that in conditions of uncertainty when the risks that financial undertakings can accept (for legal, moral or whatever reasons) differ, that the result of these different views of acceptable risk may leave a gap: that certain sorts of ventures may fail to attract support because they involve a kind of risk which is not regarded as acceptable by a sufficient number of personal or corporate lenders and investors. It is this kind of situation which has led, in a number of countries, to the establishment of special institutions, sometimes in the public sector, to fill this gap. There is nothing objectionable about the creation of such businesses provided that the motive for so doing is kept clear and provided that one effect is not to make risks appear acceptable which, on any rational, economic ground would be regarded as unacceptable.

Related to this point is another factor which can be of considerable practical importance. The activities which some firms can undertake—and this is particularly true in the financial field—can be limited because it is their function to act as agents rather than principals. They may be in a position to evaluate risks; to be more likely than others to make a correct estimate of the outcome of a certain venture; and so on. Nevertheless, as agents they may not be in a position to sponsor this venture unless a principal retains them to act. There can be situations where, though there may even be a general acceptance that a certain venture, investment or other undertaking, ought to be pursued, no-one is in a position to act as principal and start the process on its way. It is equally arguable here that it might be desirable to create an institution which would have all the expertise of agents in this field but would be entitled to act as a principal. Again, the need to be clear about motives is important. Without in the least implying that one motive is better than the other, it is particularly necessary to keep separate the economic factors from any political or social factor that may be operating in these circumstances.

The object of this paper so far has been to look at some of the more important factors which may influence actual decisions taken under conditions of uncertainty. It has been no part of the paper's purpose to imply that theory has suggested that only the arithmetic counts, or that business men operate partly in a kind of mathematical vacuum. Rather, it has been to suggest how the impact of surrounding factors, some of which might not at first glance appear relevant to the subject of uncertainty, interact with the arithmetic to produce decisions—and sometimes decisions which might themselves be deemed surprising if only the arithmetic is taken into account.

The argument has followed the Shackle belief that where important business decisions are concerned, uncertainty or risk is more likely to be present than absent. Therefore, it should perhaps be stated that while uncertainty is thought likely to exist and to be a normal feature of decision taking, it has not been suggested that uncertainty is inevitable.

Some business decisions can be taken where the element of risk or uncertainty is so small that it can, for all practical purposes, be ignored. Thus, major investment decisions can be taken under the unconditional guarantee of a Government contract which includes specified cost-price features. Again, an investment may be undertaken to support a technical innovation, far ahead of its time, which is adequately protected by patent. In these, and a number of other circumstances, there is quite a sufficient degree of certainty that at least an acceptable margin is going to be earned for a sufficient length of time for the elements of uncertainty (at least at the time the decision is taken) really to be quite unimportant. Indeed, anyone who wanted to argue that uncertainty was a less pervasive influence in business decisions than is accepted here, could well turn the argument on its head and say that uncertainty only becomes relevant when the certain facts of the situation are not enough to guarantee that at least an acceptable return will be achieved.

This presentation again implies that business men are frequently much more concerned with focus loss than with focus gain—or that what might seem a disproportionately large focus gain has to be offered by a possible venture if the prospect of this gain is to outweigh the possibility of a loss, and hence if the focus outcome as a whole is to have a chance of being attractive enough to lead to a positive decision to go ahead with the project. It is, in fact, difficult to over-emphasise the extent to which, in looking at possible investments, business men are inclined to be particularly concerned with the minimum expected return. Indeed, except for equity investors in ordinary shares, many business men would probably refuse to consider further any potential investment which had associated with it a positive focus loss. It may or may not be logical but, in some way or another business men do appear to take the view that the capital gains which may accrue from profits on income account are, as it were, bonuses which should not be included in estimating the attractiveness of the revenue likely to accrue from a project, whereas they regard as part of the primary loss itself, any prospect that a revenue deficit may lead to a capital loss.

The acceptability of varying levels of focus loss has already been discussed in terms of the legal or other situation in which a business is placed, including both the ultimate relationship between outcome and the owner's own equity capital, and in relation to the varying responsibilities which the managers of a business may have externally—in relation for example to depositors, other creditors, and so forth. This still leaves the question of how a manager, for example, fixes on the figure which he then quotes as the focus loss (or focus gain)—the lower extreme of the range of outcomes which he regards as sufficiently possible to have to be kept in mind. This question relates not to the size of the focus loss, but to what must presumably be called the possibility of the possibility which must be taken into consideration.

One practical criterion can be suggested. When a man is asked by his superior in the business what is the least profitable outcome he expects, the answer the man gives is perhaps most likely of all to be dictated by the fact that his career prospects in this field will largely depend on his being right in his forward estimate. Therefore, he may well himself suffer if, in fact, he gives a focus loss forecast which turns out in the event to be more favourable than the actual outcome—provided that no changes have taken place since his forecast, which he could not have foreseen and which reasonably could be held to have invalidated his forecast. Equally, the man may suffer if he consistently forecasts focus losses which prove to be way below the actual outcome—particularly if, as a result of his forecast, a decision is taken not to proceed with a project; that project is undertaken by a rival firm, and proves to yield a thoroughly acceptable return. If this argument seems a trifle circular, it is because in one important respect the success of a business man consists simply in being right in his forecasts when he has to guess (on whatever informed a basis) because he is still faced with a degree of uncertainty.

In one respect, however, the situation facing an individual business man or a body of directors in a decision-making session collectively is not as difficult as this may make it seem. This is because while it is convenient to make an artificial simplification that a decision is something taken at a point of time, the actual decision-making process is, in fact, something which is much more frequently continuous, and takes place over a period.

So far as decision-taking goes, businesses do not typically spend long periods in a state of inactivity, taking decisions at infrequent intervals and then, as it were, instantaneously. The train of events which leads up to a decision to go ahead with a significant investment is much more likely to be long. It can often be difficult to see at which point a decision—or the crucial or irrevocable point in the decision—was reached. Most businesses, except when they are constrained by total illiquidity (or their incompetence), are fairly continually searching for ways in which they can improve their profitability. While profits can be increased, to some extent, by the successful search for greater efficiency in a technical cost-cutting sense, or their revenues improved by better selling, most major changes in profitability are likely to arise as a result of a successful new investment.

In the early stages of the decision that leads to this investment, the degree of uncertainty is unimportant because, at that stage, no capital will have been allotted to it, even by implication. The only costs involved will probably have been the time, salaries and other expenses of one or two people. The pursuit of this investment possibility can therefore, in this first stage, continue without difficulty, so long as there still seems a possibility that it will turn out to be profitable and provided that the firm has not also found too large a number of other schemes worth pursuing—in which case, the least promising will have to be discarded, not for any reason necessarily concerned with the uncertainty element, but simply because in the last resort, resources are scarce. It is not sensible to pursue more than a certain number of possible new projects at the same time.

Assuming, however, that a possible investment continues to be investigated beyond the early stage, then, on the one hand, the costs involved will begin to mount and, on the other hand, the area of uncertainty should gradually be reduced. In a sense the process of continuing towards a decision is likely to be pursued as long as the cost involved in the continuation is more than balanced by the narrowing of uncertainty—provided that the area bounded by this uncertainty continues to involve a minimum expectation which is above the level of acceptable return.

By contrast, a potential investment will presumably be abandoned if and when the expenditure of further money does not succeed in reducing the amount of uncertainty involved with the scheme or if, as the result of greater knowledge, it becomes unlikely that an acceptable return would accrue if the investment were actually made.

Thus the critical point in the decision-making process may come (everything having gone well so far) when it is felt that uncertainty

Acceptable Risk

has reached an irreducible minimum. If the range of uncertainty that remains then is acceptable, and if the lowest level of return kept in consideration is still attractive, then it is likely to be agreed to go ahead and undertake the project itself.

Inevitably, this is both less precise and more complicated a picture of the process of taking decisions under conditions of uncertainty than is—or to some extent can be—presented in a theoretical form, particularly if that form is some kind of mathematical model. To say that reality can be less precise than a model is not in the least to criticise the model. It is as well, however, to remember that reality is likely to be more complicated. Moreover, if business decisions could always be reduced to equations or other formulations which could be programmed on to a computer, then business would be a very much less interesting occupation that it is in fact.

Expectations, Uncertainty and the Term Structure of Interest Rates

J. L. FORD and J. C. DODDS

University of Sheffield

The great difficulty in the social sciences ... of applying scientific method, is that we have not yet established an agreed standard for the disproof of an hypothesis. Without the possibility of controlled experiment, we have to rely on interpretation of evidence, and interpretation involves judgement; we can never get a knock-down answer.

JOAN ROBINSON

1

There are at least three competing "theories" to explain the term structure of interest rates, namely: (1) the traditional, expectations, theory; (2) the liquidity preference–liquidity/risk premium theory; and (3) the relatively new theory advanced by Malkiel (1). Some writers might include as a fourth, distinct theory, "the market segmentation hypothesis"; or as others, such as Malkiel ((1), p. 26), might call it "the hedging-pressure theory" or "the institutional theory". The chief advocate of this theory is Culbertson ((3), (4)).*

Despite the lengthy protestations against the traditional, expectational, theory in favour of the institutional theory by Culbertson, that theory does not appear to have gained any significant measure of support. It is in effect a theory which extends risk-aversion to its

---

* Although he should not be regarded as the originator of the theory: for without performing detailed historical research on the origin of the theory, we can find it, for example, in the work of Sir Ralph Hawtrey (5), many years before Culbertson wrote, as Kessel ((41), p. 11) for example, has pointed out.

limit in the market, and we could regard it as a kind of extreme version of (2). The theory, in a nutshell (running the risk of oversimplifying) asserts that the aim of participants in the market is to match the time-dimensions of their assets with the time-dimensions of their liabilities. *Ceteris paribus*, if there are several different kinds of (major) institutions in the market, that is, each having its own time-horizon, then the theory suggests that the markets for securities of given life will essentially be segregated: securities will not be (effective) substitutes for one another. In equilibrium, supply and demand in each market will determine each security yield: so that, *ceteris paribus*, it is the relative supplies of the various securities which determine the structure of yields; expectations have no part in influencing that structure. The tests performed by Culbertson to substantiate this viewpoint about the determination of the term structure are open to doubt, and rely mainly on the production of (invalid) negative evidence in support of the theory, evidence which to his mind destroys the main theory in the field, namely, the expectational theory. But it has even been contended by Michaelson (56), for example, that the "evidence" Culbertson has assembled is favourable to the traditional theory, not to the institutional theory. One of the most thorough tests of the importance of the relative supplies of "debt instruments" on the term structure, that by Modigliani and Sutch (55), casts doubt on the importance of these supplies in accounting for the term-structure.

In this paper we do not consider this theory: although it cannot be dismissed until more empirical work has been done on it. At the moment, we do not have any adequate data to enable us to embark on that task. Neither have we offered any theoretical or empirical observations on theory (2). This was not because we believe that that theory has nothing to offer: Professor Shackle for one, for example, appears implicitly to accept its fundamental ideas (see (21) Chapter X). For, despite the immense theoretical and empirical difficulties associated with attaching a precise meaning, and measure, to liquidity premiums themselves, the substantial work of, for example, Kessel (41) has come out in favour of the notions embodied in the theory. We must leave discussion of theory (2) to another occasion.

In this essay then we have chosen to give some consideration to theories (1) and (3). The one is perhaps "the" theory of the term structure, while the other is a newer theory, but it is a theory that contains within it the essentials of the traditional theory. In discussing these theories at the theoretical level we have partly "surveyed" (necessarily, we feel) existing ideas but we have also introduced some new slants and ideas; whilst at the empirical level all of the results reported here are new ones, in one respect or another. The contents of the paper are organised as follows: Section 2 contains some comments on the traditional theory, and the empirical testing of it. Partly because analysis of that theory exists throughout the literature and partly because of limitations on space, this is a relatively small section; Section 3 sets out and comments briefly on the Meiselman hypothesis related to theory (1), and presents some of the empirical results we have obtained on it for the U.K. and for Italy; Section 4 attempts a summary of the Malkiel theory, without too much of a critique of it, and it contains empirical results from testing Malkiel's ideas on the data we have for the U.K. and Italy; Section 5 attempts to summarise some of the broad conclusions that emerge from the paper.

2

The expectational theory of the term structure of interest rates is often labelled the Hicks–Lutz theory. For simplicity we shall frequently refer to the theory in that way. But in some respects it is not correct to suggest that 'the expectational theory' and 'the Hicks–Lutz theory' are synonymous. Two main reasons for this viewpoint are these: (a) the Hicks and Lutz approaches themselves should not be grouped together: for the Hicks ((6), Chapter XI) and the Lutz ((7) and also (8)) assessment of expected rates of interest are different, and the Hicks theory becomes eventually the liquidity preference/risk premium theory of the term structure;* (b) the essential ideas conveyed in the theory can be found, as can the basic Lutz formula epitomising his view of the expectational theory, in the work of Irving Fisher (9) and of Keynes (10).

But for our purposes there is no necessity to follow up these points; rather we acknowledge that the theory exists, and that it encompasses an accepted body of doctrine. The basic assumptions of the Hicks–Lutz theory are quantitatively very small but qualitatively extremely powerful. In the words of Lutz himself:

* The view (a) has been expressed by, amongst others, Luckett (11) and Ford (2).

In our approach to the problem of the relation between long and short-term rates, we shall start out, . . ., by making three assumptions: (1) everybody concerned [in the financial asset market] knows what the future short-term rates will be, i.e., there is accurate forecasting in the market; (2) there are no costs of investment, either for lenders or for borrowers; (3) there is complete shiftability for lenders as well as for borrowers [i.e., between the various assets in the maturity spectrum] . . . ((7), pp. 499–500).

Although these assumptions are removed *seriatim* by Lutz the possibility always remains that the term structure can still be influenced by expectational factors. The emphasis throughout is naturally on those factors; and the implications of the expectational approach are naturally drawn-out on the supposition that *effectively* the assumptions of the model are upheld.

The crucial ideas underlying the expectational theory of the term structure follow from the fact that these assumptions are sufficient to equalise *the expected holding-period return* from investment in any type of combination of assets. Thus, if we have an investor with a holding or investment period of one unit length, his return from his investments over that period will be the same regardless of whether, for example, he places his resources in an asset of one unit length to maturity or one (or several) which has (have) longer to go before it (they) is (are) redeemed.

The reason for this equalisation of holding-period returns can be, shown in several ways. We need not say too much about it since it has been adequately covered elsewhere.* However, an alternative and simple way of seeing why equalisation must materialise is to recall that all investors are confronted by the same information in the market, and so we can study the market (meaningfully) as a market. We can then apply portfolio theory† in the simplest possible way under the assumption of rational economic behaviour by the market to discover that *unless* all combinations of investment for a given holding period do produce the same (expected) holding period return then the market will not hold all the securities that are available, or placed, on the market. The essential point is that under the assumptions made here (for example, no risk/uncertainty attached to investment) the only variable that influences the investment behaviour of

---

* See, for example, Malkiel (1), for a good explanation of the equalisation process.

† Of the kind introduced by Markowitz (12), (13), and developed by, amongst others, Tobin (14), (15) and Sharpe (25).

the market is the expected return from any period of investing it might be contemplating. Any individual will naturally be led to select that asset (should there be just one such asset) which promises the highest expected return: the latter will, in effect, be the (percentage) holding-period return from his wealth; here we have the classic Bernoullian situation.* An asset can (will) only be *held* if it gives the promise of the same return in the future as any other asset.†

From the portfolio approach, *ceteris paribus*, it is also easily demonstrated that, in the given circumstances: the yields on the available financial assets are independent of their supplies; therefore making relative asset-yields independent of the relative supplies of the given assets; it is impossible to deduce, in equilibrium, how wealth will be apportioned among the assets held in the (optimum) portfolio of an individual investor, or of the market.

As with any piece of theory so with the Hicks–Lutz theory: alter its assumptions *individually* and there is every likelihood that its basic notion, the equalisation of expected holding-period returns, will be destroyed or require amendment. Although there is always the possibility that if its assumptions are adjusted, to more "realistic" (whatever meaning we might attach to the latter) ones, *collectively*, the fundamental notion of the theory will not be rescinded, remaining effectively as it was when developed in the confines of a supposedly "simple" model.‡ Unfortunately, we have not enough space to develop these lines of argument fully in respect of the Hicks-Lutz theory in this particular essay. But we may note, for example, that altering Lutzian assumption (1) by introducing "risk"§ into the model, and utilising a simple portfolio model based upon the expected utility hypothesis of Von Neumann and Morgenstern (23)¶ together with the newly introduced Hicksian "marginal advantage curve" ((17), Essay 6)‖ of investment, it can be demonstrated that

* On this see, for example, Hicks (17), Essay 6; Champernowne (18), Chapter 2; and Borch (19), Chapters III, IV and VI.

† Johnson (16), Introduction, has also invoked this idea as a rationale for the equality of holding-period returns.

‡ It is well known that Friedman (20), Part 1, for example, has always maintained that it is not appropriate, or valid, to evaluate a theory by tests, of what we might call a theoretical intuitive–empirical nature, of its assumptions, for this reason.

§ On the question of risk see, for example, J. Tobin (14), (15), and for a critique of work on this topic see, for example, K. J. Arrow (26), especially pp. 30–36.

¶ See also, for example, Friedman and Savage (24); Markowitz (13).

‖ The essential idea behind marginal advantage is contained in Hicks's classic essay "A Suggestion for Simplifying the Theory of Money", *Economica*, 1935

expected holding-period returns need not be equal. It can also be shown, provided we have the conditions for consistent aggregation of investors' demand functions, that the yield-structure depends upon the relative supplies of the given financial assets; further, it is possible to deduce how investors will divide their wealth amongst the available assets.

However, given the assumptions of the Hicks–Lutz theory, or more "realistic" assumptions concerning risk and, say, transaction costs which cancel out and produce *in toto* the same result as the traditional theory, we have the central proposition that expected holding-period returns from any feasible investment strategy will be identical. Given this equalisation theorem, as we might label it, we can set-out this formula:

$$(1+R_{nt})^n = (1+R_{1t})(1+{}_{t+1}r_t)(1+{}_{t+2}r_t)\ldots(1+{}_{t+n-1}r_t) \quad (2.1)$$

In writing this (Hicksian) expression we have adopted the kind of notation introduced by Meiselman (28). Thus: R_{nt} is the *actual* return on a bond/asset having, at the beginning of t, n periods, say years, remaining to the date when it is to be redeemed; ${}_{t+1}r_t$, for example, is the return expected, at the outset of t, to obtain on a one-period, say one-year, bond (or loan, if we like), at the beginning of period $t+1$.

This formula expresses the equality of holding-period returns in terms of a given holding-period, n periods/years in duration, in terms of the two *limits* of an investor's choice in such circumstances. Thus, he can either invest in an n-year bond and hold it until it matures or he can invest consecutively in one-year bonds. Any investment strategy for any given length of holding-period can be summed-up by considering the two extreme choices confronting an investor: investment in a bond whose length of life equals the investor's holding-period, or investment in a series of one year bonds/loans for the duration of the holding-period.*

So we deduce from equation (2.1) that any 'long-term' rate of return depends upon the one-year spot rate and the relevant expected

---

* That is to say even if the investor does *not* choose *either* an *n*-year bond or a series of one-year bonds; this is so, of course, irrespective of the holding-period. Arbitrage in the market (given the assumptions of the analysis) will see that this is so (on this, see again, Malkiel (1)).

---

reprinted as Essay 5 in (17). That essay is the forerunner of modern portfolio theory.

one-year returns.* Long-rates depend upon future expected rates of interest; indeed by equation (2.1) they are a geometric average of the spot rate and relevant expected rates. It is then possible to deduce the familiar relationships between 'interest rates'.† For example:

(i) If *all* one-year rates expected in the future should equal the present one-year rate (R_{1t}) then all rates of interest actually obtaining at period t, namely, $R_{1t}, R_{2t}, \ldots R_{nt}$, will be identical. The result is a horizontal yield-to-maturity curve (for t).‡

(ii) (a) Should *all* one-year rates expected in the future exceed the present one-year rate, we find that any given long-term rate is greater than "the" short-term or one-year, rate: that is, $R_{jt} > R_{1t}$, $j = 2, \ldots, n$.

(b) Furthermore, if it happens that all future (expected) rates rise monotonically, that is $_{t+j}r_t > {}_{t+1}r_t$ ($j > 1$), and, $_{t+1}r_t > R_{1t}$, the yield-to-maturity curve will be upward-sloping to the right. For we shall find that $R_{1t} < R_{2t} < \ldots < R_{nt}$.

(iii) (a) As a corollary of (ii) (a): if all future (expected) one-year rates are lower than R_{1t}, then any given "long-rate" is lower than R_{1t}.

(b) Analogous to (ii) (b): if it should happen that all future (expected) rates fall monotonically and $_{t+1}r_t < R_{1t}$, then the yield curve (for t) will be downward-sloping to the right.

The above statements relate to the relationship between interest rates at a *point in time*.

At least one deduction can be made about the course of interest rates, or market yields, *over time*. Thus:

(iv) Long-term rates will be less volatile than short-term rates: where "volatility" of, or fluctuations in, the various interest rate series can be measured by, say, their coefficient of variation over a given time-span.

It is not such an easy matter as might be thought *prima facie*, to add additional propositions about the "time structure" of interest rates.§ But it would seem possible for us to make at least two further

---

* Hence the analogy with a commodity futures market as brought out by Keynes (10), pp. 142–144 and Hicks (6), Chapter XI. In the Lutz–Fisher version of (2.1) R_{1t} is replaced by the first period forward/expected rate.

† See, for example: Lutz (7), and (8), Part Four; Conard (28), (29); Newlyn (30); and Malkiel (1).

‡ Where, conventionally, yield is measured along the vertical axis, and time-to-maturity is measured along the horizontal axis, of a Cartesian diagram.

§ As, for example, Lutz (8), p. 214, would have us believe: there Lutz has made the mistake of supposing that expectations are static, static in a way that, by

suggestions concerning the course of interest rates over time, namely:

(v) When there is an expectation that (all) short-term rates will be higher in the future than they are at the present time, "long-term" rates will rise. That is to say, any given long rate will be higher at t than it was at $t-1$; and its corollary:

(vi) When the expectation in the market is that (all) short-term rates will be lower in the future than they are at the present, the result will be that any given long-term rate will be lower at t than it was at $t-1$.

Accepting the framework of the Hicks–Lutz theory, *the* question to ask ourselves is: What kind of testable hypotheses can we formulate from the theory? and, furthermore, is it possible to devise a scheme of tests that would allow us to state that the theory could, or could not, explain, or account for, the structure of interest rates in the real world?

Prima facie, it might be thought that we have already, in part anyway, answered our own question, in that we have laid down the above propositions, derived from the Hicks–Lutz approach. However, it would seem that not all these propositions *are* testable *unless* the data we use on expected interest rates or market yields, are what we might call true or observed or independently given data.

However, the data that investigators of the term structure have used have been obtained from yield-to-maturity curves. The latter, at any moment of time, contain within them a set of *implied* expected one-year rates (labelled, in the literature and here, *forward* rates): this, of course, is nothing other than a tautology. So, from given yields we can write, using the Hicksian equation (2.1) and using forward one-year rates (the ϕ's) rather than "true" expected one year rates (the r's), for example, these equations:

$$(1+R_{1t})^1 = (1+R_{1t}) \qquad \text{(a)}$$
$$(1+R_{2t})^2 = (1+R_{1t})(1+{}_{t+1}\phi_t) \qquad \text{(b)} \qquad (2.2)$$
$$(1+R_{3t})^3 = (1+R_{1t})(1+{}_{t+1}\phi_t)(1+{}_{t+2}\phi_t) \qquad \text{(c)}$$

Dividing (b) by (a) we find ${}_{t+1}\phi_t$; and by dividing (c) by (b) we find ${}_{t+2}\phi_t$. So in general:

---

implication, rules out the Meiselman hypothesis. He also made the error in his earlier publication (7) as Conard (28), pp. 312–314 has implied.

$$_{t+n-1}\phi_t = \frac{(1+R_{nt})^n}{(1+R_{(n-1)t})^{n-1}} - 1 \qquad (2.3)$$

Whence we have all 'expected' one-year forward rates.

It is these forward rates which, as a consequence of the work of Meiselman (27), have been employed as expected rates—not even as their proxies. It is assumed that, to use Meiselman's own terminology, forward rates are *unbiased* estimates of expected rates (that is, liquidity premiums, *inter alia*, do not exist). Even if they are of this nature, the expected rates are only implied rates, they are not independently given expected rates.

We shall return to the latter point in the following paragraphs. But now we must note a further fact about data based on yield-to-maturity curves, namely: the actual yields given by them (for $R_{1t}, \ldots, R_{nt}$) will not, except in special circumstances, be true holding-period yields or returns. However, it can easily be shown that these circumstances are that the coupon payments on the given bonds should be zero throughout the life of the bond.* This is precisely the condition implied in equation (2.1), the Hicksian equation.

Yet we can reduce the data-problems somewhat by recalling that besides the Hicksian formula or basic equation (2.1), we have the Lutzian or Fisherian formula expressing the idea of equalisation of holding-period returns. Although all contributions to the literature in this field, except for a recent paper by A. Buse (31), have relied upon the Hicksian formula to derive a set of forward/expected one-year rates from yield-to-maturity data, it seems worthwhile to make the most of our limited kind of data and to calculate a set of forward/expected rates on the Lutzian formula. A set of such rates will differ from the Hicksian rates; of course the Lutzian rates will also be in error.†

Given that the data available on "expected" rates, whether or not they are subject to errors of measurement, are derived from yields-to-maturity, let us return to considering the empirical evaluation of the Hicks–Lutz theory; and, to be precise, the propositions we have listed hitherto concerning it. Consider propositions (i)–(iii) first of all.

* On the relationship between yields-to-maturity and holding-period returns see, for example: Malkiel (1), Appendix to Chapter 2, where Malkiel draws heavily on the unpublished work of Neil Wallace: Fisher (32), (33).

† For a comparison of the properties of Hicksian and Lutzian forward rates see Buse (31).

It is pertinent to draw our attention again to the fact that those propositions are features of the term structure of interest rates *at* a point in time. If, for example, we "deduce" from the existing structure of interest rates at point t, that all forward one-year rates rise monotonically and that $_{t+1}\phi_t$ exceeds R_{1t}, we shall also "deduce" that $R_{1t} < R_{2t} < \ldots < R_{nt}$. Via proposition (ii) (b) then we might be tempted into concluding that the expectational theory has scored a point in its favour. However, we are not entitled to make such an inference. For, if the yield curve slopes upward to the right then it follows arithmetically, that the implied one-year rates rise monotonically. If it is assumed that the implied one-year rates at our disposal are a correct expression of the market's views about expected interest rates, and we assume that the market acts rationally upon these expectations, then we could test the expectational theory of the term structure by reference, *inter alia*, to propositions (i)–(iii). But, such a test would effectively be worthless: the theory would, indeed must, always pass the test with flying colours.

By analogous arguments we can see that matters are not much improved either when we consider propositions (v) and (vi), either as they now stand or in developed form, using the kind of data at our disposal (although this is not as obvious as it is for propositions (i)–(iii)). Clearly, however, we can test proposition (iv): it is a proper test of the theory. It is a well-known and oft-observed fact, that interest rates over time exhibit the characteristics depicted in proposition (iv). This is certainly true of the data so far available on the term structure of interest rates for the U.K., the U.S.A., and Italy.*

It would seem then that the Hicks–Lutz theory, in terms of the provision of empirically verifiable hypotheses, is an empty box, as others have argued, unless we have *independent* evidence on the market's view of expected interest rates at every point in time relevant to our inquiry into the structure of interest rates.

Once such information had been collected the tests of the Hicks–Lutz theory would have to follow the general lines laid down in the numbered propositions catalogued previously.† Naturally the theory would have to prove successful on all counts. But even if the theory

---

* See: Grant (34); Durand (35); S. Homer (36); Masera (37).

† Most previously executed tests of the traditional theory, such as those by Hickman (38) and Walker (39) have erroneously tested the theory by its success or failure in successfully predicting interest rates. The spirit of these tests has been condoned, however, by Conard (28), p. 290.

did perform well in all the tests we could be left, as with tests involving any theory, with a "negative conclusion". That is to say, we might only be able to claim justifiably, along with the sentiment expressed by Meiselman (27) about his own work, that the Hicks–Lutz theory had "efficiently described" the workings of the market. We might be able to demonstrate that although the market may not consciously act according to the canons of the expectational theory, it can be described as if it did so.

3

Meiselman's work introduced an entirely new dimension into the investigation of the empirical properties of the Hicks–Lutz theory. Appreciating the crucial role that expectations play in it, Meiselman concerned himself in effect, specifically with the market's expectations of interest rates. However, his model is one that endeavours to account for revisions that the market makes to its views about expected rates, rather than a model which purports to explain (the all-important question) what determines the level of expected rates in the market, as Telser (40), for example, has noted.

The Meiselman model does not introduce any independent evidence on expectations; as indicated in Section 2, it takes the implied forward rates in the market as (unbiased) estimates of expected rates. It then attempts to offer an explanation of how the market changes its expected rates of interest. It is an error-learning model, as Telser has stated, of the same genre as the adaptive expectation models of the kind we shall utilise in Section 4 below; and since it is of that type it bases the revisions, rather than levels, of expectations on the error in forecasting or predicting the present period's (one-year) rate of interest.

The basic premise, of course in any error-learning model, be it in economics or psychology, is that the agents in the model or experiment learn from experience. They form their view of the future from past evidence; they are continually looking for knowledge to aid them in their task of forecasting the future. One part of knowledge that should not be ignored is that of the most up-to-date kind, namely, how accurately were forecasts for this instant in time? Indeed the error-learning hypotheses are more dogmatic in that they all assert that this kind of information or knowledge will not be ignored, will indeed be noted and acted upon; and furthermore, acted upon in a very special (mechanical?) way. To be specific: if the forecasts are too high expectations are revised downwards, if they are too low they are revised upwards.

We interjected the word "mechanical" in the above because although the error-learning models, and the Meiselman one included, seem to offer intuitively appealing ideas, at the general level, as it were, it is not at all clear why these ideas should be couched in such a rigid framework. For it appears, for example, that no allowance, explicitly or implicitly, is given for the circumstances surrounding the error in forecasting. These economic and/or political factors will be seen by the market as providing it with information or knowledge, on which to evaluate the future: they will be as much a part of its experience and "factual-equipment" as the error in forecasting itself. It may make the judgement that the circumstances that caused it to err at the given time were of an ephemeral nature: having disappeared they make the market feel that its other forecasts will be correct. They might not, therefore, be adjusted; although one could obviously argue the matter incessantly. For example, it could be contended that no matter how the market assesses the factors that caused it to make an error of judgement, it will fear the worst, or if we like, play for safety and make the appropriate (i.e. upward or downward) adjustment to its previous expected market rates in the belief that although it feels with certainty that the given factors have played themselves out, it had better make an allowance just in case it just might be proved wrong again.* The essential point about error-learning models, whether they be of the type used later, or of the Meiselman variety, is that they *implicitly* assume that the circumstances that caused the errors to be made in forecasting will continue in the next period—even if not to the same degree.

It is worth bearing in mind some of the objections that can be levelled at such models. However, we must also acknowledge that it would not be a simple matter to re-formulate them in the way required, say, for econometric analysis; and one could further justify their present use by suggesting that perhaps they are valid "on the average". They have embodied in them the belief that: individuals act upon, and learn from, experience; in evaluating their

---

* It is interesting to note that this important point is judged by Carter (essay in this volume) to be the one of the key factors in decision-making under uncertainty.

experience they are heavily influenced by their most recent experiences, and are somewhat myopic in applying that experience. They provide schemes for adapting expectations.

Professor Shackle, for example, in his psychologically-based theory, finds them germane to his own analysis of "the basis of change of expectations"* Thus we may quote this relevant and pointed remark:

> The judgement by which the decision-maker assigns degrees of potential surprise to hypotheses concerning the value which some variable will assume at some specified future date is necessarily based on values which he knows this or other variables have assumed in the past ((22), p. 216).

If we were to read subjective probability for potential surprise—although Professor Shackle would not condone this substitution—and consider own-variables as "basis-variables" we have, with a qualification or two, the ingredients for a Friedman-type error-learning model. Professor Shackle develops the above quotation mainly in terms of two separate variables, a "basis variable" and an "outcome variable"—even though as stated in the above quote the two variables can be synonymous. He calls the basis variable x, and the outcome variable J and:

> $y_{0,2}(J)$ will stand for the viewpoint potential surprise curve formed at date 0 concerning the value which J will assume at date 2, and $y_{1,2}(J)$ for the potential surprise curve, of shape unknown at the viewpoint, which he will form concerning J when the value of x becomes known to him at date 1. We will also write $y_{0,1}(x)$ for the potential surprise curve which, at the viewpoint date 0, the decision-maker forms concerning the value which x will assume at date 1 ... [and] When a new viewpoint is reached at date 1 a recorded value x_1 of x will become known and will be related in some way to $y_{0,1}(x)$. ... Thus we take it as an *axiom* that if the particular degree of potential surprise, $y_{0,1}(x_1)$, which has up to date 1 been associated with the particular value x_1, is greater than zero, then the curve $y_{0,2}(J)$ will at date 1 be *reconsidered* and given a *revised* form as $y_{1,2}(J)$ ((22), pp. 216–17; italics not in the original).

Shackle then proceeds to consider the areas of revision and non-revision of the "potential surprise functions". He argues that it is fallacious to suppose that if x_1 falls inside the inner range of $y_{0,1}(x)$ (i.e. has zero potential surprise) the decision-maker "will not feel any need to revise $y_{0,2}(J)$". The area of non-revision that he

* This is the title of Chapter XXV of (22).

defines and elaborates seems to be such that if we regard the basis and outcome variables as synonymous except with respect to time (as in the present context of the Meiselman model) then if the inner range happens to be a point, and x_1 has a different value from it, the potential surprise curve for future periods will be revised.

In the present context we could argue that since the Hicks–Lutz perfect foresight model produces an expected one-year rate for a given period in the future, the market is implicitly assigning zero potential surprise to its occurrence. We might also be allowed to stretch a point and add further that, since it is absolutely certain that only one one-year rate will obtain in a given period, the market attaches greater than zero potential surprise to the occurrence of any other one-year rate. So the inner range *is* a point; and if the one-year expected for period t should not equal the actual one-year rate at t, this will *definitely* occasion a revision at t by the market of all future one-year rates that it had formulated at period $t-1$. All potential surprise curves are adjusted; although in the Hicks–Lutz model the potential surprise curve would have to be T-shaped. Even then since we are concerned with expected yields on one-year bonds/loans we could only use the right-hand half of the T (it being related to positive numbers).

We have not done—and could not do so in such a short space—justice to Shackle's imaginative scheme and its applicability to revision of expectations models in economics, but despite this and the fact that there are difficulties in applying Shackle's framework of thought in the present context it is clear that his approach would sanction the basic idea behind the Meiselman model.

Meiselman, it will be recalled, takes as his estimates of expected one-year rates of interest the one-year forward rates revealed on the market. He supposes that these rates are embodied in the yield-to-maturity curves and that they can be pulled out from that curve via the Hicksian method. As we know, from the yield curve at a given moment of time there will emerge a set of forward-expected one-year rates of interest. Thus at time t there will be such a rate of interest for (the beginning of) periods $t+1$, $t+2$, ... $t+n-1$; or we may say with more clarity, along with Meiselman and his followers, that there will be rates of interest expected to be in evidence 1, 2, ... $n-1$, periods ahead of time t. In time $t-1$, for example, there will be expected rates held by the market for: $t-1+1$, $t-1+2$ ... ; that is for $t, t+1, \ldots t+n-2$.

Thus consider (the beginning of) period t. At $t-1$ there will be a $_tr_{t-1}$, which is the forward/expected rate for period t held at $t-1$. Meiselman's error variable is then: $R_{1t} - {_tr_{t-1}}$; that is the difference between the actual rate of interest on a one-year loan at the beginning of t and the rate expected to obtain on such a loan for that period (therefore, formulated at $t-1$). The dependent variables in the model are the changes made to the one-year rate expected for *a given period*, between two adjacent time-periods. Thus, in general, Meiselman's error-learning model can be represented by the following equation:

$$_{t+n}r_t - {_{t+n}r_{t-1}} = a + b(R_{1t} - {_tr_{t-1}}) \tag{3.1}$$

This is often written in this "difference" form:

$$\Delta_{t+n}r_t = a + b\, E_t \tag{3.2}$$

It is postulated that the expected value of a in any statistical equivalent of (3.1) or (3.2) is zero. So if expectations should be fulfilled, in this instance, if $_tr_{t-1}$ should equal R_{1t}, there would be no revision of expected rates of interest for specified dates in the future. Additionally, b should be positive.

In the following paragraphs we present the results of applying the Meiselman hypothesis to the data for the U.K. and for Italy. The data for the U.K. are those compiled by J. A. G. Grant (34); although those data have come in for some censure from Fisher, it is by no means certain that Fisher's own data are superior to those of Grant. But, in any case, rather than use the whole of Grant's data (stretching back to 1933) as, for example, Malkiel and Buse have done, we have only used his data from 1952 onwards. Those data seem to be virtually free of the strictures raised against them by Fisher: they are quarterly data and they terminate in the third quarter of 1963. There are numerous difficulties with the construction of yield-to-maturity curves upon which the expected rates of interest rely, and it is almost impossible to be dogmatic about the quality of such data, but those of Durand for the U.S.A. (extended by Homer) seem to be the most dubious,* while those of Masera for Italy are perhaps the most

---

* It is perhaps worth repeating what other commentators have noted, namely, that Durand realised the weaknesses in his yield curves and never intended them to be used for the testing of such models as Meiselman's. See also Masera (37); there a detailed account of the construction of yield curves will be found. Masera points out the difficulties about using the Italian data, especially where attempts are being made to explain the *level* of interest rates, because of the special institutional set-up in Italy.

reliable (although limited to data for 1 to 9-year bonds). The Italian data are on a monthly basis for 1957–1967 inclusive.

The data for this study were used on the time-basis on which they were published. Results using the Italian data on a quarterly basis so that a proper comparison can be made between the U.K. and Italian results, and results based on an annual time-period for both the U.K. and Italy, will be made available in a forthcoming publication.

Two sets of forward (expected) rates were calculated for both sets of data, the one based on the Hicksian method, the other based on the Lutzian method.* The results of testing the Meiselman hypothesis are reported in Tables 3.1–3.3. Although the Italian data allow us to calculate more forward rates than do the U.K. data, to maintain symmetry in the presentation of the results we have used only five forward rates ($n = 4$) for both sets of data.

Table 3.1 is for the U.K. and Table 3.2 is for Italy; both tables being based on the Hicksian forward rates. Table 3.3 is for Italy when the Lutzian rates are used; there is not a similar table for the U.K. since no aspect of the results was worth quoting.

In presenting the econometric results in this paper we have followed our normal practice. So the standard errors of given parameter estimates appear under those estimates, and the significance of the estimates are indicated by the following system of asterisks: one indicates that the estimate is significantly different from zero at the one per cent level or better; and two that it is significantly different from zero at the five per cent level or better. (This system might seem the reverse of what one would expect, but it has the advantage of economising on the number of asterisks used!) $\bar{R}^2$ is the coefficient of determination, adjusted for degrees of freedom; r is the simple correlation coefficient; d is the Durbin–Watson statistic used to test for serial correlation in the residuals; and ρ is Orcutt's coefficient being the value of ρ in a first-order auto-regressive scheme of the actual residuals (u_t) (in the equation $u_t = \rho u_{t-1} + \varepsilon_t$: where ε_t is a random error term).

Let us now make a few comments about each of the above tables; taking them first of all, *seriatim*. In Table 3.1 although the constant terms are numerically different from zero, statistically speaking they are not; and so we can conclude that over our sample period for the U.K. part of the Meiselman model is not contradicted by the avail-

---

* Lutzian forward rates have been calculated by a method that is, for example, implicit in the work of Buse (31) on Lutzian rates.

Table 3.1

Equation No.	Value of n	Intercept	Slope coefficient	r	$\bar{R}^2$	d	ρ
3.3	1	0.0986 (0.145)	−0.322 (0.19)	0.26	—	0.99	0.48
3.4	2	−0.018 (0.113)	**+0.328 (0.15)	0.33	0.089	1.1	0.4
3.5	3	−0.277 (0.15)	−0.22 (0.2)	0.17	—	0.93	0.53
3.6	4	−0.112 (0.176)	*+0.502 (0.20)	0.32	0.085	1.45	0.26

Table 3.2

Equation No.	Value of n	Intercept	Slope coefficient	r	$\bar{R}^2$	d	ρ
3.7	1	0.006 (0.027)	*+0.097 (0.023)	0.34	0.114	1.5	0.24
3.8	2	0.039 (0.022)	*−0.068 (0.018)	0.301	0.09	0.71	0.62
3.9	3	*0.067 (0.022)	*−0.069 (0.018)	0.32	0.094	1.21	0.36
3.10	4	*0.0784 (0.023)	+0.0033 (0.02)	—	—	1.47	0.24

able facts. Only two slope coefficients have the correct *a priori* sign, and are significantly different from zero. The overall relationship between changes in the expected rates of interest and the error term is extremely tenuous (a — indicates that statistically speaking $\bar{R}^2 = 0$). Furthermore, there is no systematic relationship between the slope coefficients as there has been in some other studies of the Meiselman-type, and the $\bar{R}^2$'s also do not decline sytematically. In all equations except (3.6) there is evidence of strong positive serial correlation in the residuals (although this is of no consequence in view of the poor overall fit of equations (3.3)–(3.5)).

The results catalogued in Table 3.2 are somewhat more favourable to the Meiselman hypothesis. But they do not present strong or systematic evidence to support its contentions. The overall fits are better than for the U.K., and there is more of a sensible pattern in these goodness-of-fits too. But the slope coefficients in equations (3.8) and (3.9) have their wrong signs, and those coefficients are highly significant (even allowing for the positive serial correlation in the residuals). Furthermore, the constant terms in equations (3.9) and (3.10) are also highly significant, thus vitiating the Meiselman hypothesis, and leading to the further possibility that liquidity premiums may exist.*

Use of the Lutzian rates for the U.K. produced worse results than those contained in Table 3.1. Not one coefficient appeared to be significant in any of the equations; and all overall fits were statistically speaking zero.† However, as can be seen from Table 3.3, even though it is a truncated version of Table 3.2, the Meiselman hypothesis fares better for Italy with Lutzian rates than it does with Hicksian rates. At least, up to a point it does! The results of $n = 3$ and $n = 4$ were worthless. For $n = 1$, equation (3.11) provides a better overall fit than equation (3.7) together with a satisfactory value of d and an insignificant constant term: however, its slope

* The fact that liquidity premiums may exist in the market even if the intercept terms are zero is now well established in the literature, thanks largely to the work of Wood (42).

† The error term could be expected to be virtually the same whether Hicksian or Lutzian forward rates are used. Since we would expect in theory (see Buse (31)) that the variancies of the Lutzian forward rates, for a given period, would be greater than those calculated by the Hicksian method, we would also expect that, in terms of the Meiselman hypothesis, the Hicksian rates produce better answers. The empirical data for the U.K. bears the said characteristics and has produced the results that follow therefrom: for the Italian data the picture is not so uniform.

Table 3.3

Equation No.	Value of n	Intercept	Slope coefficient	r	$\bar{R}^2$	d	ρ
3.11	1	0.025 (0.051)	−0.127* (0.027)	−0.38	0.14	1.73	0.125
3.12	2	0.047 (0.03)	−0.137* (0.016)	−0.61	0.37	0.9	0.52

Table 3.4

Equation No.	Value of n	Intercept	Slope coefficient	r	$\bar{R}^2$	d	ρ
3.14	1	−0.018 (0.114)	*+0.847 (0.19)	0.57	0.31	1.75	0.043
3.15	2	−0.129 (0.1)	*+0.526 (0.17)	0.44	0.18	1.59	0.13
3.16	3	*−0.34 (0.14)	−0.246 (0.24)	−0.16	—	0.96	0.52
3.17	4	−0.271 (0.17)	+0.277 (0.29)	−0.13	—	1.28	0.35

Table 3.5

Equation No.	Value of n	Intercept	Slope coefficient	r	$\bar{R}^2$	d	ρ
3.18	1	−0.0525** (0.025)	−0.131* (0.053)	0.22	0.04	1.24	0.37
3.19	2	0.079* (0.02)	−0.075 (0.04)	—	—	0.65	0.66
3.20	3	0.101* (0.02)	+0.063 (0.042)	—	—	1.09	0.42
3.21	4	0.078* (0.02)	+0.12* (0.04)	0.25	0.054	1.35	0.3

coefficient has the wrong sign for the "validity" of the Meiselman hypothesis. This same fault mars equation (3.12) which produces, so far, the best overall fit; and although there is evidence of strong positive serial correlation in the residuals there can really be not much doubt about the significance of the slope coefficient; again the intercept term is effectively zero.

A simple alternative to the Meiselman hypothesis is the Hickman-like inertia hypothesis (see reference 38) in the present circumstances this takes the following form:

$$_{t+n}r_t = a' + b'(R_{1t} - R_{1t-1}) \quad (3.13)$$

Here the new error term, which we may label E'_t, differs from E_t in that it is postulated that market has a static expectation of the one-year rate for each period: thus, $_tr_{t-1} = R_{1t-1}$.

Equation (3.13), of course, with the usual random disturbance term added to it, produced, using Hicksian rates, the results given in Tables 3.4 (for the U.K.) and 3.5 (for Italy). Consider the results for the U.K. first of all. Except for $n = 4$, no equation is worse than the comparable equation with E_t as the independent variable (Table 3.1). Equations (3.14) and (3.15) are decidedly better, in all respects, than their counterparts, equations (3.3) and (3.4), respectively. In both equations (3.14) and (3.15), the constant term is statistically speaking zero; the slope coefficient is highly significant; the values of d are satisfactory at the 5% level; and the $\bar{R}^2$ are highly significant, and not unduly low. An examination of the results for Italy indicates at a glance that Table 3.5, for the inertia hypothesis, loses out to Table 3.2, except with respect to the equations for $n = 4$.

How does the inertia hypothesis compare with the pure Meiselman hypothesis if Lutzian rates are employed in the equations? The answer to this question can be gathered explicitly, and implicitly, from Table 3.6. We say implicitly because it will be appreciated from a comparison of the extent and structure of Table 3.6 with that of the previous tables that three equations for the U.K. and two equations for Italy produced results of no value at all. Equation (3.22) for the U.K. is superior to its partner, equation (3.14), based on Hicksian rates. For Italy we discover that comparisons of Tables 3.6 and 3.5 yield no discernible pattern in the results: furthermore, now, as hitherto, the error variables have significant coefficients (though that in equation (3.24) might well be insignificant making allowance for the correlation in the residuals), but their signs are negative. A

Table 3.6

Equation No.	Value of n	Intercept	Slope coefficient	r	$\bar{R}^2$	d	ρ
3.22	1 : U.K.	0.088 (0.18)	+0.812* (0.30)	0.37	0.13	1.55	0.16
3.23	1 : Italy	0.14* (0.04)	−0.634* (0.084)	0.55	0.30	1.22	0.43
3.24	2 : Italy	0.174* (0.03)	−0.276* (0.064)	0.36	0.12	0.55	0.72

comparison of the inertia hypothesis using the Hicksian and Lutzian forward rates reveals no clear-cut answers either. For, in the case of the U.K. the Hicksian-rate equations have victory of the Lutzian-rate equations by a very substantial margin: while the reverse is true for the Italian interest rate structure.

Nothing very conclusive has emerged from empirical analysis of the U.K. and the Italian interest rate structure on any of the individual points that are being scrutinised in the process of applying Meiselman-type equations to the data. Thus, for example: it may or may not be accurate to posit the existence of liquidity premiums in either market; such premiums may or may not be an increasing function of n (as is often suggested; and as one might expect to be the situation, *a priori*); the idea of inelastic expectations may or may not provide a better instrumental variable than that of elastic expectations for accounting for revisions in future expected one-year rates of interest; even where it appears that an error-learning hypothesis has a too-large-to-be-ignored influence on revisions of expectations it is not certain that that effect occurs in the same direction as those who advocate this kind of hypothesis, Meiselman himself included, would like.

However, taking all factors into consideration it is apparent that not much support, either of a systematic or unsystematic kind, can be found for the Meiselman hypothesis. This, to invoke a well-worn argument in the assessment of much of applied econometric work, could be attributed to the quality of the data against which the hypothesis has been tested. To pursue the question of the reliability of variously constructed yield-to-maturity curves would be a lengthy task and would probably admit of no clear answer. However, what is possibly of some (or more) importance is the question of the length of data-period. Most, but by no means all, studies of the Meiselman kind have used annual data. For a number of reasons, statistical as well as economic, it is likely that such data, especially if they cover a long period of time, will produce better results, *ceteris paribus*, than the use of quarterly or monthly data. But, given the data, the hypothesis should produce good results against all periods of observation.

But there does remain the substantial point that the two series of expected rates we can calculate from yield-to-maturity data are subject to error, in that they should be derived from holding-period returns. This could well be the reason why the results of the Meiselman hypothesis are so unsatisfactory; and this is an important data problem that should not be forgotten. However, it is an empirical matter as to how far out, say, Hicksian forward rates are from the "true" forward rates on the market: it could well turn out, of course, that the true rates might be so systematically different from the Hicksian rates that the results of testing the Meiselman hypothesis would be largely unaffected by the introduction of the new, "true", rates or yields. But little work has been done on this matter; and like the construction of yield-to-maturity curves it is an arduous, tedious, and time-consuming task even when appropriate data on the coupons on, and prices of, bonds have been tracked down.

It is a sufficiently important point to bear repeating, in a slightly different form, that it does not matter for the expectational theory if the basic* Meiselman hypothesis is not supported by the facts. For it is only an hypothesis—of how expectations are revised. The forward rates may well be unbiased estimates of expected rates, and also may well determine the rate structure as the Hicks–Lutz theory suggests, and in the precise ways that it suggests, even though expectations are not revised in line with Meiselman's hypothesis. Even if the basic Meiselman hypothesis is seen to be empirically important, and the evidence is that forward rates are unbiased estimates of expected rates, it will only allow us to conclude that, when errors in forecasting are made, expectations will be (uniformly) raised or lowered, so that if the expectational theory is correct, the yield curve, or structure of rates, will move upwards or downwards (cf. the propositions detailed in Section 2 above).

Granted that we do not have independent evidence on expectations, and ignoring the data problems resulting from the application of yield curves, what appears to be called for, *inter alia*, is more investigation of possible causes in changes in expectations as given by yield curve data. This could best come about by devising schemes of, say, a distributed lag–adaptive expectations kind, which seek to explain the *level* of expectations: then it would be a simple matter to account for changes in expectations. It is not possible to report on our work along these lines here, but we might note that even the simple idea utilised by Wood (43), which does not involve distributed lags, namely, that each expected rate at t is a function of the R_1 at t, has obvious appeal and produces good empirical results.

---

* We have referred to the basic Meiselman hypothesis, this is simply because this is the main, but by no means the only, hypothesis he developed and tested.

4

In the preamble to his 'alternative' formulation of the expectations theory, Malkiel comments as follows:

This study takes the position that the traditional expectational approach is, in principle, correct and of substantial importance in understanding the actual behaviour of market interest of securities with different terms to maturity ((1), p. 50).

But in developing his own theory Malkiel states that "a short planning period will be substituted for the long-run horizon implicit in the received analysis" (ibid.). To explain his theory Malkiel introduces and elaborates on "Three building blocks which serve as the foundation of the analysis: (1) the mathematics of bond-price movements; (2) the assumption that investors have an expectation of a 'normal range' of interest rates; (3) expectations proper, that is a belief by investors that a particular course of future interest-rate movements is likely" (ibid.).

The centre-piece of Malkiel's theory is undoubtedly (2), the use of a normal range of interest rates. The idea of normal interest rates is, of course, not a new one; nor is the idea of a normal range of interest rates. However, the formal use of such a range, and certainly the way that range is used, to present a picture of how the long–short yield gap is determined in the market is novel. It is the postulated existence of a short planning horizon for investors that, taken with the notion of a normal range of interest rates, enables Malkiel to deduce his term-structure hypothesis.

To develop his concept of the normal range of interest rates *per se* Malkiel naturally enough uses a simplified example which, although requiring slight modification when the other factors in his analysis are brought into play, nevertheless portrays the essential part that the range has in determining the rate-structure. The assumptions made are that: investors have in mind a normal range of interest rates that is expected to hold in the future; interest rates on all securities are the same (they all carry the same coupon, and are assumed to be selling at par); investors make no judgement about expected interest rates as such; the portfolio planning period is short, say one year. Then since investors can now be supposed to wish to seek to equalise the (mathematical expectation of) gain they obtain from investing in any of the available securities (since coupons are the same—should be the same for term-structure analysis): given the existence of the normal range, if interest rates are near the upper bound of the normal range, for the one-year period, "investors will have more to hope than fear in terms of the possibilities for capital gains and losses" ((1), p. 65).... "Alternatively, if the interest rates are near the lower bound of the normal range, investors will have more to fear than hope" (ibid.). In the former situation "long-term bonds will be more attractive than short-term securities... long-term securities must yield less than short" (ibid.); in the latter situation, that is near the lower limit of the normal range, "an ascending yield curve will result" (ibid.).

These two deductions about the slope of the yield curve, hence about the structure of rate at a point in time, follow partly from the application of Malkiel's building block (1), "the mathematics of bond-price movements", to, for example, the assessment of relative (possible) capital gains on long and short bonds when the current interest rate (there is effectively only one interest rate in the model) is near the upper boundary of the normal range. Thus, it can be shown ((1), pp. 50–57) that, for example, as interest rates fall towards the lower bound of the normal range, with the absolute and percentage changes in interest rates for long rates being equal to those for short bonds, that long-bond prices will fluctuate more than short-bond prices. Investment in long bonds, in the given circumstances, will yield, for a given interest rate change, a higher capital gain, than will investment in short bonds.

Naturally it is the choice of investors to invest in one kind of asset or another that determines the rate-structure in the model. That choice itself will depend upon the view they hold about the likelihood that interest rates initially near the upper bound of the normal range will approach it or deviate from it. This likelihood also plays a part with building block (1) in allowing statements to be made about the rate-structure given the existence of Malkiel's normal range. Malkiel's way of handling this issue is to suppose that investors evaluate their strategy (via the mathematical expectation of gain of investing in either short or long bonds) by focusing attention on the likelihood of rates actually being *at* the lower limit or the upper limit of the normal range. The probability of either limit being attained is set at 0.5: hence the above results on the term-structure.

In a way, this explanation of the possible influence of the existence of a normal range of interest rates on the long–short yield-gap, does contain within it "expectations proper". However, the latter factor, item (3) in Malkiel's building blocks, is a neutral factor in the above analysis. For Malkiel: "By expectations proper ... we simply mean that investors may believe that *a certain course of interest-rate movements is more likely than any other*, or they may make specific forecasts of future interest rate" ((1), p. 65; italics not in original). It is possible to argue, for example, that if the current rate of interest is near the upper limit of the normal range the likelihood/probability that it will fall would be judged to be greater than the probability that it would rise. In such a case the yield curve would be steeper than before, but it would still be an ascending one. But, clearly, expectations could be of such a nature that they produce a descending yield curve.

The suggestion that there exists a normal range of interest rates, together with "the mathematics of bond-price movements" *and* the supposition that bond holders typically have a short planning horizon, enables, without the aid of expectations proper in Malkiel's sense, deductions to be made concerning the term structure of interest rates. Since the supposition is made throughout by Malkiel that investors are motivated in the monetary sense in the same way as they are in the Hicks–Lutz theory, so that they seek, for their holding-period, to maximise the returns (gains or yields, depending upon how interest rates compare at the outset of the portfolio decision periods) it is clear, as Malkiel himself has shown, that a set of forward rates similar to those for the Hicks–Lutz theory are generated by his approach. Luckett ((1), pp. 75–77) has then been able to show that the Malkiel theory contains within it the Meiselman hypothesis. Taking, as Malkiel did, 'the long rate' (R) as representative of the general level of interest rates, his basic hypothesis concerning the rate-structure can be written in this fashion:

$$(R-S)_t = f\left(\frac{R-R_{LN}}{RN_R}\right)_t \tag{4.1}$$

Here: S is 'the short rate'; R_{LN} is the lower bound of the normal range (of the long rate); RN_R is the normal range of R.

To use equation (4.1) it is necessary, *inter alia*, to specify exactly how the normal range is to be calculated. Malkiel suggests that "investors form their expectations ... of the normal range as if they took the average of rates over some period in the immediate past and added a specific number of standard deviations to either side of the average" ((1), p. 84). He assumes that number is constant. Thus, since, for example, the lower bound of the range is equal to "the average" plus a constant (k) times σ (the standard deviation) equation (4.1) becomes:

$$(R-S)_t = f\left(\frac{R-R^n+k\sigma}{2k\sigma}\right)_t \qquad (4.2)$$

where R^n is the average long-term rate (*the* normal rate in our ensuing analysis). An approximation to equation (4.2) is then:

$$(R-S)_t = F(R-R^n)_t \qquad (4.3)$$

Linearising this equation produces Malkiel's basic equation:

$$(R-S)_t = a+b(R-R^n)_t \qquad (4.4)$$

To which we add, before estimating, the usual random error term (u_t). We expect *a priori* that a will be greater than, while b will be less than, zero.

It is necessary and vital as a preliminary to empirical investigation of equation (4.4) and similar equations, to have at our disposal some means of assessing R^n_t, if we wish it to be entered as if it were an observed variable. Here we can only report on the utilisation of one particular method of evaluating R^n_t: this method requires little elaboration because it is a familiar method in applied econometric work; and another point in its favour is that it is similar to one of the methods adopted by Malkiel to evaluate his "average" long-term rate of interest.

In effect, our approach here is to let R^n_t be a geometrically declining weighted average of previous actual long-term rates of interest, it being postulated that the weights sum to unity. This hypothesis can be expressed in this way:

$$R^n_t = \sum_{i=0}^{n} \lambda^{i+1} R_{t-(i+1)}, \quad 0<\lambda<1 \qquad (4.5)$$

For the weights to sum to unity as n approaches infinity, it follows that $\lambda \equiv 0.5$.

Should we change (4.5) so that it becomes:

$$R^n_t = \sum_{i=0}^{n} \lambda(1-\lambda)^i R_{t-(i+1)}, \quad 0<\lambda<1 \qquad (4.6)$$

we see that the weights sum to unity irrespective of the value of λ. But clearly if $\lambda = 0.5$, equation (4.6) will become equivalent to equation (4.5). Although equation (4.6) has often been employed in recent work on "adaptive expectations" in econometric research,* the notion that lies behind it is, as one would instinctively expect, also implicit in equation (4.5); so that they both represent possible, though by no means exhaustive, representations of the idea of adaptive expectations.

That kind of idea, we know, underlies Meiselman's hypothesis. The difficulty, of course, in using it, and any particular representation of it, is that it *is* only an idea; its operational value must be judged in this light, leaving aside the problems associated with the added notion that we can define and use this idea at the market level. The results we obtain from using any particular method of assessing the normal rate could naturally also be influenced by the choice of method actually used. In effect, in using scheme (4.5) we have let $\lambda = 0.5$ for reasons to be noted later, and we have let $n = 15$. Although this is—it always must be—an arbitrary decision, it is in line with some of Malkiel's own work, and it means that the sum of weights is effectively equal to unity.

Let us leave these preliminaries for now and turn to the empirical properties of the Malkiel theory. We shall, for reasons of space and of difficulty of comparison, only quote some of the results we have obtained from the U.K. data, leaving aside those obtained from the Italian data. Along with Malkiel we shall for the present let the standard deviation be invariant with respect to time; the long rate of interest we shall take to be the yield on $2\frac{1}{2}\%$ Consols (R_t); and the short rate of interest we shall take to be the yield on a one-year bond (S_t).

It is clear that if we estimate equation (4.4) as it stands the regression coefficients are likely to be biased and inconsistent. However, since it is the basic Malkiel equation it seems worth while to see how it does perform empirically; and as it happens the degree of bias in the coefficients (using the variance of the residuals as the variance of the true/hypothetical errors) is quite small. In fact, the statistical counterpart to equation (4.4) is:

$$(R-S)_t = \overset{*}{1.024} - \overset{*}{(1.1465)} (R-R^n)_t \qquad (4.7)$$
$$(0.107) \quad (0.14)$$
$$\bar{R}^2 = 0.18, \quad d = 0.77$$

* As an example see the excellent work of Feige (44).

The very unsatisfactory value of the Durbin–Watson statistic, which is accompanied by a (significant) value of 0.61 for Orcutt's co-efficient, indicating serious positive auto-correlation of the residuals, one could argue has arisen because the equation is "mis-specified", that is, the hypothesis is not a powerful one. However, because of this serious correlation in the residuals the standard errors of regression coefficients in equation (4.7) will be wrongly evaluated. But all things considered it is likely that (though, of course, we cannot be dogmatic about this) the parameters a and b will be significantly different from zero, have the correct signs, and have values not too different from those indicated above.

Obviously we can circumvent the bias and possible inconsistency involved in estimation of equation (4.4) by estimating its "reduced forms":

$$R_t = \frac{a}{1-b} - \frac{b}{1-b}R_t^n + \frac{1}{1-b}S_t + \frac{1}{1-b}u_t \qquad (4.8)$$

$$S_t = -a + bR_t^n + (1-b)R_t - u_t \qquad (4.9)$$

We can, on the conventional assumption about the error terms legitimately estimate either of these equations by ordinary least squares (OLS); assuming, that is, *inter alia*, that S_t is exogenous in (4.8) and endogenous in (4.9), and vice-versa for R_t.

However, it is not possible to unscramble the parameters in the estimation of equations (4.8) and (4.9) so that *unique* estimates are obtained of the structural parameters in the model, namely, a and b. The reason for this is easy to see: both equations are over identified. However, we know that the "compound parameters" in the equations will be unbiased and consistent; and that if we estimate the equations via a restricted least squares (RLS) technique we can obtain *directly* unique, consistent, estimates of the "structural" parameters. Malkiel used only equation (4.9): we shall give some consideration to both equations; either one of which can be used to determine the rate structure.

The OLS statistical counterparts to equations (4.8) and (4.9) for the U.K. are as follows:

$$R_t = \underset{(0.21)}{0.3448} + \underset{(0.056)}{0.7705}^{*} R_t^n + \underset{(0.037)}{0.2131}^{*} S_t \qquad (4.10)$$

$$\bar{R}^2 = 0.93, \quad d = 1.0$$

$$S_t = -1.147 + 2.15 \overset{*}{R_t} - 1.1246 \overset{*}{R_t^n} \quad (4.11)$$
$$(0.64) \quad (0.37) \quad (0.387)$$
$$\bar{R}^2 = 0.67, \quad d = 0.77$$

In terms of goodness-of-fit these results are vastly superior to equation (4.7), as one would expect. However, both equations exhibit strong positive serial correlation of the residuals, with (significant) values of Orcutt's coefficient of respectively, 0.5 and 0.6.* This will probably not affect the likelihood of the coefficients in equation (4.10) being different from zero, since their t-values are now fairly high, and their estimates are unbiased ones. Also there was no evidence of multi-collinearity in equation (4.10) to complicate the estimation of the variances of the estimates.

If we unscramble the estimates in equation (4.10) we find that we can have three values, all appropriately negative, for b. However, equation (4.8) upon which equation (4.10) is based, contains non-linear restrictions on the parameters, or the linear restriction that the slope coefficients sum to unity. When the restriction is imposed upon the estimates of equation (4.10) we obtain a unique value of b, which we can discover by dividing the coefficient on R_t^n by that on R_t. In the present case, since the restriction on equation (4.8) is virtually satisfied by the data, the truest way of calculating b is by supposing that the restriction is exactly fulfilled, so that b should be taken as -3.616. Then the "structural" equation becomes:

$$(R-S)_t = 1.59 - 3.616 (R-R^n)_t \quad (4.10)(a)$$

From equation (4.11) a unique estimate of a is found; a being equal to 1.147, b then now has two values: since the restriction on equation (4.11), from equation (4.9), that again the two slope coefficients

---

* If we suppose that Orcutt's coefficient provides us with the correct means of transforming the data to remove this auto-correlation then the transformed equations produce these results, both having satisfactory values of d:

$$R_t - 0.5 R_{t-1} = 0.265 + 0.2\overset{*}{0}5 (S_t - 0.5 S_{t-1}) + 0.7\overset{**}{3}6 (R_n - 0.5 R^n_{-1}) \quad (4.10)'$$
$$(0.176) \quad (0.05) \quad (0.37)$$
$$\bar{R}^2 = 0.813, \quad d = 1.86$$

$$S_t - 0.6 S_{t-1} = 0.375 - 0.418 (R_t^n - 0.6 R^n_{t-1}) + 1.\overset{*}{4}24 (R_t - 0.6 R_{t-1}) \quad (4.11)'$$
$$(0.47) \quad (0.4) \quad (0.36)$$
$$\bar{R}^2 = 0.38, \quad d = 2.02$$

Tests showed that the restrictions on the slope coefficients were satisfied.

should sum to unity is almost fulfilled, we should perhaps take the coefficient on R_t^n as the better estimate of b. So, for example, the structural equation is:

$$(R-S)_t = 1.147 - 1.246\ (R-R^n)_t \qquad (4.11)(a)$$

We have already noted that if we apply RLS to equation (4.11), with the relevant linear restriction on the slope coefficients, that we shall obtain a unique, and the "proper", value of b. The RLS estimate of equation (4.11) is so similar to equation (4.11) itself that we shall not quote it; as would be expected an F-test revealed that the restriction was valid, the error sum of squares for equation (4.11) and the with-restriction-on equation (there also being only one restriction, of course) differing by only 0.01. Also once the restriction was imposed upon equation (4.8) it produced, again as would be expected, virtually the same value of b as did equation (4.10)—b can be estimated by restricted least squares and by, say, the "Taylor's series linearisation" non-linear technique.*

In view of the fact that R_t^n is a distributed lag function of R it is not surprising, even though R_t^n is regarded as, and entered as, an observed quantity, that equation (4.10), with R_t taken as the dependent variable, produces superior results to equation (4.11). In "classical" monetary theory it will often be found that the view is held that the long rate, is led, in a certain way, by the short rate or expectations about it, and the normal and/or expected long rate of interest. However, in the present case no firm evidence, even in the context of the model being utilised, can be offered on the question of whether, in the process whereby the term structure is generated, the long rate or the short rate is the lead variable in the market.

To substantiate the view implicit in the above reduced form results that the long rate is the rate that is leading the market would probably require that equations (4.8) and (4.9) be estimated by a simultaneous estimating technique. However, it is by no means clear how this could be done: for it is imperative to maintain the restrictions on the parameters in either equation; so that to keep within the economic bounds of the model the equations must be seen to justify the existence of those restrictions. But furthermore, we have the complicating fact that there are non-linear restrictions that must be placed

---

* On non-linear techniques, results from the application of which we have noted later in the text, see, for example, Malinvaud (46), Draper and Smith (45).

on the parameters *through* the equations to obtain consistent and unique estimates of a and b.*

We shall content ourselves with the conclusion that the true values of a and b probably lie within the bounds given in the above equation; so too does the explanatory power of the simple hypothesis used so far; and so too does the elasticity of the yield gap with respect to the "normal rate gap".† But it is clear that even within those limits the basic hypothesis is a reasonably powerful one, under the assumptions made. Changing the latter could change the empirical results on the yield gap, as we shall, in fact, see. For we know that the success of the hypothesis in whatever form is a *joint* success of both the hypothesis and of the way the relevant variables are calculated. The latter remark leads us naturally on to the next line of argument.

So far we have utilised the hypothesis by assuming that the normal rate of interest is something we can observe by means of an "expectation generating" equation of the kind epitomised in equation (4.5). But we have gone further than this in that we have predetermined the value of λ at one-half. Now we shall examine some alternative empirical equations to (4.8) and (4.9) on the supposition that the scheme detailed in equation (4.5) is appropriate to the problem on hand, but that the specification of the weights is something that should be left undetermined, to be determined for us, if at all possible, by the econometric analysis itself. If into equation (4.4) we substitute equation (4.5) and carry out the Koyck transformation, upon simplifying we have these equations:

$$R_t = a_0 + a_1 R_{t-1} + a_2 S_t + a_3 S_{t-1} + w_t \qquad (4.12)$$

where:

$$a_0 = \frac{a(1-\lambda)}{1-b}; \; a_1 = -\left[\frac{\lambda a}{1-b} - \lambda\right]; \; a_2 = \frac{1}{1-b}; \; a_3 = -\frac{\lambda}{1-b};$$
$$(4.12)(a)$$

$$S_t = b_0 + b_1 R_t + b_2 R_{t-1} + b_3 S_{t-1} - w_t \qquad (4.13)$$

where:

$$b_0 = -a(1-\lambda); \; b_1 = (1-b); \; b_2 = (2b\lambda - \lambda); \; b_3 = \lambda; \; (4.13)(a)$$

---

* Even though another difficulty is that we do not have a proper model in the econometric sense, there is very little literature on the identification problem even in such models when restrictions exist (see, for example, Fisher (47)). But restrictions must help to identify previously under-identified equations.

† For those readers who are interested in working out the elasticities we report that at the point of sample means the ratio $(R-S)$ to $(R-R^n)$ was 0.958.

to which we may add:

$$(R-S)_t = a(1-\lambda) + bR_t - 2b\lambda R_{t-1} + \lambda(R-S)_{t-1} + w_t \quad (4.14)$$

For all equations:

$$w_t = u_t - \lambda u_{t-1} \quad (4.15)$$

The econometric problems related to the estimation of these equations via OLS are familiar enough (we may ignore (4.14). Both equations (4.12) and (4.13) contain lagged dependent variables which will lead to biased estimates: and the situation is made even worse if we make the usual assumption that the error term in equation (4.4), u_t, is such that $Eu_t u_{t-i} = 0$. We then have $ER_{t-1} w_t \neq 0$; w_t is an auto-correlated error term: the estimates of the regression coefficients will also be inconsistent.*

However, it will be possible, or (we should more correctly state) it will be legitimate, to use OLS to obtain consistent estimates of the regression coefficients in, say, equation (4.12) if we can argue that, on the contrary, it is true that:

$$u_t = \lambda u_{t-1} + \varepsilon_t, \; E\varepsilon_t = 0, \; E\varepsilon_t \varepsilon_{t-i} = 0 \quad (4.16)$$

for then it follows immediately that $w_t = \varepsilon_t$, a *random* error term. Indeed the results of applying (4.4) to the data indicate that u_t might reasonably well be described by a first-order autoregressive scheme as in (4.16). If we conveniently find that (4.16) is the correct scheme (of course, we can never tell whether it is, for it is meant to apply intrinsically to the *hypothetical* errors (u_t) in (4.4)) then the error term in the to-be-estimated equations bear the usual random characteristics. So we have ruled out—assumed away!!—the existence of any covariance between the lagged dependent variables and the error term.

---

* See, for example: Goldberger (48), Chapter 6; Klein (47); Koyck (50). The Klein–Koyck method of handling the possibility of inconsistent estimates from OLS estimation of equations (4.12) and (4.13) has been challenged by Liviatan (52) whose method of dealing with the inconsistency problem is simpler than the Klein–Koyck method. However, it suffers from the (economic) disadvantages of a two-stage least squares procedure. In the present case we used Liviatan's technique in two different forms (the second way was to add an extra "instrumental" variable for each first stage equation) but the results were disappointing. Too high a price seemed to be paid for the dubious attainment of consistent estimates.

On this supposition we can accept the OLS estimates as being unbiased and consistent. The OLS estimates, in effect, were as follows for equations (4.12) and (4.13)

$$R_t = 0.27314 + 0.8642^* R_{t-1} + 0.2029^* S_t - 0.098 S_{t-1} \quad (4.17)$$
$$(0.195) \quad (0.06) \quad (0.05) \quad (0.058)$$
$$\bar{R}^2 = 0.944, \quad d = 1.84$$

$$S_t = -0.0477 + 1.414^* R_t - 1.1836^* R_{t-1} + 0.7252^* S_{t-1} \quad (4.18)$$
$$(0.527) \quad (0.357) \quad (0.33) \quad (0.11)$$
$$\bar{R}^2 = 0.82, \quad d = 2.35$$

Both equations have satisfactory values of the Durbin–Watson statistic—although there is a tendency for this statistic to be biased towards 2 with the present kind of equations—and Orcutt's coefficient for both equations is absolutely small, being 0.015 and -0.18 respectively, and is statistically speaking zero. So there is some reason to suppose that the error term in (4.17) and (4.18) might be a random one.

Although in terms of overall performance equation (4.18) is to be preferred to equation (4.11), equation (4.17) produced the same result as did equation (4.10). Since R_t^n, in equation (4.10) contains within it, with a high weight, the term R_{t-1}, one could argue that equation (4.17) differs from (4.10) by the mere addition of another explanatory variable, S_{t-1}. This in itself would increase the value of R^2: but the using-up of an extra degree of freedom has meant that the two equations have essentially the same explanatory value.

It would likewise be expected that the overall performance of equation (4.11) would be improved by the addition of a lagged dependent variable. However, if we are prepared to accept the view that our assumption about the error term in (4.12) and (4.13) is correct then if we wish to use the basic hypothesis (4.4) to explain the spread of interest rates via the level of the short rate it is equation (4.18) that we should use. All the slope coefficients in (4.18) are highly significant, they all have their correct *a priori* signs. From which we deduce that, as required: $\lambda > 0$; $a > 0$; $b < 0$.

Again, however, one fundamental disadvantage of (4.18) estimated via OLS, and similarly of (4.17), is that it does not enable us to unscramble its estimated parameters and arrive at *unique* estimates of the basic parameters in the model. Both equations are over-identified. Non-linear estimating techniques are called for.* Such techniques produced a value of -7.275 for b and of -0.229 for λ. Both, as far as one can make this kind of judgement in the present context, appear to be highly significant estimates: but that for b seems extremely large while that for λ is clearly unacceptable since it is negative. Although it is not strictly legitimate to argue in this fashion with non-linearities present in the model, one could argue that with a $\bar{R}^2$ of 0.94, and therefore, with an error sum of squares virtually equivalent to that for equation (4.13), the non-linear estimates indicate that the restrictions on the present equation are fulfilled.† If this is so then since λ is negative, the "model", as it results in these kind of estimating equations may be incorrectly formulated. The non-linear results from equation (4.13) were no more encouraging: and in any event there remain the difficulties associated with the lack of a simultaneous estimation of the parameters in the two equations.

Although the possibility of estimating, say, λ from the model itself is intuitively appealing, we must be very wary about accepting the value of numerical estimates of basic parameters given to us via non-linear techniques. In the present work which, *inter alia*, extended the above equations to allow the possibility that the assumption about the error term should have been of the form $w_t = \rho w_{t-1} + v_t$, the results using the Taylor's series method and the Gauss–Newton method of non-linear estimation produced some very odd and dubious results. On one occasion numerous runs on the computer suggested that use of the above-stipulated error term in the model indicated that b was effectively zero, but could assume *any* value without affecting the overall results!!‡

Thus all things considered it is probably better to call a halt at the "reduced form" equations (4.17) and (4.18), which together give

* Equations (4.12) and (4.13) are estimated subject to (4.12)(a) and (4.13)(a), the non-linear constraints on their parameters.

† We can partition the sum of squares in non-linear regression on the supposition that the solution we have obtained is "the" solution, that is, it is equivalent to that that we would have obtained had we solved (been able to solve) the normal equations.

‡ All too frequently we fail to examine the validity of error-term and other restrictions in applied econometric work, getting carried away by the techniques we are using, without bothering to ask ourselves if we need to use them in the first place. Cf. for example, Laidler and Parkin (51), where the nature of the error term assumption, i.e., the "reduced form model" finally estimated, might be completely inappropriate (so too might the "structural model"). This is just one among many examples: and we are all guilty of such misdemeanours somewhere or other.

excellent results. The fact that we cannot estimate the structural parameters is not too much of a drawback. However, we must always bear in mind that equations (4.17) and (4.18) can only be regarded as estimates of the value of the Malkiel hypothesis if the constraints on the parameters in the equations are satisfied. In all the "good" non-linear estimates of the equations the constraints appear to have been satisfied by equations (4.17) and (4.18): although the constraints resulted in our obtaining the negative value for λ reported above. If λ had been positive, we would have less difficulties: but because of the doubts about non-linear estimation we would have to perform some mental gymnastics to assume that we had "the" answer.

So far we have indicated some of the empirical results we obtained from applying Malkiel's basic hypothesis to the U.K. data. Since we have been concentrating our attention on equation (4.4) we have taken the Malkiel view that σ is constant, and that $2k\sigma$ is the size of the normal range. Since R_t^n is changing, whether measured in the way we have chosen to measure it for the market, or in the way that Malkiel himself chose to measure it, the standard deviation itself should be regarded as changing. For it must be regarded as a simple kind of risk-factor associated with the given value of the normal rate. So for every period, if there is a different value of the normal or average rate of interest, there could be a different normal interest rate range.

We shall now consider letting the standard deviation be a variable, doing so in one particular way, and furthermore making k in equation (4.2) equal to unity. The method of estimating the standard deviation that we have chosen to report on in this paper is to calculate the normal rate by the approach adopted above, say by scheme (4.5), choosing the weights such that they do sum to unity. In this event we can regard the weights as *probabilities*;* so that the value of R^n calculated by this method for any period of time is regarded as the mathematical expectation of the long rate for that period, being the sum of the rates of interest in $t-i$ each multiplied by their appropriate probability of occurrence. σ is then obtained as the standard deviation of the series of actual (possible) interest rates for t, that are involved in the formation of the normal rate at t, around the normal rate. It is then further assumed that the rates that are used to form a given normal rate are part of a normal distribution, so that the

* Griliches (53) in his excellent survey has discussed the weights as probabilities—but in a different way from us.

The Term Structure of Interest Rates

only necessary measure of "risk" is the spread/range of the normal rate.*

The "reduced form" equivalent of equation (4.4) in the present circumstances produced this result:

$$R_t = \overset{*}{2.81} - 0.326\ X + \overset{*}{0.573}\ S_t \qquad (4.19)$$
$$(0.276)\quad (0.271)\quad\ \ (0.072)$$
$$\bar{R}^2 = 0.61, \quad d = 0.47$$

where

$$X = \left(\frac{R_t + \sigma_t - R_t^n}{2\sigma_t}\right)$$

The crucial coefficient, that on X, is not statistically significant: also the low value of the Durbin–Watson statistic indicates serious positive auto-correlation of the residuals, a fact further enhanced by noting that Orcutt's coefficient is 0.7 and significant. Equation (4.19) should contain the *restriction* that the coefficient on S_t is unity. An F-test (F is 35), causes us to reject the hypothesis that the S_t coefficient is unity. But we cannot dismiss the hypothesis on such flimsy grounds, because we have not been able to impose enough restrictions on equation (4.19) to make it conform to the basic hypothesis. The reason for this is not hard to find: we cannot transfer R_t *per se* from the r.h.s. of the equation to the l.h.s.

In this specification of Malkiel's hypothesis the best results are obtained with the short rate as the dependent variable. The equivalent of equation (4.19) is:

$$S_t = \overset{*}{-1.82} + \overset{*}{0.964}\ X_t + \overset{*}{1.059}\ R_t \qquad (4.20)$$
$$(0.65)\quad (0.343)\quad\ \ (0.135)$$
$$\bar{R}^2 = 0.66, \quad d = 0.78$$

In equation (4.20) all the parameters are highly significant—even if

---

* Tests so far carried out indicate that this is a reasonable assumption. But we shall have to await further work before we can be even remotely dogmatic on this issue. What we have done in calculating the standard deviation *could* be expressed in this fashion: in assessing the normal rate, in terms of the conventional probability approach to decision-taking under uncertainty, we have assumed that for each possible "state of nature" (15 in all for each t) there is only *one* possible yield.

we make some (arbitrary) allowance for the presence of serial correlation in the residuals—and they have their correct *a priori* signs, with b being negative and virtually speaking unity; a now having a positive value of 1.82. If the basic hypothesis is correct then, *inter alia*, the coefficient on R_t in (4.20) should statistically speaking be no different from unity, and this is the case. The two slope coefficients in (4.20) should also be equal: RLS estimate of (4.20) confirms that this is so (F being virtually zero once more).

In the nature of things it was not possible to develop the equation in the same way as we did for equation (4.4), neither was it possible to let the normal rate be entered as a distributed lag function rather than as an "observed" number. So, at best, these latest results can legitimately only be compared with those for equation (4.4) where the normal rate is entered in the latter fashion. It then transpires that it is impossible to choose between the short-rate equations, but that the long-rate equations are superior where the standard deviation is regarded as being *constant*. The relative importance of the two types of equation changes: for with the standard deviation constant the long-rate equations are the best, while for variable standard deviation the short-rate equations are best.

Thus, given the basic hypothesis, and given the method of estimating the normal rate of interest we can deduce that either (i) Malkiel's view that the standard deviation of return can be viewed as constant has some merit or (ii) the standard deviation needs to be assessed in a different way from the method reported on here, or possibly another risk-factor has to be brought within the scope of the analysis.

The basic Malkiel hypothesis can be further extended, in many ways, for example, by inclusion of more explicit recognition of expectations. The work of de Leeuw (54), which had a strong influence on the study by Modigliani and Sutch (55), is worth noting in this context. He used, *inter alia*, the Keynesian normal rate hypothesis ((59), pp. 201–204), with a constant standard deviation this is effectively the normal range hypothesis of Malkiel, which embodies in it the way that the market feels that interest rates are likely to move: but he did so together with the hypothesis advanced by Duesenberry (58). He suggested that "It would not ... be surprising if it turned out that a rise in rates led to an expectation of a further rise and vice versa" ((58), p. 318). So, expectations of capital gains, central to the Keynesian theory concerning the *level* of interest rates (about which Duesenberry was writing), and to de Leeuw's and Malkiel's hypothesis on the term-structure, could be influenced, so it is suggested, by both ideas, but influenced in opposite directions.

In using this additional expectational variable we did not follow the approaches adopted by de Leeuw or Modigliani-Sutch. We took the equations discussed earlier, and those not reported on here, and added to them in their "mathematical" form, variables such as R_t, R_{t-1}, R_{t-2}, ..., to catch the influence of recent changes in the long rate on the yield gap. However, on an equation-by-equation basis, no systematic results emerged; and for the most part the earlier results were as good as, if not better than, the new equations. More work is being done on this topic; and variables have been experimented with to indicate the time-dimension of expectations related to the extra expectational variable. So far the results have been disappointing. This could be because of data deficiencies, or improper choice of time-dimension variables: but it is most likely to be due to the fact that so very little room for improvement remains for explaining the yield gap when the long-rate equations are used. De Leeuw found that both the normal rate variable and the Duesenberry-type expectational variable were significant influences on the term-structure. But, leaving aside data considerations our results are not directly comparable to his. Also they are not strictly comparable to those obtained by Modigliani and Sutch, for they combined the normal rate hypothesis and the Duesenberry idea into one variable, and furthermore, in considering the "average" or normal rate of interest they use the Almon lag (57), which we, of course, have not; although it is doubtful if our results would be much changed if we were to use that lag, even if we were to feel that it was economically superior to the Koyck-type lag.

5

We must now offer a few brief concluding remarks:

(1) A simple portfolio approach enables us to see the essence of the traditional theory and to point out its deficiencies. However, given the assumptions of the theory, and despite what one might feel about it, it is possible to deduce many (appealing) propositions that, in principle, are testable. However, unless we have independent evidence on expected rates of interest, not one of these propositions can, in fact, be tested.

(2) Given the nature of the data at our disposal, the only tests related to the Hicks–Lutz theory that can be undertaken are those devised by Meiselman. However, it is not at all certain that for all times such an error-learning model of the Meiselman kind is apposite; despite the acceptance of models of that nature in economics. Also, although we must bear in mind the (possible) deficiencies in the data we have used, the Meiselman hypothesis is not a very powerful, or a universally acceptable, one for the financial markets in the U.K. and Italy, for the periods of our enquiry. However, it is clear that we cannot make any firm judgement about the presence of liquidity premiums; and therefore about the wisdom of ignoring the traditional theory in favour of the risk-premium theory.

(3) The Malkiel theory, although not at variance with the traditional theory (or the Meiselman hypothesis), is a theory which, starting with slightly different premises from the traditional theory, allows a straightforward theory to be formulated on the term structure, and in terms of the long–short yield gap itself. This it can do because the nature of interest rates is such that the whole spread of rates, or the changes in yield spreads, can be highlighted by concentration on one yield differential, say that between the longest- and the shortest-dated stock in existence (this is basically true for our data).

Although there are some theoretical problems involved in accepting the Malkiel hypothesis, most of the problems associated with it concern its empirical testing, especially the proxying of the variables in the model. There is the added difficulty of not being able to obtain a simultaneous solution to the basic parameters of the model. Having said all this, if we retain certain ways of assessing the variables in the model it appears that, at least using the long-rate as the dependent variable, we can produce good results for the term structure. Also it then appears that, using one method of measuring the normal range, Malkiel might well have been right, on the whole, to ignore the range *per se* and to rely on the relationship between the long rate and the normal rate to capture the (Keynesian) influences he felt were at work. However, if we attempt to explain the term-structure from the short end of the market it seems that it could be worthwhile to attempt to include explicitly a measure of the range.

(4) We have partly indicated some of the econometric difficulties involved in testing a hypothesis such as that advocated by Malkiel: but we must never allow ourselves to forget those difficulties: we must be hesitant about drawing firm conclusions from our work. We

must also always bear in mind that we are continuously not just testing the basic theory itself, but also ways of measuring normal rates, and so on. Before conclusions can be deduced on those issues numerous other hypotheses have to be considered and followed-up.

REFERENCES

1 B. G. Malkiel, *The Term Structure of Interest Rates*, Princeton, Princeton University Press, 1966.

2 J. L. Ford and T. Stark, *Long and Short Term Interest Rates*, Oxford, Blackwell, 1967.

3 J. M. Culbertson, 'The Term Structure of Interest Rates', *Quarterly Journal of Economics*, November 1957, pp. 485–517.

4 J. M. Culbertson, 'The Interest Rate Structure: Towards Completion of the Classical System', in F. H. Hahn and F. P. R. Brechling (eds.), *The Theory of Interest Rates*, London, Macmillan and Co., 1965.

5 R. G. Hawtrey, 'A Rejoinder', *The Manchester School*, October 1939, pp. 156–158.

6 J. R. Hicks, *Value and Capital*, Oxford, Clarendon Press, 2nd ed., 1946.

7 F. A. Lutz, 'The Structure of Interest Rates', *Quarterly Journal of Economics*, November 1940, pp. 36–63. This is reprinted in the American Economic Association, *Readings in the Theory of Income Distribution*, Homewood, R. D. Urwin, 1946, pp. 499–529. References to Lutz are to this reprint.

8 F. A. Lutz, *The Theory of Interest*, Dordrecht-Holland, D. Reidel Publishing Co., 1966.

9 I. Fisher, *The Theory of Interest*, New York, Macmillan and Co., 1930.

10 J. M. Keynes, *A Treatise on Money*, Volume II, London, Macmillan and Co., 1930.

11 D. G. Luckett, 'Professor Lutz and the Structure of Interest Rates', *Quarterly Journal of Economics*, February 1959, pp. 131–144.

12 H. Markowitz, 'Portfolio Selection', *Journal of Finance*, March 1952, pp. 77–91.

13 H. Markowitz, *Portfolio Selection: Efficient Diversification of Investments*, New York, Wiley, 1959.

14 J. Tobin, 'Liquidity Preference as Behaviour towards Risk', *Review of Economic Studies*, February 1958, pp. 65–86.

15 J. Tobin, 'The Theory of Portfolio Selection' in F. H. Hahn and F. P. R. Brechling (eds.), *The Theory of Interest Rates*, London, Macmillan and Co., 1965.

16 H. G. Johnson, *Essays in Monetary Economics*, London, Geo. Allen and Unwin, 1968.

17 J. R. Hicks, *Critical Essays in Monetary Theory*, Oxford, Clarendon Press, 1967.

18 D. G. Champernowne, *Uncertainty and Estimation in Economics*, Volume 3, Edinburgh, Oliver and Boyd, 1969.

19 K. H. Borch, *The Economics of Uncertainty*, Princeton, Princeton University Press, 1968.

20 M. Friedman, *Essays in Positive Economics*, Chicago, Chicago University Press, 1953.

21 G. L. S. Shackle, *Uncertainty in Economics* (1st edition), Cambridge, Cambridge University Press, 1953.

22 G. L. S. Shackle, *Decision, Order and Time in Human Affairs* (1st edition), Cambridge, Cambridge University Press, 1964.

23 J. von Neumann and O. Morgenstern, *Theory of Games and Economic Behaviour* (3rd edition), Princeton, Princeton University Press.

24 M. Friedman and L. J. Savage, 'The Utility Analysis of Choices Involving Risk', *Journal of Political Economy*, August 1948, pp. 279–304.

25 W. F. Sharpe, 'Capital Asset Prices: A Theory of Market Equilibrium Under Conditions of Risk', *Journal of Finance*, September 1964, pp. 425–442.

26 K. J. Arrow, *Aspects of the Theory of Risk-Bearing*, Yrjo Jahnssonin Saatio, Helsinki, 1965.

27 D. Meiselman, *The Term Structure of Interest Rates*, Englewood Cliffs, Prentice-Hall, 1962.

28 J. W. Conard, *An Introduction to the Theory of Interest*, Berkeley, University of California Press, 1959.

29 J. W. Conard, *The Behaviour of Interest Rates*, New York, National Bureau of Economic Research, 1966.

30 W. T. Newlyn, *The Theory of Money*, Oxford, Clarendon Press, 1962.

31 A. Buse, 'Hicks, Lutz, Meiselman and the Expectations Theory', *Review of Economic Studies*, July 1970, pp. 395–406.

32 D. Fisher, 'The Structure of Interest Rates: A Comment', *Economica*, November 1964, pp. 412–419.

33 D. Fisher, 'Expectations, the Term Structure of Interest Rates, and Recent British Experience', *Economica*, August 1966, pp. 319–329.

34 J. A. G. Grant, 'Meiselman on the Structure of Interest Rates: A British Test', *Economica*, February 1964, pp. 51–71.

35 D. Durand, *Basic Yields of Corporate Bonds 1900–1942*, New York, National Bureau of Economic Research, 1942; and also, 'A Quarterly Series of Corporate Basic Yields, 1952–1957; and some Attendant Reservations', *Journal of Finance*, September 1958, pp. 348–356.

36 S. Homer, *A History of Interest Rates*, New Brunswick, Rutgers University Press, 1963.

37 R. S. Masera, 'Least-Squares Construction of the Yield Curves for Italian Government Securities, 1957–1967', *Banca Nazionale del Lavoro*, Part I, December 1969, pp. 347–371; Part II, March 1970, pp. 82–102.

38 W. B. Hickman, 'The Term Structure of Interest Rates: an Exploratory Analysis', New York, National Bureau of Economic Research, mimeographed 1943.

39 C. Walker, 'Federal Reserve Policy and the Structure of Interest Rates on Government Securities', *Quarterly Journal of Economics*, February 1954, pp. 19–42.

40 L. G. Telser, 'A Critique of Some Recent Empirical Research on the Explanation of the Term Structure of Interest Rates', *Journal of Political Economy*, December 1967, pp. 546–561.

41 R. A. Kessel, *The Cyclical Behaviour of the Term Structure of Interest Rates*, New York, National Bureau of Economic Research, 1965.

42 J. H. Wood, 'Expectations, Error and the Term Structure of Interest Rates', *Journal of Political Economy*, April 1963, pp. 160–171.

43 J. H. Wood, 'The Expectation Hypothesis, the Yield Curve, and Monetary Policy', *Quarterly Journal of Economics*, August 1964, pp. 457–470.

44 E. Feige, 'Expectations and Adjustments in the Monetary Sector', *American Economic Review*, papers and proceedings, May 1967, pp. 462–473.

45 N. R. Draper and H. Smith, *Applied Regression Analysis*, New York, John Wiley and Sons, 1966.

46 E. Malinvaud, *Statistical Methods of Econometrics*, Amsterdam, North-Holland Publishing Co., 1966.

47 F. M. Fisher, *The Identification Problem in Econometrics*, New York, McGraw-Hill, 1966.

48 A. S. Goldberger, *Econometric Theory*, New York, John Wiley and Sons, 1964.

49 L. R. Klein, 'The Estimation of Distributed Lags', *Econometrica*, October 1958, pp. 553–565.

50 L. A. Koyck, *Distributed Lags and Investment Analysis*, Amsterdam, North-Holland Publishing Co., 1954.

51 D. Laidler and J. M. Parkin, 'The Demand for Money in the United Kingdom 1956–1967: Preliminary Estimates', *Manchester School*, September 1970, pp. 187–208.

52 N. Liviatan, 'Consistent Estimation of Distributed Lags', *International Economic Review*, January 1963, pp. 44–52.

53 Z. Griliches, 'Distributed Lags: A Survey', *Econometrica*, January 1967, pp. 16–49.

54 F. de Leeuw, 'A Model of Financial Behaviour', in J. S. Duesenberry, G. Fromm, L. R. Klein and E. Kuh (eds.), *The Brookings Quarterly Econometric Model of the United States*, Chicago, Rand McNally and Co., 1965.

55 F. Modigliani and R. Sutch, 'Innovations in Interest Rate Policy', *American Economic Review*, May 1966, pp. 178–197.

56 J. B. Michaelson, 'The Term Structure of Interest Rates: Comment', *Quarterly Journal of Economics*, February 1963, pp. 166–174.

57 S. Almon, 'The Distributed Lag Between Capital Appropriations and Expenditures', *Econometrica*, January 1965, pp. 178–196.

58 J. S. Duesenberry, *Business Cycles and Economic Growth*, New York, McGraw-Hill, 1958.

59 J. M. Keynes, *The General Theory*, London, Macmillan and Co., 1936.

Uncertainty and Dynamic Axioms

SIR ROY HARROD

Formerly of Christ Church, Oxford

It was a great pleasure to me to be asked to write in this volume; and I esteem it an honour also. Shackle has made many illustrious contributions to economics; among these his work on uncertainty has pride of place, and it may well constitute the most important work done on that subject in our generation.

In one way, therefore, it seems appropriate to offer something within that field for this volume. From another point of view, however, it may be regarded as presumptuous! Accordingly, I hasten to add that I propose to restrict myself to a particular theme, namely the relation of uncertainty to certain formulations in pure growth theory that I have propounded.

In his *Years of High Theory* Shackle has reviewed some of these in very generous terms. At the same time he has found a good many difficulties. He holds that some spring from my reluctance to use *ex-ante* concepts, as commonly understood; and he doubts whether the matters in question can be properly sorted out without any analysis of time lags. Also he holds, rightly, that one cannot get to grips with the subject without taking into account the state of mind of those who place orders at the time when they place them, including their uncertain expectations about the course of events to come.

In my own mind the paramount importance of uncertainty in relation to the basic dynamic axioms has always been present. I have to admit that I may not have spelt this out for readers, and, worse admission, that I may not have spelt out my background assumptions sufficiently fully to myself. On the other hand, there is an extensive treatment of uncertainty in my essay on Profit (*Economic Essays*,

Macmillan, 1952). It is difficult in the complex subject of economics not to take certain reasonable assumptions for granted; but it may nevertheless be dangerous not to re-inspect them, for their relevance to a particular issue, and even not to wander away down certain by-paths, in order to make quite sure what is there. So, this seems to be a suitable occasion for me to spell out the assumptions about uncertainty that were, or ought to have been, in my mind.

A preliminary point, suggested by Shackle's critique, is whether we should define the growth rate of an economy at a particular point of time as the rate of growth of orders, or the rate of growth of the net domestic product. Incidentally, what is a product? A residential dwelling is usually regarded as one. So are "consumer durables". Once the consumer has paid his price or signed his lease or hire purchase contract, that is considered to be the end of the matter.

The question may be more difficult in the case of purchases or acquisitions by non-consumers. It seems necessary to introduce an arbitrary time limit, like a year. We usually define the capital/output ratio as per annum. The methods of national income statisticians in defining what outputs should or should not be regarded as part of the N.D.P. in a given year may be accepted provisionally—always, of course, subject to the possibility of criticisms from time to time.

It is presumably conformable with Shackle's intention that, in considering the growth rate of orders, we should subtract any increase in the number of orders placed in respect of a single unit of N.D.P., e.g. because of a splitting up of the productive process into a greater number of stages, each undertaken by separate businesses. Conversely, if there is vertical integration, the value of the consequent reduction in all orders placed for a unit of product should be added to the recorded value of orders placed in respect of that unit. In other words, the concept we need is the growth in the value of orders net of any change in that value that is due to a change in the number of orders placed between the inception of the process of producing a certain unit of N.D.P and the completed production of that unit.

Orders collectively resulting in a unit of N.D.P., as defined by the statisticians, are scattered over the successive processes of production. As regards the forms of the objects ordered there is usually a backward procession in time away from objects most closely resembling the unit of the N.D.P. in question towards what may be called ur-objects. A purchase in a retail store may cause a deflation in its stock, leading to its stepping up the size of its order on the next occasion of placing one. So backwards through the wholesaler, if any, to the producer of the object in its final forms and backwards again to the producers of components and raw materials; and along the path there may be by-products in the form of orders for an enlargement of capital equipment, whether shop premises, extra factory plant for one or other of the stages of production of the finished articles and, finally, factory plant for the producers of the factory plant aforementioned.

Many of these orders may be for goods of value far in excess of the extra unit or units of N.D.P. proposed to be produced at a given point of time. But we may suppose that, subject to systematic disturbances shortly to be discussed, and to chance, the cases where the value of capital goods (or extra inventories) ordered greatly exceeds the value of the increment of final product required are balanced by cases where, for the time being, no orders for capital equipment (or additions to inventories) need be placed in relation to the increased sales of final products. Estimates of the value of all orders should always be seasonally adjusted.

If there is any growth at all in an economy, the value of orders placed at a given point of time will exceed the value of the N.D.P. at that point of time. Most orders relate to parts of the N.D.P. that will accrue at a future time. Since the total N.D.P. will be greater at a future time, the value of orders at a given time will be higher than the value of the total N.D.P. at that same time.

In what follows I set out three basic relations between an equilibrium ("warranted") growth rate of orders and an equilibrium ("warranted") growth rate of output. The "warranted" growth rate is, of course, different from the actual growth rate, to which I shall presently come, and also from the "natural" growth rate. The "warranted" growth rate of the N.D.P. is determined by the savings ratio and the capital/output ratio, while the "natural" rate is determined by the increase of manpower resources and technological progress.

1. If the savings ratio and capital/output ratio remain constant, the warranted growth rate of orders will be identical with that of the N.D.P.

2. If the saving ratio is rising, the (rising) warranted growth of the N.D.P. and that of orders will be identical.

3. But if the saving ratio remains constant and the capital/output ratio falls, the warranted rate of growth of orders will rise at the same

rate as the warranted growth of N.D.P. rises, but will stand continuously at a lower level.

The reason for this is that as Cr (required capital/output ratio) declines, the average time-span between orders and completions also declines. If x stands for the fraction by which the time span declines per annum and the warranted growth rate of N.D.P. is equal to Sd/Cr, which rises continually because Cr is declining, that of orders will be $(Sd/Cr)(1-x)$. The two fractions clearly rise at the same rate, but the fraction showing the warranted growth rate of orders stands continuously below that for N.D.P. This entails that the proportionate excess of orders over N.D.P. continuously declines. But it must remain in excess for so long as there is a positive time-span, which, in effect, means always. Conversely if Cr is rising, the growth rate of orders will be continuously above that of N.D.P.

In the foregoing we have been considering continuing growth rates and continuing accelerations or decelerations, and second order differentials can be brought in also. There has been no reference to discontinuities or inflections in the curves. If any have occurred within the relevant backward time horizon, the relations of the curves will be different, and would have to be studied by reference to the theory of time-lags. I have always recognized this.

But I have taken the view that I should use what powers I have to establish the interrelations between growth rates proceeding continuously before going on to the subject of discontinuities. It is my impression that the study of discontinuities will continue to be ineffective, so long as we lack a set of propositions showing the interrelations between continuing growth rates of the various elements. To establish such propositions seems to me to have first priority. More still remains to be done in this area.

It may be objected that the actual world is fraught with so many discontinuities that a study that ignores them is very unrealistic. That may be so; but it is not quite relevant. Understanding of the interrelations between continuing growth rates (including accelerations etc. if and when such obtain) is needed to provide the intellectual foundation for the analysis of the consequences of discontinuities of various kinds.

If a certain value of orders is placed at a given point of time, one must not expect a continuing stream of activity in consequence of these orders of equal amount until the accrual of what is ordered. In most cases there is more likely to be a humped curve with activities starting at a fairly low level, reaching its maximum well before the end of the period, and then relapsing to a low level towards the end of the period. The curves, of course, need not always be of this shape. There will be a variety of patterns. It does not follow that aggregate activity will at the point of time in question be less than that shown in the formula, because the activity due to orders previously placed will probably be above average in relation to the whole course of time following those orders.

There may often be an interval between the placing of an order and the start of work due to it. Such intervals may be divided into two classes. On the one hand, the interval may be due to the operation of ordinary administrative machinery. In this case, the zero activity in the period following the placing of the order may be regarded as part of the shape of the humped curve already mentioned. This phenomenon should not disturb the regular relation between the warranted growth of orders and the warranted growth of activity concurrently proceeding.

The second case is when there is a greater time-lag between the receipt of the order and the inception of work than is normal. This may be due to orders being at such a level that there is not sufficient capacity to start activating them as quickly as usual. In this case, the level of orders must be above its "warranted" level; it will be a symptom of excessive aggregate demand, i.e. "inflationary pressure".

We have been considering the properties of an equilibrium growth rate of orders and its relation to an equilibrium growth rate of the N.D.P. It is when we turn to the actual growth rate of orders that uncertainty comes into the picture, and indeed into the foreground of it.

The totality of orders at a given point of time is the sum of individual orders at that time. Every person and every firm that places an order has to take a forward look, to determine the size of the order and, indeed, whether it is wise to place an order at all. Each entrepreneurial unit will be confronted with a number of uncertainties about the future course of events. These may be divided into the specific and the generic.

The specific uncertainties relate to the specific character of the goods or services that the ordering agent wishes to make available. They depend on such matters as changes of taste on the part of the buying public, which may be favourable or unfavourable to the would-be supplier. There is also the possibility of changes of technology, which may make it expedient for a producer to delay for a period before installing new equipment, although he may need it at once, owing to the danger, which may be a probability, nearing unity, that it may become obsolete before he has got worthwhile work out of it. Technological developments may affect the designs of consumer goods also, and, if events are on the move, it may be expedient not to plunge heavily into plans for producing more of the old designs. The producer has to think also of his own competitive strength. Will he be able to gain a larger share of the market for what he produces, or will his share inevitably decline? Some of these problems may be partly soluble by means of market research. But the validity of the findings of that research may still be uncertain. Or again, the reduction of uncertainty by such research may in some cases not seem to the producer worth the money that the research would cost him. It is not necessary in this place to attempt to cover the whole ground of specific uncertainties. It is obvious that the list of them would be very long indeed.

These uncertainties confront a very large number of producers, more broadly, of orderers, in an economy of reasonable size. Each and all of them will be endeavouring to make the best guess that he can. It would be a sort of miracle if they all got the right answer in relation to what was to come. Would it be reasonable to think that, on the average, over a very large number of independent decision-makers, errors would cancel out? Would those who overestimated possibilities balance those who underestimated them? If this were so, the general level of decisions over the whole economy would conform to the warranted value of them. This would be a rather precarious assumption, even if the economy were very atomistic. If errors of judgement in the same direction happen to be made by a few firms that bulk large in the total economy, these errors could affect the average overall estimate in the economy of what should be done. However, if uncertainties were confined to specific matters, there might be at least some tendency to the cancelling out of errors.

Then we come to the generic uncertainties. These concern the question as to whether the economy as a whole is likely to be booming or quiescent. The answer to this will clearly affect the judgement of each entrepreneur about the right number of orders. Whether the economy is booming or quiescent will affect a wide range of end products, although not of course in the same degree. There are certain staple goods, "necessities", for which the demand will not fall much in times of depression nor rise much in times of boom. Then there may be new type articles coming into use, which may be destined to rank as "semi-necessities" at some future date, for which the demand is growing rapidly; such a demand may go on pushing upward through a period of quite severe depression. One may think of wireless sets during the great slump after 1929. Then again there may be other new goods of a luxury type, for which the demand will increase rapidly only in fair weather. Since goods differ from one to another in these respects, producers have to consider how their own will be affected. In part, it is true, this belongs to the realm of "specific" uncertainties, but behind them is the generic uncertainty of whether the economy is in fact going to be booming or stagnant. And here we have a high degree of uncertainty. While specific uncertainties may be reduced in part by additional expenditure on market research, much less can be done to reduce uncertainty by a study of the wider forces affecting the general condition of the economy. It is true that we now have highly-priced "forecasting" services, and these are being assiduously marketed. It would be interesting to know if the forecasters of the general state of the economy can make a reliable forecast of the demand for their own product. These forecasts are not very trustworthy. The reason is, not so much a lack of efficiency on the part of the forecasters, as the fact that the causes of the generic movements of the future are insufficiently understood by the world's greatest experts—no doubt there will be continuing improvement in this respect. It might even be argued that the causes are sometimes in principle unknowable, since they depend on the decisions of politicians, which in turn may be geared to some quite extraneous circumstances. To get things straight, forecasters might have to go right outside the field of economic forces, and to make a study in depth of the psychology of politicians.

Thus there is all the difference between the specific areas where more detailed study could give greater accuracy and the generic area where the question of what will happen is much more difficult to answer and where the matter may indeed be indeterminate. In this generic sphere it is much less likely that errors will cancel out. Symptoms may influence a wide range of representative entrepreneurs in the same way; and yet the conclusions flowing from this influence may well be incorrect.

If the entrepreneurs each and all adhered to the warranted growth rate, that would make them feel that they had done the right thing.

If they made errors that cancelled out, so that total orders and total activity added up to the warranted growth rates, the upward corrections made by those dissatisfied with their position would cancel the downward course made by others and the economy as a whole would stay on its warranted growth path.

But if total activity at a given point of time is not equal to the warranted level, corrections will not bring it back there. I now come to what I have called my "instability" principle. I submit that this has its place and importance, but it is only one aspect of my growth theory. Some commentators on my work have written (incorrectly) as though it constituted the major part of my growth theory. Furthermore there have been gross exaggerations. For instance some writers have referred to a "knife-edge", which is really a caricature of my whole position. It is true that, if one is balancing on a knife-edge, one is certainly in a position of unstable equilibrium. But so one would be if sitting at the top of a fairly flat shallow dome. I have not attempted any measurement of the likely gradient of the declivity, on either side of the warranted rate. But, as an example of what might be possible I wrote in my original essay on 'Dynamic Theory' (*Economic Journal*, March 1939) about "the reaction time... required for an undue accretion or depletion of capital goods [capital goods here include inventories] to exert its influence upon the flow of orders—if this reaction time is six months." An object that it takes six months to disturb can hardly be said to be on a knife-edge. The question is how long it is before a disturbance prompts an entrepreneur to reconsider his ordering policy. While definitely repudiating the idea of a knife-edge, I think that "six months" errs in the other direction, making the representative entrepreneur seem more set in his ways than he normally is.

While uncertainty about the future has to be taken very much into account in analysing what influences decision, present experience must have some influence also. Let G = actual growth, G_w = warranted growth, s the actual saving ratio, C the actual incremental capital/output ratio and C_r the required incremental capital/output ratio. If $G > G_w$, then either $s > sd$ or $C < C_r$ or both. In this case we may take the question of the capital/output ratio first. In this simple and basic formulation fixed capital is lumped together with circulating capital. In the situation presented the weighted average of all entrepreneurial experience is a shortage of capital. If their experience had been that their level of capital was just about right and they had made certain decisions about what orders to place in the light of their guesses about the future, then the presumption is that their present experience of a shortage of capital will cause them to order more than if their present experience was of a sufficiency of capital. How great the uncertainty about the future is will differ from case to case. The importance of current experience in governing the amount of orders placed will also vary from case to case. But it may surely be taken as axiomatic that on the overall average somewhat more orders will be placed if on the overall average the present experience is one of a shortage of capital, fixed or circulating. Whether it takes a week, or, as in my original article, six months, for the average entrepreneur to be influenced by present experience, will also doubtless differ from case to case. The converse proposition also holds; if the actual rate is running below the warranted rate, present experience will be that capital, fixed or circulating, is redundant, and this will tend to push actual growth further below the warranted rate.

There will be similar perverse adjustments on the side of the saving ratio. Here again, there will be interplay with uncertainty. If a company finds its profit, and thereby its de facto reserve, running above what it needs on its existing policies, it may decide to distribute more, which will be a force tending to make shareholders increase expenditure (though doubtless they will save some part of the extra dividend), or it may review its policies and decide to be more ambitious, whether in the production of the goods in which it specializes or perhaps by planning mergers and takeovers. The latter policy might leave the output plans of the parent company exactly where they were; but it is reasonable to suppose that on the overall average the takeovers will lead to some increase of output. Conversely, if the firm finds itself subject to a profit squeeze, it may be under a *force majeure* to cut back on its previous plans. Here too the excess or deficiency of saving tends to move plans and orders further from the equilibrium growth rate. And this will have a further perverse effect.

In the above, I have repeated some things that I have written before. It was expedient to do so in order to show how closely the instability principle is intertwined in all respects with the uncertainty of expectations. I now pass to another aspect of the role of uncertainty, where it plays a most important part. I refer to the question of the rate of interest.

There is a view commonly associated with the name of Irving

Fisher, but also to be found in Marshall, that the market rate of interest will tend to be equal to some "natural" rate (however defined) plus the rate at which prices are known to be going to rise during the relevant time horizon, or minus the rate at which prices are known to be going to fall. This view has been extremely widely held, especially in the recent years of painful inflationary experience. It may be secretly welcomed by some central bankers in quest of an alibi, when blame for high interest rates is laid on the faults of the international monetary system or excessively tight domestic monetary policies on the part of the central banks themselves.

Keynes entirely repudiated this doctrine.* I was convinced by Keynes's reasonings at the time and have always included his repudiation in my standard lectures on this subject. He did, however, hold, and this seems correct, that the expectation of inflation would reduce the yield of equities, real estate and objets d'art—the yield of the last mentioned being the pleasure given by them—relatively to the yield of fixed interest bonds. This theory has been manifestly verified during recent years. Cash and fixed interest bonds are denominated in money, and neither has a hedge against inflation. The rate of interest constitutes the rate at which bonds and cash exchange for each other. As neither of these assets has a hedge against inflation, it is logically impossible for the rate at which they exchange against each other to be altered by the knowledge that there will be more (or less) inflation than was previously presupposed. What is logically impossible must not be included by a lecturer in his exposition of economic theory. However, in this stance one is conscious of a conflict with an overwhelming private opinion. "Is it not obvious", people say, "that the expectation of inflation is having its effect on current interest rates?"

The conflict may, I submit, be resolved by reference to uncertainty. In the foregoing I used the rather strong word "knowledge" advisedly, with reference to expectations about inflation. "Very strongly and almost universally held opinion" might for practical purposes come to the same thing. It is necessary for the Fisher doctrine that there should not merely be a view that there will be inflation, but also a view about how much the inflation is going to be. Otherwise the Fisher doctrine would merely affirm that, if the natural rate were 4%, the actual rate would be somewhat in excess; this is rather vague,

* See, especially, *General Theory of Employment, Interest and Money*, pp. 140–143.

and in examples of the effect of inflation on the rate of interest a definite rate of inflation is usually inserted.

The argument is entirely transformed, if we posit uncertainty about what the rate of inflation is going to be. The doctrine that uncertainty about the rate of inflation may raise the actual rate of interest is logically tenable and conforms quite well with recent experience and with common sense. Thus here uncertainty plays a primary role.

If it is known for certain what the rate of inflation will be within the relevant time horizon, the asset holder will distribute his assets between those having a hedge against inflation (equities etc.) on the one hand, and those not having any hedge against inflation, namely bonds and cash, on the other hand. If it is known what the rate of inflation will be, there will be no need for any subsequent redistribution of assets within the time horizon. Depending on the rate of inflation, the asset holder will decide how much current income he is prepared to sacrifice in order to have his hedge against inflation. The sacrifice acceptable may not be quite as large as the future rate of inflation, as there may be a greater risk in regard to all non-money-denominated assets than there is in the case of Government bonds; indeed, in former times, when the expectation of inflation was absent, the yield on even first-rate equities, apart from those related to sectors with supernormal growth rates, usually stood above the yield on bonds.

Then, as between bonds and cash, neither having a hedge against inflation, the asset holder would distribute his holdings between the two with reference to the amount of liquidity he required. This is Keynesian doctrine and still holds. In the overall aggregate, the relative amount of cash and bonds available is mainly determined by the monetary authorities. If for any reason asset holders wish to become more liquid, then, unless the monetary authorities thoughtfully increase the amount of cash and decrease the amount of bonds on the market, the rate of interest will go up. It may rise or fall from time to time, according to the circumstances of the case, when the rate of inflation expected remains constant.

But now introduce uncertainty as regards what rate of inflation there is likely to be in the period ahead. In deciding what present income to sacrifice in order to go into assets with a hedge against inflation, the asset holder has presumably to make some approximate guess about what the rate of inflation will be in the immediately coming period. He may also entertain the belief that within a fairly short timespan it may become evident that the rate of inflation is going to be worse than he initially feared, or, alternatively, that the rate of inflation will be less severe. For instance, a General Election may return a Conservative Party to power, which many believe likely to take sterner measures against inflation than their predecessors. There may be a drop in what is considered likely to be the forthcoming rate of inflation. Then, if it appears that the Conservative Government does not take any manful measures, pessimism about the rate of inflation will increase. The situation will have become worse, because, before the Election there was at least the possibility of a Government coming into power that would take sterner measures against inflation, but after it it seems that there is no hope of either party taking firm measures. This example is given only as an illustration of what might happen. It is to be hoped that before these words are published it will have been found that the Conservative Government that came into power in 1970 will have proved to have taken strong and effective measures against inflation.

If uncertainty is present to an important extent, the asset holder may feel that, having made the best guess that he can at the moment for the short term, he may quite soon have to revise his views on the future course of inflation. There is a constraining force all the time on the amount of capital that he invests in assets having a hedge against inflation, because, by doing so, he loses income. He may judge, for instance, that he gets a nice balance between a hedge against inflation and a loss of current income by investing three-quarters of his capital in equities, etc. But, he may have had at the back of his mind, that, if the inflation gets worse, he may wish to go further than this, and sacrifice current income in respect of seven-eighths of his capital. It is important that he should be free to do this if the situation seems to demand it in the fairly near future.

And now we come to the relation between cash and bonds. Neither has a hedge against inflation. In regard to that, one is indifferent about which one holds; bonds have the advantage of yielding interest. But the uncertainty about how inflation is going to develop in the future makes the asset holder desire to keep liquid. If he goes too much into bonds, and then, after all, soon afterwards, wishes to increase the share of equities in his total capital, he may have to sell bonds at a loss. Uncertainty about the future course of inflation makes him desire to keep more liquid than he otherwise would. This drives up the rate of interest of the bonds. This is the pure Keynesian doctrine of liquidity preference, and it appears to cover the case of uncertainty about the future of inflation. Keynesian theory and the theory of uncertainty are happily married. The views currently held by the man in the street may be revised as follows. If he affirms that inflation at a known rate may simply be added to the natural rate of interest to determine the market rate of interest, he is wrong. His hunch that inflation has something to do with high interest may be justified, always provided that it is understood that what sends the rate of interest up is not a known prospective rate of inflation, but uncertainty about what that rate of inflation will be.

There may be extreme cases in which inflation alone can drive up the interest rate without uncertainty playing a great part. Inflation may be so great that the individual would seek rigidly to confine his holdings of money-denominated assets to the kind required for immediate transactions. He does not want bonds at any price. But someone has to hold the bonds. This may drive their value down to a very low level indeed. A classic instance of an astronomic rise of interest rates when inflation was very severe was in Germany in 1923. So averse were people from holding money-denominated assets that many, on payday, after doing the necessary shopping, came into banks to invest their small change in equities, even although they knew that they would have to sell them again within a week or two. Judgement about the German case is complicated by the fact that in the period of rampant inflation the total money supply in real terms fell to a very low level. People who have seen a billion Mark banknote (1923) may not appreciate this, and suppose that at that time there was an orgy of note issue. This was not the case; the note issue lagged way behind the price increases. This would tend to drive the rate of interest up on Keynesian principles.

We may conclude that in extreme cases of rampant inflation, when people do not want to hold any bonds, the mere fact of inflation, apart from uncertainty, can drive up the interest rate. Actually, such a case does not tend to help the Fisher doctrine because, when inflation is rampant, people have little idea about its probable precise rate, so that there is no definite rate that they can add on to the natural rate of interest on Fisher lines to yield an appropriate current market rate of interest. The rate of interest soars up because people desire to reduce their money-denominated assets to an absolute minimum, namely that required for immediate cash transactions.

But for more normal levels of inflation rates, the uncertainty doctrine holds. Within the realm of fairly moderate inflation, if there were certainty about what the rate of inflation would be, the prospective inflation would have no effect on the rate of interest. The greater the uncertainty, the higher will be the interest rate.

Liquidity, Uncertainty, and the Accumulation of Information*

JACK HIRSHLEIFER

University of California, Los Angeles

In the standard economic theory of value, market-clearing prices exist for all commodities. In such a model, all commodities are equally and perfectly "liquid". Clearly, the problem of imperfect liquidity arises only when one or more of the ground rules of the neoclassical model no longer obtains.

1. SOURCES OF ILLIQUIDITY†

The most obvious source of illiquidity is the fact that commodities are not in general perfectly and costlessly *marketable*, i.e., transaction costs exist in real-world asset markets. For one thing, limitations of information may prevent buyers and sellers from finding one another. Or, through misunderstanding or stubbornness, they might not succeed in arriving at a bargain even when a mutually advantageous trade between them is possible. Then an individual transactor will find himself in the position of balancing the conjectural net advantage of further search and consequent negotiation against the alternative

* The research underlying this paper was undertaken while the author held a National Science Foundation Fellowship at the Catholic University of Louvain. Research and clerical assistance were provided by the Centre for Operations Research and Econometrics at Louvain. Further clerical assistance was provided by the Western Management Science Institute, UCLA. Thanks are particularly due to Jacques Drèze for corrections and suggestions.

† For a related discussion, see J. Marschak, "Role of Liquidity under Complete and Incomplete Information", *American Economic Review*, Papers and Proceedings, May 1949, esp. pp. 182–183.

of accepting the best available offer now in hand. Since the costs and likely benefits of search and negotiations are in part a function of the nature of the commodity (its degree of standardization, its storability, portability, etc.), assets will vary in marketability. Marketability may also be affected by considerations other than the physical nature of the commodity. Tax provisions represent an obvious example: exchanges of some commodities, but not others, may be burdened by transaction duties—sales taxes, capital-gains taxes, etc. There may also be impaired marketability where a personal element attaches to an asset's productivity. In the case of a business firm whose success is associated with the personality of the proprietor, the sale-price of the physical assets of the firm will be low relative to the capitalization of the income yield to the present owner.

In the present paper, however, this entire range of phenomena is set aside. It will be assumed that costless competitive markets *do* exist, so that all commodites are perfectly marketable. The purpose behind this unrealistic assumption is to facilitate the analysis of another distinct source of illiquidity, quite apart from impaired marketability. This second source of illiquidity is connected with inability to revise plans for consumption and investment in the light of later and better knowledge. Such a loss of flexibility will be accepted, and illiquid assets held, only if (as will be seen below) these investments have an offsetting advantage in productivity, i.e., less liquid assets will be associated with a higher rate of yield.

The source of illiquidity considered here is associated with the length of the period to "maturity" of the asset. Maturity is an unambiguous concept only for assets possessing a *point-input point-output* payment pattern. Examples include some financial assets, such as bills sold at discount (but not stocks or interest-bearing bonds), and some physical assets, such as trees grown for timber (but not trees grown for fruit). The central principle involved will stand out most clearly if we deal here only with such assets, with their unique encashment dates. Illiquid assets then are those characterized by a relatively large discount for "premature" realization; this corresponds to a relatively high time-rate of return if the asset is held rather than so realized. It remains to be shown just what are the underlying forces making this come about, and in particular why the time-rate of discount is greater on long-maturity assets—so that these tend to earn a higher rate of yield than short-maturity assets.*

* For evidence on this point, see R. A. Kessel, *The Cyclical Behavior of the*

In examining this question, a connection will be shown between *physical* illiquidity and *market* illiquidity. However, it is essential to distinguish the two in considering investments. A recently planted tree will be a highly illiquid asset in the physical sense, for it may be many years before any significant fraction of the ultimate timber yield can be realized even by early cutting. But it may be that the asset has perfect market liquidity—if title to such a tree can be immediately converted into money at a price representing only a normal time-discount of the future value at maturity.

2. INTERTEMPORAL CHOICE UNDER UNCERTAINTY

A time-state model of choice under uncertainty* will be employed to examine the forces determining the liquidity "premiums" enjoyed by short-maturity assets in market equilibrium. The bearing of the following necessary conditions will be elucidated: (1) *Uncertainty*, of a type that is at least partially dispelled by the unfolding of events over time. (There must also, of course, be market aversion to uncertainty). (2) *Ability to defer* consumption-investment decisions, so that the reduction of uncertainty (accumulation of information) can be utilized. (3) At least partial *physical irreversibility* of longer-maturity productive investments, so that only the shorter-maturity investments can fully benefit from the possibility of reconsideration.

The time-state model used here has, as illustrated below, four marketable commodities: certain claims c_0 to consumption at time-0 ("the present"); contingent claims c_{1a} and c_{1b} to consumption at time-1, such claims being valid if and only if state-*a* or state-*b*, respectively, obtains at time-1; and certain claims c_2 to consumption at time-2.† A unit of *certain* dated income will be expressed as c_0, c_1, or c_2—where any particular numerical value given for c_1 indicates that

* K. J. Arrow, "The Role of Securities in the Optimal Allocation of Risk-Bearing," *Review of Economic Studies*, April 1964; G. Debreu, *Theory of Value*, Wiley, New York, 1959, Ch. 7; J. Hirshleifer, "Investment Decision under Uncertainty: Choice-Theoretic Approaches," *Quarterly Journal of Economics*, November 1965.

† This model is that employed in H. A. John Green, "Uncertainty and the 'Expectations Hypothesis'," *Review of Economic Studies*, October 1967. Green cites an earlier version of this paper as one of his sources, while this revised version in turn makes use of certain of his ideas.

Term Structure of Interest Rates, National Bureau of Economic Research, Occasional Paper 91 (1965).

both c_{1a} and c_{1b} have that same numerical value. The very special nature of this model is not really as restrictive as appears. The principles remain the same if the number of uncertain states is increased or if uncertainty is admitted at a number of future dates up to some terminal horizon.*

$$\begin{array}{c} \text{Date: } 0 \quad 1 \quad 2 \\ \hline \\ \text{Commodities: } c_0 \quad \begin{array}{c} c_{1a} \\ \\ c_{1b} \end{array} \quad c_2 \end{array}$$

At this point a formal definition of liquidity-premiums can be provided. Let P_0, P_1, and P_2 symbolize the prices of unit claims to certain incomes at the respective dates, all these prices being determined at $t = 0$. Let c_0 be the numeraire commodity, with $P_0 = 1$. A premium (which may or may not be a *liquidity*-premium) on the shorter-maturity asset will be said to exist at $t = 0$ if the ratio P_1/P_0 exceeds the ratio P_2/P_1—or, equivalently, if $(P_1/P_0)^2$ exceeds P_2/P_0.

The same relationships can be translated into interest-rate equivalents, where "riskless" interest rates (the only rates to be considered here) are defined in terms of prices of certain incomes of the various dates.

$$P_1 = \frac{1}{1+r_1}$$

$$P_2 = \frac{1}{(1+r_2)(1+r_1)} = \frac{1}{(1+R_2)^2}.$$

(1)

Here the lower-case symbols represent "short-term" interest rates, $1+r_1$ being the discounting factor translating certain income at time-1 into its equivalent at time-0 and $1+r_2$ the factor translating certain income at time-2 into the immediately preceding time-1. The upper-case symbol represents a "long-term" rate, $1+R_2$ being the discounting factor which (when properly compounded) translates income at time-2 into present income at time-0. Then a premium on the *prices* of short-term assets would correspond to a premium on the pecuniary *yields* of the long-term assets, so that R_2 exceeds r_1—or, equivalently, the "deferred" short-term rate r_2 would exceed the current short-term rate r_1.

Finally, we can define P_{1a} and P_{1b} as the prices of the respective contingent claims at time-1, where

* Green, *op. cit.*, p. 388.

$$P_1 = P_{1a} + P_{1b} \tag{2}$$

since a unit certain claim at a given date is obtained only by purchasing unit contingent claims covering each contingency at that date.

By an extension of the familiar Neumann–Morgenstern procedure to intertemporal risky choices, a cardinal function $v(c_0, c_1, c_2)$ spanning consumption at different dates and satisfying the expected-utility rule can be established.* Then:

$$U = \sum_{s=1}^{S} \pi_s \, v(c_{0s}, c_{1s}, c_{2s}) \tag{3}$$

where s is an index running over the S possible *sequences* of time-states, π_s is the probability of the sequence, while c_{ts} is the consumption at time-t associated with the sequence-s. In the particularly simple model used here, there are but two such sequences: c_0, c_{1a}, c_2 and c_0, c_{1b}, c_2. The sequence-probabilities correspond simply to the state-probabilities at time-1. These may be denoted π_a and π_b. So the utility function specializes to:

$$U = \pi_a v(c_0, c_{1a}, c_2) + \pi_b v(c_0, c_{1b}, c_2) \tag{3a}$$

To carry the analysis further, let us assume that a community of "representative individuals" with identical tastes and opportunities exists—each having the same endowment vector $(y_0, y_{1a}, y_{1b}, y_2)$ over the four commodities. Let us suppose initially the world is one of pure exchange, excluding all intertemporal productive possibilities. Among the excluded possibilities is simple storage, which (as a way of moving real income forward over time) represents one type of intertemporal productive transformation. In the absence of productive possibilities, a "sustaining" price vector must emerge making each representative individual just willing to hold his endowment combination—thus, no exchange actually takes place. The sustaining prices, with $P_0 = 1$, are given by:

$$\begin{aligned} P_{1a} &= \left.\frac{\partial c_0}{\partial c_{1a}}\right|_U = \frac{\pi_a v'_{1a}}{v'_0} \\ P_{1b} &= \left.\frac{\partial c_0}{\partial c_{1b}}\right|_U = \frac{\pi_b v'_{1b}}{v'_0} \\ P_2 &= \left.\frac{\partial c_0}{\partial c_2}\right|_U = \frac{v'_2}{v'_0} \end{aligned} \tag{4}$$

* The procedure involved is illustrated in J. H. Drèze and F. Modigliani, "Epargne et Consommation en Avenir Aléatoire," *Cahiers du Séminaire d'Econométrie*, 9, 7–33, 1966.

where the derivates are to be evaluated at the endowed quantities.

Consider the following numerical example. Let the v-function of (3a) be:

$$v(c_0, c_1, c_2) = \sum_{t=0}^{2} \ln c_t. \tag{5}$$

Then

$$U = \pi_a(\ln c_0 + \ln c_{1a} + \ln c_2) + \pi_b(\ln c_0 + \ln c_{1b} + \ln c_2) \tag{6}$$
$$= \ln c_0 + \pi_a \ln c_{1a} + \pi_b \ln c_{1b} + \ln c_2.$$

Let $\pi_a = \pi_b = \frac{1}{2}$, and the endowment vector $(y_0, y_{1a}, y_{1b}, y_2) =$ (100, 150, 75, 100). With $P_0 = 1$, the sustaining prices are $P_{1a} = 1/3$, $P_{1b} = 2/3$ (so that $P_1 = P_{1a} + P_{1b} = 1$), and $P_2 = 1$ (see Table 1).

Table 1. Pure-Exchange Solution

Quantities			Prices			Marginal Utilities		
t: 0	1	2	0	1	2	0	1	2
	150			1/3			.0033	
100		100	1		1	.01		.01
	75			2/3			.0067	
				1			.01	
			Discount Rates					
			−	0%	0%			

The numerical example has evidently been constructed to make all the interest rates zero; since $R_2 = r_1$, *no liquidity premium initially exists*. That is, riskless short-maturity assets (claims to c_1) are discounted at the same time-rate (0%) as long-maturity assets (claims to c_2).

Now, continuing in the context of the numerical example, suppose that the possibility of production is admitted in the form of costless and riskless intertemporal *storage*. Thus, arrangements can be made to transform at par units of c_0 into units of c_1 or of c_2, and units of c_1 into c_2. But, any such decisions are to be made *now* (at time-0), in ignorance of which state will actually obtain at time-1. Then it is evident that no storage will actually take place, the solution remaining unchanged from that shown in Table 1. In particular, the ruling prices remain the same and, consequently, there is no liquidity premium. For, from the point of view of any individual, the possibility of physical storage transformations at par are no more favorable on the margin than the possibilities of exchange transformations already available at the price ratios $P_1/P_0 = P_2/P_1 = 1$. Or, in terms of the marginal utilities, we can see that $U'_0 = 1/c_0 = .01$, $U'_1 = U'_{1a} + U'_{1b} = \frac{1}{2}v'_{1a} + \frac{1}{2}v'_{1b} = \frac{1}{2}(1/150) + \frac{1}{2}(1/75) = .01$, and also $U'_2 = 1/c_2 = .01$—all the marginal utilities being already equal, there is no point in storage transformations.

The situation is quite different, however, if it is possible for the individual to defer the decision as to storage transformations between time-1 and time-2 until *after* learning which of the contingencies has been realized at the former date. It is then evident that if the better-endowed state-*a* obtains at time-1, storage would take place—in the example of Table 1, if y_1 were known to equal 150, we would have $U'_1 = v'_{1a} = 1/150 < U'_2 = 1/100$ instead of $U'_1 = \frac{1}{2}v'_{1a} + \frac{1}{2}v'_{1b} = .01 = U'_2$. On the other hand, if state-*b* obtains, there is no incentive for storage since $y_{1b} = 75$ as against $y_2 = 100$, and $U'_1 = 1/75$ would be greater than U'_2. The possibility of taking advantage of later information thus lends a certain flexibility to time-1 claims (short-term assets) viewed at time-0. We would expect that, for the original decision at time-0, individuals would desire to transfer consumption from both c_0 and c_2 toward c_1. But, since storage is one-directional over time, the transformation from c_2 to c_1 cannot physically take place. The lessened desire to hold c_2 should then reveal itself in a fall in P_2 relative to P_1—i.e., in a liquidity-premium for the shorter-maturity claims. On the other hand, since storage from time-0 to time-1 is possible, we would expect such storage to occur—minimizing the tendency of the price P_1 to rise relative to P_0.

These relationships can be illustrated by obtaining a solution for the numerical example when storage is permitted. Note first that c_2 being no longer immutable, we must respecify the sequences entering into the calculation of utility as c_0, c_{1a}, c_{2a} and c_0, c_{1b}, c_{2b}—where c_{2a} benefits from storage transfers from time-1 when state-*a* obtains. Then:

$$U = \pi_a \, v(c_0, c_{1a}, c_{2a}) + \pi_b \, v(c_0, c_{1b}, c_{2b}). \tag{7}$$

Now, it is evident from the symmetry of the *v*-function in the form (5) that the storage transfers that take place at time-1 when state-*a* obtains will be such as to equalize c_{1a} and c_{2a}. If we symbolize storage at time-0 by z_0, and storage at time-state-1*a* by z_{1a}, we know that $z_{1a} = \frac{1}{2}(y_{1a}+z_0-y_2)$. Hence the optimum may be found by maximizing utility with respect to the single variable z_0.

$$\frac{dU}{dz_0} = v'_0 \frac{dc_0}{dz_0} + \pi_a v'_{1a} \frac{dc_{1a}}{dz_0} + \pi_a v'_{2a} \frac{dc_{2a}}{dz_0} + \pi_b v'_{1b} \frac{dc_{1b}}{dz_0} + \pi_b v'_{2b} \frac{dc_{2b}}{dz_0}.$$

Since $dc_0/dz_0 = -1$, $dc_{1a}/dz_0 = dc_{2a}/dz_0 = \frac{1}{2}$, $dc_{1b}/dz_0 = 1$, and $dc_{2b}/dz_0 = 0$, we obtain:

$$v'_0 = \tfrac{1}{2}\pi_a(v'_{1a}+v'_{2a})+\pi_b v'_{1b}.$$

This says that storage z_0 takes place up to the point where the marginal utility of c_0 equals the indicated weighted average of the marginal utilities of c_{1a}, c_{2a}, and c_{1b}.

Table 2. Solution with Storage, Deferrable Decisions

	Quantities			Prices		
t:	0	1	2	0	1	2
		126.65	126.65		.382	.382
	96.7			1		
		78.3	100		.618	.483
					1	.865

Discount Rates		
—	0%	7.5%

Making the numerical substitutions,* the optimal storage at time-0 is approximately $z_0 - 3.3$. The implied prices and quantities are shown in Table 2. Thus, $1 = P_1/P_0 > P_2/P_1 = .865$, so that a liquidity-premium exists. In terms of interest rates, $r_1 = 0\%$ while $R_2 = 7.5\%$.† It will be noted that even though the relative values of P_{1a} and P_{1b} change, their sum remains equal to unity. This is of course imposed by the possibility of storage transfers at par between c_0 and c_1.

We can now review the three conditions indicated earlier as being necessary for the emergence of a liquidity-premium.

Uncertainty: Evidently, without uncertainty there would be no need for flexibility.

* Here $v'_0 = 1/(y_0-z_0) = 1/(100-z_0)$; $v'_{1a} = 1/(y_{1a}+z_0-z_{1a}) = 1/\frac{1}{2}(y_{1a}+z_0+y_2) = 2/(250+z_0)$; $v'_{2a} = v'_{1a}$; $v'_{1b} = 1/(y_{1b}+z_0) = 1/(75+z_0)$; and $\pi_a = \pi_b = \frac{1}{2}$.
† $1/(1+R_2)^2 = .865$ implies $R_2 = .075$.

Ability to defer decisions: In the absence of this condition there could be no flexibility, however great the need. We saw above how, in two models otherwise exactly alike, a liquidity-premium arose only in the one permitting the deferring of decisions.

Physical irreversibility: The necessity of this condition was not underlined above, and it is rarely noted in the literature. But its implications are quite interesting. We could indeed imagine a world in which investment transfers in the form of storage could not take place, but where the reverse of costless storage—anticipatory physical

Table 3. Time-state Sequences

	With Storage Only			With Reverse-Storage Only		
$t:$	0	1	2	0	1	2
		125	125		150	100
	100			100		
		75	100		$87\frac{1}{2}$	$87\frac{1}{2}$
Marginal Utility	.01	.0107	.009	.01	.009	.0107
Direction of Desired Transfer	$\longrightarrow$			$\longleftarrow$		

realization of future claims at par—could be engaged in.* The time-state-sequence implications of the storage versus the "reverse-storage" assumptions are illustrated in Table 3. The table shows two comparable situations, where consumptions are balanced by storage or reverse-storage respectively between time-1 and time-2 (on the basis of the information as to which state obtains at time-1) but without going through the computations necessary to optimize consumption at time-0. However, the marginal utilities at each date indicate the direction of the optimal transfer to be made at time-0.

The situations are close to mirror images of one another. With the indicated disparity of the marginal utilities in the storage situation, transfers via storage from time-0 to time-1 were called for. In the reverse-storage situation, transfers from time-1 to time-0 would be

---

* In such a world the individual might be endowed with a set of perishable dated rations, so constituted that any unit can be consumed equally well before the specified date—but if it were attempted to defer consumption until after that date, the ration would be useless.

optimal. Furthermore, under reverse-storage the "liquidity-premium" would evidently attach to the time-2 claims: P_2/P_1 will exceed P_1/P_0!

We are rather more interested, however, in comparing storage alone with a situation where *both* storage and reverse storage would be possible. This is shown in Table 4, again before any adjustment of consumption at time-0. Note that in the numerical example allowing both storage and reverse-storage, there is only a very slight discrepancy in the marginal utilities—calling for a small transfer of consumption to time-0. There is no liquidity premium, since all the prices would equalize at unity after this transfer.*

Table 4. Time-state Sequences

	With Storage Only			With Storage and Reverse-Storage		
t:	0	1	2	0	1	2
		125	125		125	125
	100			100		
		75	100		$87\frac{1}{2}$	$87\frac{1}{2}$
Marginal Utility	.01	.0107	.009	0.1	.0097	.0097

3. CONCLUSIONS

The implication of all this is that the physical irreversibility of claims to future incomes—the comparative unavailability in the real world of reverse-storage transformations or, *a fortiori*, of disinvestments yielding a net surplus at earlier dates—is a necessary condition for the liquidity premium represented by an excess of P_1/P_0 over P_2/P_1.

We may now remark on the potentialities of market liquidity as a substitute for physical liquidity. In the "representative-individual" model used up to this point, the market provided no additional source of liquidity: everyone's situation being identical, no pair of individuals could find their respective desires or resources complementing one another so as to permit trade. But in the real world, individuals and their situations are not identical. In particular, their

* The optimal transfer to c_0 is about 1.4, so that the solution would be $c_0 = 101.4$, $c_{1a} = c_{2a} = 123.6$, $c_{1b} = c_{2b} = 86.1$.

incomes for given time-states will be imperfectly correlated: one individual's poorer-endowed state might be associated with another's better-endowed state. Then the existence of markets for assets will tend to reduce the realization discounts on physical investments like trees grown for timber. For, the arrival of a set of circumstances causing one individual to seek early realization may coincide with another individual's desiring to augment his productive investments to achieve more future return. Nevertheless, we would not expect this levelling or cancelling tendency for aggregate state-incomes to work out perfectly, since there is considerable positive correlation due to widespread social events like prosperity versus depression or war versus peace. So the existence of markets dilutes, without eliminating entirely, the effect of the irreversibility of physical investments that represents a necessary condition for the liquidity premium.

The counter-balancing force, upon which we must place the bulk of the explanation as to why people do after all hold long-term assets, is *productivity*. This force was masked in our examples above, where the net yield on physical investments was fixed by assumption at 0%. But if a continuum of investments of differing yields were available, the tendency of R_2 to rise above r_1 would represent a higher marginal rate of real yield on long-term investments. (This does not mean that long-term investments are *intrinsically* more productive, in any philosophical or essential sense—but only that the cut-off rate of return will be higher on the long-terms.) In the numerical example illustrated by Table 2, at equilibrium $r_1 = 0\%$ while $R_2 = 7.5\%$. However, with storage the only productive possibility, there was no way of earning 7.5% on long-term physical investments—hence, the only transformations entering into the solution were short-term transfers from c_0 to c_1 via storage. But with a continuum of short-term and long-term marginal investment yields, consumptive sacrifice at time-0 would be distributed between "liquid" but lower-yielding short-term investments and "illiquid" but higher-yielding long-term investments.

To sum up, the great advantage of short-term assets, given risk-aversion and an uncertain world, is that they facilitate the utilization of new information about the environment as it becomes available over time. For the information to be usable, it must be possible to defer some decisions, or to reconsider tentative decisions. In order for the reconsideration opportunity to be peculiarly advantageous for holders of short-term as opposed to long-term assets, there must be limits on the *physical* reversibility of long-terms. In somewhat diluted form—due to divergences of individual tastes and opportunities, and imperfect correlation of better- and poorer-endowed states—these limits on physical reversibility pass over into impairments of market realizations of long-term assets at "premature" dates. And finally, to assure that the information is purchased at a positive price, i.e., to preclude the corner solution in which *no* long-term investments are undertaken, there must exist a real marginal time-rate of yield on long-terms greater than that on short-terms.

Uncertainty and Probability in International Economics

HARRY G. JOHNSON

London School of Economics and Political Science and the University of Chicago

In a contribution to a volume prepared in honour of my long-time friend, George Shackle, whose work interested me enough in my early teaching career at Cambridge to prompt me to construct a physical model of his "ϕ-surface,"* it would be gratifying to be able to say that his work on uncertainty, either by itself or as a distinguished component of a large literature on uncertainty and probability, had made a significant indirect contribution to the development of the field of international economics. Unfortunately, and perhaps somewhat to the discredit of the field, such a statement cannot be made. International economics has flourished in the period since 1945 without the benefit of large admixtures of the theory of decision-taking under uncertainty. This is not to say that international economists do not make frequent reference to the role of uncertainty in international economic affairs, in a literary way, where the problem arises—and sometimes to quite useful effect. But formal analysis of uncertainty and its solution has been applied to only a limited range of questions, peripheral to the main core of the subject.

The reason for this, in my judgement, lies in the difference between the context in which decision-taking under uncertainty becomes an interesting theoretical (and practical) question, and the general concerns of international economic theory. The former type of theory is essentially theory about the behaviour of the individual economic

* Harry G. Johnson, 'A Three-Dimensional Model of the Shackle ϕ-Surface,' *Review of Economic Studies*, XVIII (1950–51), pp. 115–18.

unit, in a partial-equilibrium setting—though, as with the theory of liquidity preference and portfolio-management behaviour, results achieved at this level are commonly aggregated thereafter into theories of market behaviour. International economic theory on the other hand, is necessarily concerned first and foremost with the problem of general equilibrium in the international economy, and in pursuit of this problem is generally content with the simplest and most general models of behaviour in the domestic economy—and these typically abstract from uncertainty, since recognition of the presence of uncertainty produces no simple conclusions about the difference it makes to economic behaviour, on which an analysis of international trade in the presence of uncertainty could be built that would produce conclusions interestingly and convincingly different from the conclusions of the standard certainty models of international trade.

As an illustration of this point, one may contrast the critical absence of considerations of uncertainty and probability in the pure theoretical models of international trade, with the vast amount of theoretical work that has been done in recent years on a problem that is very similar in some essential theoretical respects, namely the influence of "distortions" of various kinds—taxes, subsidies, union wage differentials, urban–rural wage differentials, tariffs on imported raw materials—in reducing the economic welfare of an internationally trading country below the first-best attainable level, and the nature of the "second-best" policies required to minimize the welfare cost of distortions that cannot be eliminated, for one reason or another.*

A parallel treatment of uncertainty would have to start by establishing a standard for determining how far, if at all, differences in uncertainty among alternative economic activities (assuming on the basis of casual empiricism that they exist) constitute a "distortion" of the workings of the competitive system away from the attainable

---

* The classic article is J. Bhagwati and V. K. Ramaswami, 'Domestic Distortions. Tariffs and the Theory of Optimum Subsidy,' *Journal of Political Economy*, LXXI, No. 1, February, 1963, pp. 44–50, reprinted in R. E. Caves and H. G. Johnson (eds.), *A. E. A. Readings in International Economics*, Volume XI, Homewood Richard D. Irwin, 1968, Chap. 14, pp. 230–39.

See also Harry G. Johnson, 'Optimal Trade Intervention in the Presence of Domestic Distortions,' in Baldwin et al., *Trade, Growth and the Balance of Payments, Essays in Honor of Gottfried Haberler*, Amsterdam, North-Holland Publishing Company, 1965, pp. 3–34; reprinted in Harry G. Johnson, *Aspects of the Theory of Tariffs*, London, Allen and Unwin, 1971, Chap. 4, pp. 119–53.

Pareto optimum. Correctable distortions due to uncertainty might exist if *either* the uncertainty were attributable in part at least to faulty institutional arrangements for collecting and disseminating relevant knowledge, which could be improved by an investment of resources that would be privately unprofitable but socially profitable, *or* the prevailing private procedures for taking decisions in the face of uncertainty led consistently to socially sub-optimal results, which assumption implies that these procedures could either be improved by investment in public education in techniques of decision-taking under uncertainty or be counteracted by various kinds of tax-subsidy arrangements. In either case—in contrast to the "distortions" analysis, in which both the imposition of new countervailing distortions and the removal of old ones is assumed to be economically costless—the appropriate remedy would require investment of public resources (except in the case of the tax-subsidy remedy for socially inferior private decision-taking) and therefore call for a cost–benefit analysis of the policies concerned.

The foregoing hypothetical construction of a theoretical analysis of the trade and welfare effects of uncertainty bears a close similarity to contemporary analysis of the ancient infant-industry argument for protection. Indeed, the alleged or presumed incapacity of the private market to take decisions in the face of uncertainty that one accepted as or believed to be socially optimal constitutes one of the main contemporary arguments for infant-industry protection, especially in its popular modern form of governmental underwriting of the research and development programmes of technologically-advanced and high-risk industries. Recent theoretical explanations of the infant-industry argument for protection, however,* have shown that the theoretical specification of a valid argument are so narrow that little if anything remains of it as a practically relevant problem, while the experience of the developing countries with protection to their industries granted on that ground has been one of shocking economic waste.† Since the theoretical difficulties of coming

* See for example R. E. Baldwin, 'The Case Against Infant Industry Protection,' *Journal of Political Economy*, LXXVII, No. 3, May/June, 1969, pp. 295–305. and Harry G. Johnson, 'A New View of the Infant Industry Argument for Protection,' Chap. 5, pp. 59–76 in J. A. Macdougall and R. H. Shape (eds.), *Studies in International Economics: Monash Conference Papers*, Amsterdam North-Holland Publishing Co., 1970.

† See for example I. Little, T. Scitovsky, and M. Scott, *Industry and Trade in Some Developing Countries: A Comparative Study*, Oxford, Oxford University Press, 1970.

to grips with uncertainty as a possibly distorting factor in international trade are so much greater by comparison with the easily observable distortions international economists have so far been analyzing, it seems highly unlikely that any conclusions useful for policy-making would emerge from the effort. Probably the most reliable statement that can be made at present is that the haphazard current efforts of governments to compensate various export- and import-competing industries for undertaking risk and uncertainty or to assume part of the burden themselves are very unlikely to improve the efficiency of allocation of resources or to promote economic growth in any meaningful sense. But without a reliable theory constructed on the lines outlined above, even this statement is both uncertain in validity and risky in presentation.

As mentioned above, once one descends from the heights of general equilibrium theorizing about the fundamental explanation of patterns of international trade to more concrete and practical problems susceptible of discussion either in a partial equilibrium context or in an empirically specifiable general equilibrium context, references to risk and uncertainty and the implications of their presence become much more common, though as also mentioned the treatment of them is generally literary or logical rather than formal. A few major exemplary problems will be discussed here. For this purpose, it is convenient to follow the customary distinction between "real" international economics (comparative costs and commercial policy) and international monetary economics, though some of the problems cut across this borderline, which is artificial in any case.

On the side of comparative cost theory, as already mentioned, uncertainty plays an important role in the contemporary version of the infant industry argument in the less developed countries, it being commonly asserted that private entrepreneurs will overestimate the risks involved in establishing new industries, and hence will require insurance in the form of protection—frequently in the extreme form of a state-conferred monopoly of the market—before they will undertake socially profitable new investments. One dimension of this argument, that brings in all the complexities of knowledge as a public good, is that if the risk-taker or uncertainty-bearer is successful, his methods will quickly be imitated by others so that he will lose part or all of the return he should legitimately expect to make on his investment. Protection in this case is clearly an inferior alternative to public subsidization of the costs of risk-taking. But the argument begs the questions whether competitive entrepreneurs in less developed countries habitually overestimate the risks of new enterprises, and need subsidies to induce them to arrive at socially optimal decisions, and whether they cannot capture sufficient gains from successful risk-taking to make their private incentives to risk-taking approximate to the social gain from it. The same question arises in a sharper form with respect to subsidization of high-technology industries in developed countries, where the large corporations involved might be expected to be at least as rational as governments in their assessment of the commercial attractions of takings risks (naturally, of course, no natural risk-taker would be averse to letting someone else underwrite the possible losses from the risks he is undertaking anyway).

Risk and uncertainty also play an important role in the standard arguments for policies of promoting the industrialization of less developed countries, that the variability of the prices of primary product exports and the resulting uncertainty about export income and import capacity make stable development and development planning difficult if not impossible, and (though this is an argument from *a priori* certainty that the market's decisions are wrong rather than from uncertainty *per se*) that there is a long-run tendency for the terms of trade to turn against primary-product exporters. Neither the adverse consequences of price variability nor the fact of the long-run trend of the terms of trade have been satisfactorily established thus far; but the assumption that uncertainty is a bad thing in itself continues to play a powerful role in thinking about commercial policy in the less developed countries, even though it has become increasingly clear with experience that one of the major sources of private entrepreneurial uncertainty in such countries is the government itself, and specifically both arbitrary changes in import licensing and industrial control policies and uncertainty about the degree to which government is willing to resort to inflationary finance.

To turn to an issue of more recent concern, the international activities of the multinational corporation, risk and uncertainty enter the analytical picture in at least four significant ways.

In the first place, there is the important question as to why corporations become multinational by establishing production facilities in foreign markets, rather than by exporting or alternatively by leasing their productive knowledge to local entrepreneurs and, why, when they establish production facilities abroad, they seem to prefer the wholly-owned or majority interest subsidiary to the joint venture or minority participation. Various explanations have been advanced, but the common threads among them involve the theme of uncertainty: the uncertainty of relying on exports to the market which may be arbitrarily discriminated against by governmentally-imposed tariffs or complete embargos, or discriminated against more subtly by governmental favouritism to and subsidization of domestic enterprises; and the uncertainty of taking into effective minority or majority partnership foreigners whose concentration on local interests may seriously perturb the global profit-seeking objectives of the company. As against the uncertainties, the multinational corporation has to accept uncertainty about its own capacity to operate efficiently in an alien market system dominated by alien institutions. It probably tells us something about human attitude to uncertainty, something very much in the spirit of George Shackle's approach to the whole problem, that corporations are more willing to risk their own knowledge and capacity for recognizing and solving problems in an alien institutional environment, than they are to hire the services of experts in that environment, in the form either of importing agents or of local minority or majority partners, to cope with the problems for them. Better the devil you know than the devil you do not know but have heard about from your agents—or possibly his agents! In more technical language, corporations, and people generally, seem to be more willing to bear uncertainty at the cost of acquiring information about it by personal investigation than to buy insurance against unknown risks at a premium determined by people whose honesty they do not trust.

In the second place, there is the question why the multinational corporations—those in the extractive industries apart, since where they go is largely determined by geography rather than economic calculation—tend to concentrate their international operations in other advanced countries than the parent country, rather than in the less developed countries, where pure static theory suggests that their comparative advantages in terms of modern technology and access to cheap capital should pay off most handsomely. Again a large part of the answer lies in risk and uncertainty. The more developed countries are likely to have more reliable governmental policies, and more readily comprehensible social and economic institutions. Uncertainty and risk are reduced by taking one's larger leap into less obscure places rather than into near-darkness.

A third question is why the multinational corporation has a strong preference for obtaining as much of its finance for foreign operations as it can from local rather than parent-country or world-market sources and minimizing its input of outside capital. This characteristic has been a perennial source of complaint about the multinational corporation, especially in countries that have a balance-of-payments motivation for attracting foreign capital. Again, uncertainty—especially about government policy with respect to exchange rates and controls over remittances of earnings—plays a major role. If a company can manage to put in no money of its own, any returns it can get out are pure gravy. But if it puts in a large chunk of its parent-country's money and gets nothing out in return, both higher management and eventually the shareholders will be rightly critical.

The fourth question, one which arises from the side of government rather than of the corporation, concerns the relative risks and uncertainties involved in the financing of domestic investment from foreign sources by equity capital as contrasted with portfolio (fixed-interest) investment. Governments, avid for foreign capital resources to supplement domestic savings but reluctant for various reasons to accept foreign control of domestic industrial and other economic activity, have a strong revealed preference for foreign portfolio over foreign equity investment. From the standpoint of government concern about possible (or probable) balance-of-payments problems, however, there is little doubt that equity investment is less potentially troublesome than fixed-interest investment, provided that the source of the balance-of-payments problem is external and not internal. Foreign equity investors will share more than foreign portfolio investors in the profits of a (subsequent-to-investment) inflationary policy; but variation in external demand for the country's products will be reflected in variations of the profits of foreign equity enterprises, and therefore in the earnings remittances of foreign enterprises to their parent companies, so cushioning the balance of payments against external disturbances, whereas remittances of interest on foreign borrowings will be invariant to fluctuations in the country's export earnings.

On the side of international monetary economics, the problem of risk and uncertainty, in the general literature at present under discussion, has appeared mainly in connection with the long-standing argument over fixed versus flexible exchange rates, and more specifically in connection with the question of the role of speculation in the foreign exchange market.

In the latter context—to take the more technical issues first—one of the central issues has been to explain why arbitrage does not in fact typically ensure the establishment of interest rate parity—i.e., equality of the interest rate in one currency market plus the forward premium on that currency or less the forward discount with the interest rate in another currency market. The explanation entails appeal to the increasing risk involved in the provision of arbitrage funds, which allows forward exchange rates to depart from the interest rate parity under the pressure of abnormal speculation.* Under normal circumstances, speculation against a currency would naturally always pass through the forward and not the spot exchange market;* but the inelasticity of supply of arbitrage funds, associated with risk and uncertainty, by allowing the forward rate to fall to discount will make it more profitable to speculate against a currency on the spot market, thereby causing a current loss of international reserves. This analytical conclusion led a number of economists to conclude—in the mid-1950s, when the question was important for Britain—that counter-speculation by the monetary authority should take the form of intervention to support the forward exchange rate and so channel speculation into the forward market.† (Unfortunately, this is a desirable policy only if the authorities are right in believing that the exchange parity is viable, and the speculators wrong in their belief that the currency will have to be devalued—as the British monetary authorities found to their cost in 1967.)

With regard to the broader question of fixed versus floating exchange rates, one of the major issues involving the role of risk and uncertainty has always been the contention of the opponents of flexibility that flexibility would generate destabilizing exchange rate speculation. This contention rests on a specific and questionable theory of behaviour under uncertainty, namely that private decision-takers adopt the decision rule of expecting price trends to continue in the same direction, rather than that of expecting prices to converge on their long-run equilibrium value. The objection to this assumption,

---

* On the theory of forward exchange, see Egon Sohmen, *Flexible Exchange Rates*, Chicago, University of Chicago Press, 1969, and H. G. Grubel, *Forward Exchange, Speculation and the International Flow of Capital*, Stanford, Stanford University Press, 1966.

† See for example John Spraos, 'Speculation, Arbitrage, and Sterling,' *Economic Journal*, LXIX, March, 1959, pp. 1–21.

presented in Milton Friedman's classic article on "The Case for Flexible Exchange Rates,"* is that destabilizing speculation will result in losses for the speculators and so eventually eliminate such speculators. Various economists have attempted to disprove the contention that destabilizing speculation will result in losses for the speculators; but these attempts rely either on a distinction between professional and amateur speculators, or on a calculation of profits that does not require them to be realized. On the other hand, it is quite possible for speculators on the foreign exchange to earn the funds with which they speculate in the pursuit of non-speculative productive activities, and hence either to squander these funds persistently on speculation, or to recoup their losses by productive activities and then return unprofitably to the speculative fray. Hence the Friedman argument, while valid, may be well wide of the practically relevant point.

A lesser but still significant issue is the contention of the opponents of exchange rate flexibility that fluctuations of the exchange rate under a floating rate would generate additional uncertainty to a degree sufficient seriously to impede international trade and payments. This contention raises the difficult and probably unanswerable question, whether the uncertainty generated by a floating exchange rate is more or less damaging to efficient resource allocation generated by a fixed rate system in which governments may impose arbitrary controls designed to protect the exchange rate, and still have the opportunity to change the rate if circumstances require it.

These are but a few examples of the ways in which considerations of uncertainty and risk have entered the literature of international economics, although in the author's judgment the more important ones. Of them all, the debate over destabilizing speculation under flexible exchange rates has employed the most sophisticated analytical techniques.

As suggested above, however, a thoroughgoing incorporation of the analysis of risk and uncertainty analysis into international trade theory requires a technique for analyzing decision-taking in the face of uncertainty that is capable of producing results of general interest differing in important respects from those that standard theory

* Milton Friedman, 'The Case for Flexible Exchange Rates,' pp. 157–203 in his *Essays in Positive Economics*, Chicago, University of Chicago Press, 1958, reprinted in abridged form in Caves and Johnson, *op. cit.*, as Chap. 25, pp. 413–37.

based on abstraction from uncertainty would indicate. This in turn requires two things: location of problems for which concentration on the individual decision-taker is a relevant procedure, and a technique of analysis of individual decision under uncertainty that yields significant new insights. As regards the latter, the Markowitz–Tobin portfolio-selection analysis has the required characteristics—in contrast it must be admitted to the more subjective and less mathematical approach of George Shackle. As regards the former, the problem is to identify a frame of reference within which the behaviour of individual decision-takers is significantly influenced, and in predictable ways, by uncertainty of a specifiable type. Three lines of recent work in international economics conform to these specifications.

The first, and most obvious but also most important, concerns the reserve-holding behaviour of countries operating through their central banks, and specifically the optimum reserve-holding behaviour of an individual national central bank. This question is relevant not only to the judgment of the efficiency of individual nations' central bank behaviour, but more significantly to the solution of the question of optimizing the magnitude and rate of growth of international reserves. The solution is obvious, in the sense that it involves weighing the gains from holding larger international reserves against their interest cost and the costs of the alternative policies that would have to be adopted in case international reserve holdings proved inadequate.* Nevertheless, monetary theory suggests a number of alternative ways of formulating this choice and specifying the relevant parameters. There are also subsidiary questions concerning the optimum allocation of a central bank's reserve assets as among gold, dollars, and special drawing rights, not to speak of the more complex problem of preserving "credit-worthiness" with other central banks.

The second line of development concerns the question of diversification of exports in less developed countries. Traditional theory has tended to belittle the objective of diversification, as wasting investible resources. However, portfolio-balance theory shows that portfolio diversification can increase expected yield for a given risk,

---

* The standard references are P. Kenen and E. Yudin, 'The Demand for International Reserves,' in P. Kenen and R. Lawrence (eds.) *The Open Economy*, New York, Columbia University Press, 1968, pp. 339–54, and R. Heller, 'Optimal International Reserves,' *Economic Journal*, LXXVI, June, 1966, pp. 296–311.

or decrease risk for a given expected yield, so long as yields on alternative assets are not perfectly correlated. This portfolio-balance approach has been employed in defence of policies of diversification of exports in less developed countries by Brainard and Cooper.* Their contribution is especially valuable for its demonstration that some kinds of diversification produce no significant economic benefits since the prices of the various products tend to fluctuate together, and that the processing of imported raw materials for export may be less risky than it seems at first sight because the prices of the inputs and outputs do tend to fluctuate together. The case they develop for governmental intervention rests on divergence of private from social risk aversion, their assumption being that private decision-takers tend to underrate the social costs of high variability of export receipts. This assumption seems at first sight to conflict with the assumption commonly made in connection with the infant industry argument for protection, that private decision-takers overrate the risks of new enterprises; but it is logically conceivable that such decision-takers overrate their private risks while underrating the social risks because some of the latter are borne by other economic units (such as workers) or by government.

The third line of development concerns the welfare gains to investors from the availability of investment opportunities in more than one national capital market—again a matter of imperfectly correlated risks of fluctuations of prices. Herbert G. Grubel† has calculated these gains and found them substantial—though his statistical work is marred by the implicit assumption that security values in each national market fluctuate together, and the fact that they do not must reduce the potential gains from international diversification of security holdings.

To summarize, uncertainty and probability theory have not had a major influence on international economic theory because they are primarily partial and not general equilibrium theories, and so are beside the point of the central concerns of international economic theory. At a more partial equilibrium and concrete level, the importance of uncertainty has definitely been recognized, though the recognition remains at the level of alternative possibilities among which

* W. C. Brainard and R. Cooper, 'Uncertainty and Diversification in International Trade,' *Food Research Institute Studies in Agricultural Economics, Trade and Development*, Stanford University, VIII, No. 3, 1968, pp. 257–85.

† H. G. Grubel, 'Internationally Diversified Portfolios,' *American Economic Review*, LVIII, Dec. 1968, pp. 1299–1314.

economists can choose as their tastes dictate. Finally, use has been made of the tools of the theory of decision-taking in the face of uncertainty—specifically of the portfolio-balance approach to investment management—in those contexts in which these tools were clearly relevant.

Decision-taking and the Theory of Games

B. S. KEIRSTEAD

University of Toronto and University of New Brunswick

INTRODUCTORY NOTE

In a public lecture delivered in Belfast, and subsequently published, Professor Shackle referred to my concept of what he called "flow decisions". Now that was perfectly all right, except that I had not, at that time (1969) published anything about decision-taking in flow. Professor Shackle and I have discussed our work together since 1951 whenever we were able to meet and by continuous correspondence. The discussion has been definitely one-sided because I have depended far more on his suggestions and critical advice than he has on mine.

The invitation of the editors of this book has been most welcome. It enables me to participate in a work to give honor to George Shackle, and I am glad to be able to pay public homage to him. It also gives me an opportunity to put before my colleagues what I mean by decisions in flow and to relate that concept to the general theory of games.

I have had to include in this piece some preliminary material, so as to give perspective to the main thesis. Part I really sets out my attitude towards economic studies and some definitions that are essential to the latter argument. The short Part II defends a basic philosophic assumption and also introduces some rather chatty empirical stuff designed: (a) to show that the theory of decision is not confined to economics but has a general application; and (b) to create a certain bias in favor of the subsequent argument.

In Part III we come to the "hub of the matter". All deterministic theories of decision-making are unconvincing and unsophisticated save one. That exception is based on the theory of games. I have tried to present the argument in its favour as honestly as possible when one is condensing a long and difficult theory in a few readable paragraphs. I admit the possibility of the "min–max" solution to the selection of the "optimum" strategy, given the new computer technology, but I shall dispute the assumption that this strategy is regarded as optimum by decision-takers. I shall also dispute the hidden assumption that strategic decisions are calculated over intervals in play. It is notable that the great authors of the original *Theory of Games* referred mostly to chess in their few illustrative passages, though a reader will find an occasional reference to checkers or draughts and, I think, one reference to American football. All these games have one thing in common. They are all discontinuous with long intervals between play for the planning of strategy and counter strategy. We do not believe them to be representative of entrepreneurial, military or political decision-making.

I

Economics, we believe, must be considered as a useful study. Though it grew out of philosophy and retains, one hopes, essential elements of a humane and liberalizing discipline, it ought to be relevant to the issues of an institutional, phenomenal world.

The great Marshall certainly believed this. Curious, inquiring and objective he may well have been, but he thought the main purpose of his work was to provide knowledge for the relief of poverty. A great colonial governor in the early part of the nineteenth century could say, "Long may this institution stand and flourish under the royal charter I have this day conferred upon it . . . and may it ever be a center of liberal learning and useful knowledge."*

Economics as a generalised study of choice is, or should be, one of the fundamental humane disciplines, detached, urbane, liberalising. It is not, as presently professed, very useful to those who have to make the decisions on which the future material—and, to some extent, spiritual—welfare of mankind depends. It is with some sense of urgency that we appeal to rather than challenge our professional colleagues.

* Sir Howard Douglas, On Conferring A Royal Charter to the University of New Brunswick, 1829 (King's College, Fredericton, founded 1785).

Received economic theory does deal with preference and choice, but in models which are strictly deterministic and which rest on simplifying assumptions which remove from the scene the distinguishing human attributes of individuality and imagination. It is small wonder that so many of our contemporaries spend their time in refining static and deterministic models and in displaying logical and mathematical virtuosity. One may admire, as one admires the expert who can do *The Times* and the *New Statesman* crosswords in a half hour, but one can hardly regard it as useful. It is only when we allow the imaginative process of decision-taking that we may hope to develop a new economic theory which may be helpful in our contemporary society.

We distinguish between the decision-making process and "taking a decision". By the decision-making process we refer to the time consuming process of accumulating data, examining past experience, considering similar problems on which decisions had to be taken in the past—the accumulation, in a word, of all the information necessary to make the decision a rational and informed one. At some stage in this drawn-out, time-consuming process of decision-making there comes a moment, however, when someone has to *make up his mind*.*
The person charged with the responsibility—the entrepreneur in an economic concern, the top civil servant in the formation of public policy—that person charged with the responsibility of determining policy, at some point makes up his mind. When we say, "I have made up my mind", we usually refer to an instantaneous decision.†

As Professor Shackle has written: "it is difficult even nowadays to realise how deeply economic theory has lain under the spell of classical (physical) mechanics and its appropriate mathematical ways of thinking, and has accepted calculable nature as a model of human affairs".‡ It is not such a model. The area of free decision is a bounded one, but it exists. Once, in an experiment, the actor forms his purpose, understands his limits, physical or institutional, within

---

* Cf. Shackle, *Decision, Order and Time in Human Affairs*.

† Hume on "reason" and "sentiment" in the moral decision. Reasons may prepare the ground for the ultimate choice, but "virtue is more what is felt than what is judged". Thus the great rationalist stands in contrast to his predecessor, John Locke, who held that the study of moral judgments could be reduced to an "exact science".

‡ G. L. S. Shackle, Review of *Capital, Interest and Profit*, Economic Journal, LXX, No. 280, December, 1960. For a fuller development of these points see also: G. L. S. Shackle, *The Years of High Theory*, Cambridge, 1967, pp. 286–296.

which he is free to act, imagines the future possible consequences of his decision, his insight and volition are a part, an essential part, of what Karl Popper calls "the causal nexus". Causality in human affairs is a complex, not a simple, relation and the taking of decision is its distinguishing attribute.

Those who have read Aristotle will realise that the mechanical cause of early nineteenth-century science, as defined by Hume, is only one of the set of relationships to which Aristotle, and later Kant, give the name of cause. The physical scientists may wish to discard the concept of mechanical cause which they have found to be unworthy or unworkable. That is not, however, a solid reason for social scientists to give up a quite different concept of cause, one which may prove most useful in human affairs and which Aristotle, if we may be permitted a borrowed translation, called purposeful. Nor is one too far removed from Kant when one denies that *cause* can be defined as mere sequence.*

We do not deny that in human affairs, in human decisions, there is a degree of determinism. In the end, what it comes down to is what we believe to be the most useful assumption. I assume that there is meaning to the phrase "free will". I do not think anyone can dispute my right to make that assumption for purposes of argument except on the grounds that it is not a useful assumption. To defend it I submit, first, that the alternative assumption makes no sense. Men, as Locke said, become creatures of "whimsy" and can behave only "as fools" if freedom means lack of the constraint of reason. The modern defenders of the view he sought to destroy will tell us that there is no question of "whimsy", but of predictable behavior which, over the mass, can be determined by probability. Are they right? They are so often right that one's faith is shaken, but then they go gloriously astray. How many now remember the demographers' calculations of the world's population made just after the war? And then those political forecasters? Mr. Churchill (as he then was) could not be defeated in the United Kingdom: but he was. Mr. Truman had no chance of winning the presidential election of 1948—even *Time* came out with an analysis of what beat Truman, an unhappy publication post-dated to follow the election, but *Time* and all the determinists were wrong. Somehow or other American electors did not follow the determined lines. They elected Mr. Truman as

---

* Immanuel Kant, *Critique of Pure Reason*, N. K. Smith, ed., London, 1939, pp. 43–44 and 223–224.

President and while we await the final verdict of history we may suggest that they decided wisely.

These are but two examples. There are many more. Such examples, however, do not constitute an argument. Our thesis is that of the two possible assumptions about freedom of will, the assumption of freedom within bounded circumstances is preferable to the alternative assumption of determinism. Within the area of free decision, human judgment—knowledge, purpose, imagination and insight—form a part of cause. We have said that this element is the distinguishing attribute of causality in human affairs. We may go further and say that the ability to exercise it is the essential quality of man.

II

It is said that at the Pentagon building in Washington strategic decisions are taken according to computerised calculations of probabilities and the application of the theory of games. One hopes that this is pure slander, although American strategy in the VietNam war does rather appear to be based on a min–max principle. The general theory of decision ought, however, to apply as well to military decisions as to those made about investment in the private sector of the economy.

With this in mind, we turn now to the theory of strategy to observe the nature of the commander-in-chief's decision. There are three general laws or principles which should guide, but cannot determine, these decisions. We say they "cannot determine" the decision; this is because the principles may not all operate in the same direction. Each, taken by itself, might "determine" a strategy which in the particular experiment would not coincide with the strategies dictated by an application of the other principles. The commander's freedom to decide is constrained by geography, logistics, imperfect "intelligence reports", and uncertainty as to which of the possible ripostes is open to the enemy. Ideally he would try to dictate to the enemy only one choice, as does a good chess player. War, however, and in spite of many metaphors that suggest a close similarity, is not chess. Infantry units are not passive pawns, but a brilliant lieutenant or a stout-hearted sergeant may devise a tactical defense of a platoon position which may throw out the timing and development of a whole strategic evolution. Moreover, it is never possible to know the enemy's mind or to confine him to only one counter-strategy. Thus constrained by physical factors, bounded by uncertainty, guided by certain principles, the commander must make up his mind in an area of free decision. What he elects to do will depend on his understanding of the whole situation, his full insight, imagination of his enemy's mind, and his courage or will. "The theory of *la grand guerre*, or as it is called strategy, is beset with extraordinary difficulties and we affirm that very few men have clear conceptions of the separate subjects—that is conceptions carried up to their full logical conclusions. In battle most men are guided merely by the tactical judgment which hits the objective more or less accurately according as they possess more or less genius."*

The three principles of war are surprise, massing and maintaining supplies (what we should call logistical organization), and the selection of the correct objective. In speaking of the third principle von Clausewitz says it is the product of two factors, which must be clearly perceived by the commander. He must define his objective precisely, even sacrificing tactical points if the response might lead to confusion,† and he must, once concentrated and launched, "venture all". If we may alter the order of these principles we may observe how close they come to our own description of decision-making in general. The selection of a strictly defined objective is a common element of all strategic decision-making. We must know what we intend to achieve; we must have defined our purpose. Again, since we act in an experiment of bounded uncertainty, we cannot know the counter-strategies of our enemies, our competitors or opponents. We must select the hypothesis which will give them the least chance of surprising or confounding us. Our logistics must be as good as we can make them, that is to say our technicians and other expert advisors must have given us the fullest possible information about the entire situation. We decide, in our experiment, with as much knowledge and understanding of it as can be obtained. The element of surprise, so important in warfare where intelligence is limited and "appreciations" often contradictory, has no real counter-part in entrepreneurial decisions although there are occasions in competitive sectors where it has played a part in gaining at least temporary

* K. von Clausewitz, *On War* (revised English ed. 1940), p. 26.

† In the German break-through of March 1918, many British strongpoints were simply by-passed while the German attack poured through weak places in the line and severed the lines of communication and supply to those British units still firmly holding on.

competitive advantage. We might argue that it has its counterpart in innovation.

Finally, we may observe the experiment as a whole. The decision-maker in both cases finds himself in a situation of uncertainty. He amasses all the data he can. He imagines the future, the possible results of his act and the possible counter-strategies. Eventually he selects an hypothesis and acts on it. He has made up his mind and the driving force of his own will and determination is added as an element in the causal force at work. The experiment is unique; it cannot be repeated. It is crucial, for, once launched, the actor must "venture all".

III

"Venture all".... This is not the min–max solution. Of course decision-makers try to reduce uncertainty as much as they can. The experts in the civil service advise Cabinet, General Staff and Intelligence officers advise the Commander-in-Chief, engineers and psychologists and other such "experts" advise the entrepreneur. Because this is true, as we readily admit, many writers have developed in one form or another a deterministic theory of decision-taking. The "facts" —whatever that means—*determine* the decision. (So far as routine decisions are concerned, they probably are pretty much "determined" but as much by habit as by "facts". We are talking, however, about the Shackle decision, the unique, "once and once only" decision.) Now most of the deterministic theories are philosophically so unsophisticated that they do not warrant attention. One theory however, is sophisticated and challenging and deserves full and honest consideration.

This theory is based on the mathematics of the theory of games.[*] We referred earlier to the "optimum strategy". According to the fundamental principle of the theory of games the ideal strategy is that which minimizes the probability of the loss while achieving the maximum gain *consistent with the minimization of the probability of loss*. This basic principle of the theory of games is generally applicable, but it is applicable by itself, without resort to probability theory, only to the most simple two-party, three-strategy games. When the

---

[*] J. von Neumann and O. Morgenstern, *The Theory of Games and Economic Behavior*, Princeton, 1944.

players become more numerous, or the possible strategies and counter-strategies more numerous, the number of calculations becomes vast. A three-party game with six alternative strategies available to each player requires theoretically, as we recall, something like one million calculations. Obviously for a human player to select a strategy in any practical situation is virtually impossible, but the solution is mathematically determinate. Herein lies the strength of the argument we are condensing. For if it is mathematically determinate, the experiment has a determinate solution. All that prevents a practicable application is the number and complexity of the calculations which have to be made, something far beyond the capacity of a single human mind. Such calculations are not, however, beyond the power or capacity of the modern computer. Not only can the computer solve the vast array of equations set for it by the "programmer", it can solve them, if not in a flash, at least within an incredibly short space of time. Moreover, the computer has a memory, a most retentive and dependable one, so that, once the game has begun, the computer can adjust changes in data, resulting from the opening moves to the strategies which from time to time become available. This is a very impressive claim, and sceptical readers ought to realise that computers have been built which can always win at drafts or checkers, provided they have the first move, and they will win against a skilled human player who has the first move, provided he makes a single error in play. In chess, the computers have so far been unsuccessful. I understand that a well-programmed computer can win at chess provided any opening gambit is followed through without any variation from the orthodox development. The computer, you must understand, can both remember and calculate rather better than most human beings; it cannot imagine; it lacks insight.*
Almost it could be said to be the symbol of orthodoxy.

One objection, which has been made to this theory, may be dismissed. This is that the number, the mathematically theoretical number, of possible strategies and counter-strategies in any real situation of, say, a battle, or of oligopolist competition, is so vast that it would be humanly impossible to "programme" the machine, and its "min–max" solution would be probably to do nothing. I intend to enter serious objections to this theory, but not this one. As one writer has put it (I cannot enter a footnote here, because though I have a clear memory of reading this, I cannot locate where I

* For what we mean by imagination and insight see below.

did read it) of a hundred thousand mathematically possible strategies and counter-strategies, the programmer knows only about two or three dozen which are practically relevant. Even with thirty possible strategies the computer can calculate the ideal one where a man could not do so. (In passing, we might note that the neutrality of the programmer here becomes dubious. Nevertheless we are content with this; we happily allow the introduction of a little human judgment into this general theory.) If this is allowed, we should agree that there is a strong case, based on the theory of games, for a deterministic solution of the problem of the selection of the "correct" or "ideal" strategy in certain situations. It is widely believed today that these situations include almost all the strategic situations of the military command, the concern and the political policy-maker.

We hope that in this severe condensation we have done no injustice to the main postulates of the theory of deterministic decision-taking.

We do not attack this theory: it is helpful in what it explains. We simply reject it as a complete theory of decision because it is both theoretically and practically incomplete.* The reasons for this rejection are five fold and may be set out briefly in this manner:

(a) The deterministic solution allows no freedom of human choice. This is a philosophical question. One may choose to select the assumption of determinism or the assumption of free decision. It is a choice of assumptions. We have reason, other than emotional bias, to favour the assumption of free will.

(b) The ideal strategy selected by the computer is not a battle strategy, "win or lose". It is a minimum loss consistent with gain strategy. In human affairs this is too often irrelevant. One wants to win. The "ideal strategy" of the theory of games is not the strategy which would recommend itself to a commander of troops, the coach of a football team or the entrepreneur of an aggressive concern.

(c) In the computer's decision there is nothing of what Shackle calls the "creative act". There is no insight and no imagination. And no apologist for the machine has claimed these attributes for it.

(d) There is no volition. The machine cannot will. It cannot follow its selection to a maximum gain consistent with minimum loss strategy with some sort of resolution which might be summed in the words: "and I will see it done". Only the real entrepreneur, cabinet minister, or general says this, and sees it done.

* Bernard J. F. Lonergan, *Insight, A Study of Human Understanding*, Philadelphia, 1958, pp. 97–98.

Decision-taking and the Theory of Games

(e) Most real situations are *"games in flow"*, that is they are not discontinuous games in which ever new strategies can be developed. This is not a question of the shortness of time required by a computer. It is philosophically the difference between the calculus and difference equations. For real situations a better analogue than those discontinuous games such as checkers (drafts) or chess would be such games as soccer, hockey or rugger, where the *flow* of play is continuous and the playmaker, as he is called, has to initiate strategy while not only he is in motion but all opponents are in motion and the flow of play rolls on and strategies are developed, modified, resurrected, then again changed, all in a continuous flow. (One should admit they often come to no effective end.) We are less concerned, however, with our example than with the mathematical principle it illustrates. The mathematics of the theory of games is that of discontinuity: the mathematics appropriate to strategy in action is the calculus, the theory of flows.*

We do not know how far these five points need elaboration beyond statement. We shall be as brief as possible.

(a) We admit that this is merely a question of choice of assumptions. *De gustibus non est disputandum.*

(b) One has to wonder whether in any strategic dilemma the decision-maker really thinks in terms of a minimum loss, maximum profit outcome. Professor Shackle's "focus loss, focus gain" solution may appear to be similar, but it really is different. In the Shackle case the decision-maker focuses on a loss and gain hypothesis. One hypothesis has greater power to "excite the mind" than another. So the decision is taken. In the min–max solution in the theory of games, the player in the experiment does not set out to "win". He plays so that over the long period of time, after repeated experiments, he will gain. He selects the strategy now which over a period of time will

---

* Economists seem to have had to choose between discontinuous models ("period analysis") like those of the Swedish School and continuous, mechanically determinate macro-economic models, called mistakenly, we believe, "dynamic", in which there is no place for decision. This, of course, is done for simplification. Models of continuous decisions in a flow situation would be enormously complex. I am not a good enough mathematician to know if such a model would be theoretically possible. Professor Shackle, who is a mathematician, says in a letter that it would be "inconceivably" difficult. The argument in the text, however, is that, in fact, decisions are continuously taken and revised in a flow situation. This is the common experience of decision-makers. To admit that it is difficult to analyze is not the same thing as saying we shall analyze something quite different because it is easy and pretend that our analysis is relevant to real experience.

give him the maximum benefits consistent with minimum possible losses. He is a very cautious kind of guy, not the dashing entrepreneur of Schumpeterian economics, but rather the civil servant of the sort political cartoonists like to draw. As a soldier he is a Vauban, not a Marlborough; Blucher, not Wellington; the Imperial General Staff of 1917 as opposed to the tank command at Cambrai. I should like to see a place in entrepeneurial theory for the dashing, imaginative, innovating entrepreneur of whom Schumpeter speaks. While he may not be responsible for economic growth (*la croissance*) in Professor Perroux's language, this fellow is responsible for development (*le développement*).

(c) On this point I need add little to the last paragraph.

The computer, the machine, is neither creative nor imaginative. The future holds within its cloak the unknown. The machine cannot imagine what is there. It can operate only on the assumption that there is nothing new, that past data give it a clear clue to the future.* This, as Professor Shackle has argued, is just not so. The future is unknown and uncertain. It is under these conditions that decisions *now* are taken which will become effective in an uncertain future. Such decisions demand imagination, the quality that Father Lonergan calls "insight". I do not think there is any evidence to suggest that they are intuitive. I might add here that I have always thought that Professor Shackle believed in an intuitive decision, but I can find no evidence of this in specific terms either in *Expectation in Economics* or in *Decision, Order and Time in Human Affairs*. Nevertheless I still think that the Shackle phi-function implies the attribute we call intuition. I think that by "intuition" he means immediate apprehension of a fact or a proposition without intermediate datum-intervention.

(d) The idea of volition launches us on the dangerous seas of Hegelian philosophy. Is it possible, one wonders, to acknowledge, without accepting holus-bolus the idea of the Absolute Will, that human volition is an important part of taking a decision? We do not say, in fact, as a player in a two-party game, that we expect a certain outcome. We do say that we "intend an outcome". And once having made up our minds we devote every energy to bringing

---

* Professor Shackle writes: "It is novelty, I would say, which makes decisions something more than calculation. How can you programme a machine with *data* about *the essentially new*, i.e. the *essentially unknown*?" (in a letter to the author).

that outcome to pass. On this point we depart not only from Professor Simon, whose machine clearly has no intention of its own, but also from Professor Shackle whose decision-maker is a passive, intuitive agent who is surprised or not surprised by certain hypotheses. When I say, "I intend to do this, I have made up my mind", I have not only selected a hypothesis about the future, I become a part of the causal process. My intention and my will, unless irrationally directed, tend to create the realization which has been hoped for. When I say, "I intend to hoe the beans today", and then it rains, I do not hoe the beans because I know that to work among bean plants in wet weather is to invite rust. So I tie up the tomato plants or I read a detective story. The following day, shall we agree, dawns fair and bright. My wife says, "today you can hoe the beans". She is perfectly right. There is no rational reason why I should not hoe the beans. But if I lack the will to do so the beans will not be hoed. (We put aside the possibility that by masterly inactivity I can get my wife to do the job in my place.) It is only when I decide that I *intend* to hoe the beans that the beans get hoed. I have put the case most mildly, because I do not want to get caught up in the cobwebs of Prussian military philosophy.* Nevertheless we can think of many examples: coaches who tell their teams that they lack only the will to win. This, apparently, is a successful coaching device or it would not be used by so many coaches in America.† This, however, is by the way. Much more telling is the heroic case of Hannibal's crossing of

---

* Von Clausewitz, *ibid.*

† At one time I was a coach myself. I coached the McGill University Rugby Football Club for eight years. (We did not do too badly. In that period we won 29 matches, lost 6 and drew 2.) At the end of the fourth year, when my chaps had gone undefeated for four years, the coach of the McGill University Canadian Football team invited me to the dressing-room of his squad. He gave them a pre-game pep talk which consisted mostly of telling them that their opponents, Toronto, would probably excel them in skill, but he begged them to "fight, fight, fight" for "old McGill". He then, so help me, bowed down in prayer, and invited God to intercede on behalf of McGill. It seemed to me like introducing a thirteenth player; rather like the kind of interference from Olympus that the Greeks depended upon during the Trojan War. In the event, God did not really help much. Toronto beat McGill very effectively. Afterwards my chaps went out to play the Toronto Rugby Union Club. I also had a last-minute dressing-room chat with them, but I did not invoke God. I suggested that the third row forwards break fast from set scrums and smear the Toronto stand-off. He was, in my opinion, the only point of danger. My club won 27–0, without God's help. Will power, without understanding, will not win games whatever many coaches seem to believe. Some thought and analysis are necessary, and nothing in the text contradicts this.

the Alps. Once the passage had been made he fought the battle of Cannae as a model of strategic command. It has been copied, never surpassed. Whereas, however, Cannae was a triumph of technical skill and the intelligent and economic use of limited resources, the crossing of the Alps was a triumph of leadership and determination, that is to say the will of the leader.

Thus, while we do not believe for a moment that sheer determination can achieve all or anything without an intelligent appraisal of the facts, we do believe that the volitional element in decision is an important part of it. As we shall come to say "I intend" is part of the causal process in human affairs.

(e) On this point I am less sure of my ground, because I am not good enough at mathematics to engage in debate over mathematical philosophy. I think I have a cardinal point to make but it may turn out to be only a question of practicability.* It seems to me that the theory of games applies only to discontinuous games, i.e. games like checkers or chess wherein each move may be planned in the light of revealed counter-strategies. This may also be true of American field games such as baseball and American football. Baseball is a game in which the strategy of every play may be calculated by the coach both of the team at bat and the team in the field. There is ample time for such calculations, if a computer is not to be programmed, between each pitch. We have even seen the pitcher walk out of his box to consult with the catcher, the team captain or the team coach. And on every base the batting side has "base coaches" who indicate to the base runners the decisions of the team coach. It is so, also, in American football. Anyone who has watched or studied this game will remember that on every single play a round table conference is held by both the attacking and the defending teams. There they are, all in two concentric circles, their big and padded bottoms facing, shall we say, into the television cameras. They talk it over; they take their time; the coach sends in a substitute with new orders and a fresh strategy. He may or may not have a computer at work, I do not know. He certainly has "spotters" from Olympus who give him an analysis of the play. The American football coach could, I should think, use a computer with advantage. He would have lots of time, while the commercial was inserted, to choose his strategy. It is not without significance that American economists should think of strategies in games in discontinuous terms. Sociologists might give

* Bernard J. F. Lonergan, *ibid*, pp. 97–98.

thought to the fact that the great American games, baseball and football, are played solely in the United States. Games are a cultural expression and American games have never "caught on".

By contrast, ice hockey, originally a Canadian game, soccer and rugger, which in origin were British, are international games. They are played everywhere and nowhere with more vim and vehemence than in the United States. Americans, tied as they are by a kind of mystique to their own games, which are so terribly dull and serious, still do like to play games for fun. (In our opinion there is no legitimate reason for playing games, except that they are played for fun.) However, this may be, we shall look at these three international games, and when we do so we observe that they have one thing in common. There is a play-maker—the center in hockey, the center-forward in soccer, the stand-off half in rugger—and he adapts himself, and his team-mates adjust themselves accordingly, to a continuous *flow*. On the move the play-maker continuously adjusts himself, and takes decisions, as the play flows on. We submit that this is not just a practical matter of the much greater speed at which the international games are played: it is surely a question of the type of mathematics applicable to the analysis of these games. On the one hand we have the discontinuous analysis of the theory of games and difference equations, on the other hand we have the mathematics of continuous flow, the differential calculus, and we have the continuous adjustment of strategies to counter-strategies as the play, the experiment, develops. Anyone who has watched the play of the Hon. L. Kelly can see how consistently he is thinking, how persistently he follows through his pattern, how rapidly he adjusts when things "go wrong". He is the very picture—on the ice and on the television screen—of the decision-maker, a symbol of the flow of consciousness and of the intelligent conscious control of the flow of consciousness.

The play-maker in a flow game, say the stand-off or fly half in rugger, may often find himself in a position where he cannot make a positive decision and is constrained to make a negative decision, that is to postpone positive decision-taking. For example, the stand-off half may discover that his three-quarters have run across field too far before straightening their runs so that he has lost contact with them, and that the opposing forwards are swarming down on him so that he lacks playing space i.e. ground to manoeuver. The only thing he can do is kick for touch. This gets him nothing except delay.

He has postponed the positive decision in the hope that he will be able to make it in the future under more favorable conditions.

One wonders how many entrepreneurial decisions are of this nature, negative or delaying, seeking "playing space", that is, more flexibility for manoeuvre. This admission is damaging to the Shackle concept of the unique, once and once only, decision situation. It is equally damaging to the argument of this essay. The qualification must, however, be allowed; and when the postponed decision must be taken, then I think, the Shackle thesis and the argument of this essay will stand.

The Treatment of Expectations in Econometrics

L. R. KLEIN

University of Pennsylvania

1. SPECIFICATION OF ECONOMETRIC MODELS

To a large extent, econometric analysis builds on an economic theory base. This is particularly true in the specification of econometric models; whether micro or macro, whether partial or complete. The prominent role assigned to expectations in economic theory must surely carry over, then, to econometric analysis. Theoreticians like Professor Shackle have made the point in a telling way that economic units use expectations when making optimal economic decisions. In some versions of theory, economic units are assumed to optimize expected profits or expected satisfactions. These optimization schemes are planned in terms of expected market variables, such as expected output price, expected interest rate, expected wage rate or even expected tax rate. Expected income levels, expected activity levels, expected factor inputs are also highly relevant in model building.

This is all clear enough and rightfully enriches theoretical reasoning in economics, but what of econometrics, where it is not appropriate to reduce a problem to various contingencies about the outcome of expectations? In econometrics, we need definite measurement and fully testable model formulations. The trouble with expectations variables is that they are subjective, personal, and not easily measured for numerical statistical analysis.

For as long as most living econometricians can remember, an attempt has been made to introduce lags in econometric model specifications as surrogates for expectations. In my first model building venture, for the Cowles Commission in the middle 1940s, I specified the equations of the models being constructed in terms of anticipated values and used recently realized values of a variable as indicators of anticipated values.* I wrote, "... the immediate past level, rate of change, acceleration, etc., of prices would be a likely set of data on which to form expectations of future prices". Other authors, of course, had also used lags or distributed lags of variables to represent expectations and to bring other aspects of dynamics into econometric models. Apart from expectations, lags might appear in econometric equations because of construction periods, delays in decision making, adaptations to new situations, and stock/flow definitions. All lag distributions are not indicative of expectations, and, as I shall argue later, all expectations are not represented as lag distributions; nevertheless the most common way to quantify and measure expectations variables is through the use of lags.

The simplest example of a model using time lags for expectations is the familiar cob-web. This system is assumed to be descriptive of agricultural markets for perishable commodities. The model is well known,

$$q_t^s = \alpha_0 + \alpha_1 p_{t-1} + e_t \quad \text{supply} \tag{1}$$

$$q_t^d = \beta_0 + \beta_1 p_t + u_t \quad \text{demand} \tag{2}$$

$$q_t^s = q_t^d \quad \text{market clearing} \tag{3}$$

$e_t, u_t = \text{error}$

Since the commodity is perishable, by assumption markets are effectively cleared, as asserted in (3). The model states that producers supply (plant) a good (agricultural commodity) on the basis of expected price and put the whole amount (crop yield) on the market for whatever price it will fetch. Anticipated price, which forms the basis for supplier decisions, is not objectively measured, but an indicator of expected price is used instead. In the typical agricultural case, the farmer has little basis for forming expectations about price when he has to decide upon acreage and seeding. He knows the price at that time, but not at the time of marketing, because he doesn't know the volume to be marketed. In the absence of *a priori* knowledge about subsidies, price supports, or other price information, the best judgment about future price is last season's price.

* L. R. Klein, *Economic Fluctuations in the United States, 1921–1941*, New York, Wiley, 1950, p. 16.

Objective data could be collected for this model, and it could be estimated by standard econometric techniques. The estimated system would then generally imply the periodic cob-web cycle. The system need not be linear but the lag structure serving as a surrogate for expectations should be the same for a nonlinear version of the model.

This kind of dynamic system seems to fit data for many different markets in a reasonably good manner. It is, however, considered by many theoreticians to be an affront to producer intelligence and the general theory of rational behavior. If the oscillation were predetermined as it comes out of this simple model, producers would act on the oscillatory information and speculate the pattern out of existence. If we complicate the model by permitting storage and crop carry-overs, inventory speculation on the basis of expected prices might introduce a more complicated lag structure through the use of longer and more detailed lag distributions. This may also affect "expected" price in the supply equation.

Are lags, either in the simple form of last period's value or in lag distribution form, always good measures of anticipations? In the case of price, it seems that the recent historical existence of an unusual period (closing of the Suez Canal, worldwide devaluation, outbreak of war, etc.) would produce some highly atypical values that would be poor indicators of expectations in situations where it is known that the unusual factors will not be present. It seems to be wrong for the econometrician to be a "slave" to past values, no matter how unusual they are, as indicators of expectations.

The American economy has just come through a period in which previous price movements were distorted by a major strike which has been settled. The strike (General Motors, autumn, 1970) distorted the weights in forming the GNP deflator, which is often used as a general price variable in econometric models. Since the index number for cars happens to be below the average index value for all GNP and since it received a small weight during the historical strike period, this biased the whole index upward for the particular quarter. There will be a corresponding downward bias in the strike recovery period. This suggests that lagged price is a poor indicator of current price. This defect is not remedied by using an entire lag distribution instead of a simple lag value for expected price.

Another approach to dynamic economic modeling for the purpose of representing expected values was followed at an early stage by

Metzler in his construction of inventory models.* His schemes are all translated into terms of observable time series and have been statistically estimated. In simplest form, using Metzler's own notation, the system is

$$u_t = \beta y_{t-1} \quad \text{consumption function} \tag{4}$$

$$s_t = \beta(y_{t-1} - y_{t-2}) \quad \text{inventory investment function} \tag{5}$$

$$y_t = u_t + s_t + v_0 \quad \text{definition of national income} \tag{6}$$

y_t = national income
u_t = consumer expenditures
s_t = production for inventory
v_0 = exogenous investment.

In this system, consumption is made to depend on lagged income. This is a behavioral or adjustment delay. The inventory equation is based on the idea that production for inventory should be the difference between actual and normal stocks of the preceding period, where the difference in the two stock levels is determined by the difference between actual and expected sales of period $t-1$. Actual sales for consumption are

$$\beta y_{t-1},$$

while anticipated sales are

$$\beta y_{t-2};$$

therefore, production for inventory is

$$s_t = \beta y_{t-1} - \beta y_{t-2}.$$

Equations (4)–(6) make up a small self contained dynamic system, depending on observed data, since lag values have been used in place of expected values. The model has been extended by Metzler by introducing expected income (from past values) in the consumption function and making a stock adjustment form of the inventory investment equation.

Inventories and inventory models are hard to estimate and determine well, in an econometric sense, yet the Metzler model stands up as an outstanding contribution which performs as well as alternatives

* L. A. Metzler, 'The Nature and Stability of Inventory Cycles', *The Review of Economic Statistics*, August 1941, pp. 113–129.

Expectations in Econometrics

in a difficult sector. Much of the good performance of the Metzler model stems from his use of expectations in the form of lag variables.

2. TWO APPROACHES

There are two principal methods of dealing with expectations in econometrics. One is an extension of the older idea of using lagged values, as indicated in the cob-web and inventory cycle models cited above. The other is by direct measurement from sample surveys of individual respondents.

Lag distributions: The extension in the use of lagged values is the use of lag distributions. A simple but indirect way of introducing a lag distribution is to start from the assumption that expectations are formed from the adjustment hypothesis.

$$p_t^e - p_{t-1}^e = \lambda(p_{t-1} - p_{t-1}^e) \tag{7}$$

This states that the change in an expected value (price expectations in this case, p_t^e) is adjusted with coefficient $\lambda (0 < \lambda < 1)$ to the discrepancy between the previous period's actual and expected value. The integral of this finite difference equation in expected values is

$$p_t^e = \lambda \sum_{i=1}^{\infty} (1-\lambda)^{i-1} p_{t-i} \tag{8}$$

This dynamic adjustment process of expectations formulation is, therefore, equivalent to assuming that expected price is a weighted average of past prices, where the weights are proportional to the geometric series $1, (1-\lambda), (1-\lambda)^2, (1-\lambda)^3, (1-\lambda)^4$, etc. Since the sum of these terms is given by

$$\sum_{i=1}^{\infty} (1-\lambda)^{i-1} = \frac{1}{1-(1-\lambda)} = \frac{1}{\lambda}$$

we can write

$$\lambda \sum_{i=1}^{\infty} (1-\lambda)^{i-1} p_{t-i} = \sum_{i=1}^{\infty} w_i p_{t-i}$$

where

$$\sum_{i=1}^{\infty} w_i = 1.$$

If (7) is a stochastic relation, but not directly observable, with random error u_t, the integral in (8) has an error term of the form

$$v_t = \sum_{i=0}^{\infty} (1-\lambda)^i u_{t-i}.$$

The series v_t is autocorrelated. On the other hand if expectations are assumed to be formed directly as a weighted average of past prices, as in (8), with a random error term, the associated error derived for (7) will be autocorrelated.

The idea of assuming expected value to be weighted averages of past values is now common in econometric work. It is formally the same as assuming that *permanent* or *long run* values stand for expected values, where long run values are defined as weighted averages of past values. This is the idea behind the various empirical, time-series formulations of the permanent income hypothesis for saving or consumption. It is used for the specification of agricultural supply functions, dependent on *long run* price, and in the version of the quantity theory of money equation in which *long run* price and *long run* income are the joint explanatory variables that are associated with movements in the money stock.

In the theory of the term structure of interest rates, it is asserted that the long term rate is a moving average of expected short term rates. This gets expressed as

$$(r_L)_t = \alpha \sum_{i=0}^{\infty} \mu^i (r_s)_{t-i} + u_t \tag{9}$$

or in some closely related variant. Equation (9) is often estimated from

$$(r_L)_t = \alpha (r_s)_t + \mu (r_L)_{t-1} + v_t \tag{10}$$

or

$$(r_L)_t = \alpha (r_s)_t + \mu (r_L)_{t-1} + \beta (r_s)_{t-1} + v_t \tag{10}'$$

Equation (10) or (10)' is directly estimated from observed data, but interpreted as an estimate of (9). In the latter form it can be seen to have expectational content.

A similar idea occurs in the various stock adjustment formulations of economic behavior, the most celebrated being the stock adjustment form of the accelerator equation

$$K_t - K_{t-1} = I_t = \lambda (K_t^* - K_{t-1}) + e_t. \tag{11}$$

The expression in (11) implies that capital, K_t, is changed over its previous value, giving net investment, I_t, in proportion to the discrepancy between *desired* capital stock and actual capital stock of the previous period. If desired stock is proportional to output, K_t, we have

$$I_t = \lambda(\alpha X_t - K_{t-1}) + e_t \\ = \lambda \alpha X_t - \lambda K_{t-1} + e_t \qquad (12)$$

Equation (12) can also be written as

$$K_t = \lambda \alpha X_t + (1-\lambda) K_{t-1} + e_t$$

whose integral is

$$K_t = \alpha \lambda \sum_{i=0}^{\infty} (1-\lambda)^i X_{t-i} + u_t \qquad (13)$$

In this form we can interpret the right hand explanatory variable as *long run* or *permanent* production level, which determines capital stock. This is, therefore, a form of expectations explanation of

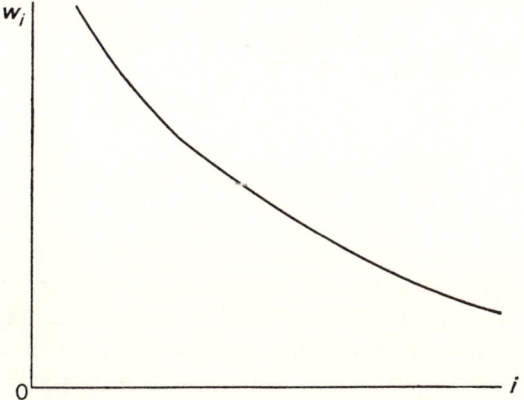

Figure 1. Geometric Lag Distribution

capital stock. The econometrician usually estimates (12) from current and lagged data, but the parent hypothesis is (13).

All the expressions used so far to represent lag distributions are of the geometric type. The typical shape is shown in Figure 1. More general lag distributions, particularly of the unimodal humped type, are also important in econometric analysis. They, too, justify interpretation in terms of expectations. In planning economic decisions that take several periods (months, quarters, years) to formulate and execute, the lag distribution is likely to be of the hump type. This is typical of large scale investment planning and is just the kind of situation in which the use of expectations analysis in the sense of Professor Shackle is most appropriate. Econometric analysis of investment now generally assumes that expectations of activity levels and market conditions at the most remote stage, when

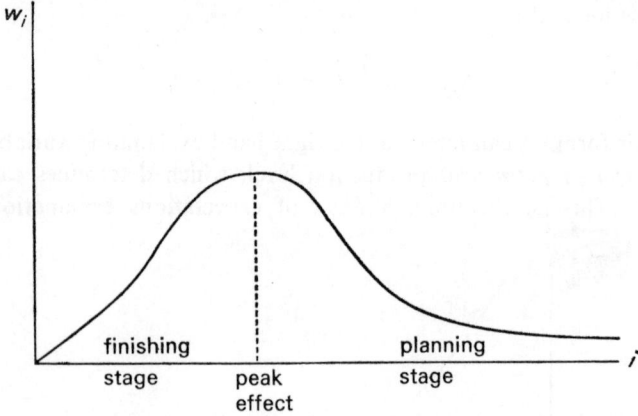

Figure 2. Humped Lag Distribution

the project is being first considered, have little weight but grow in relative significance as the time approaches for making final commitments. There is a peak (lag) period of effect and a steadily declining degree of influence as the time approaches for final delivery or installation. Since investment projects are often large and lumpy, only limited changes in the whole scheme can be instituted after a certain point of work has been passed. In the case of a building, decoration, furnishing, and equipping can be changed as the final date approaches. Expectations of market or activity conditions have some effect, but they become comparatively small as the final date approaches. The lag distribution should thus have the form in Figure 2. To illustrate this kind of lag distribution in the context of investment functions, we write

$$I_t = \sum_{i=0}^{P} w_i X_{t-i} + \sum_{i=0}^{r} q_i K_{t-i} + e_t \qquad (14)$$

where w_i and q_i follow distribution patterns with the general shape given in Figure 2. A special case, however, would be a monotonically falling distribution curve in Figure 1. Possibilities for graduation of w_i and q_i are polynomial lag functions or rational polynomials, both of which are being used in current work.*

$$w_i = \alpha_0 + \alpha_1 i + \alpha_2 i^2 + \alpha_3 i^3 \qquad (15)$$

or

$$\frac{N(L)}{D(L)} = \frac{n_0 + n_1 L + n_2 L^2 + \ldots}{1 + d_1 L + d_2 L^2 + d_3 L^3 + \ldots} \qquad (16)$$

$$L^j X_t = X_{t-j}$$

In the first case, we say that the w_i or the q_i lie along polynomials which can have a prescribed shape over a finite range. The statistical estimation of the polynomial coefficients provides a basis for calculating the weights in the lag distribution from (15). In (16) we form a ratio of two operator polynomials, where L is the lag (displacement) operator and the investment function has the form

$$I_t = \frac{N_1(L)}{D_1(L)} X_t + \frac{N_2(L)}{D_2(L)} K_t + e_t$$

The estimation of the coefficients in the numerator and denominator polynomials provides a basis for computing the weights in the relevant lag distribution.† Estimation problems are more difficult to handle for (16) than for (15), but the former distribution forms are more general.

The rational function lag distributions may appear to be quite arbitrary, but L. Taylor has tried to show how they might arise from an optimization process by an economic decision maker.‡ The geometric lag distributions are special cases of this form when

* S. Almon, 'The Distributed Lag between Capital Appropriations and Expenditures', *Econometrica*, January 1965, pp. 178–196; D. W. Jorgensen, 'Rational Distribution Lag Functions', *Econometrica*, January 1966, pp. 135–149.

† P. Dhrymes, L. R. Klein, and K. Steiglitz, 'Estimation of Distributed Lags', *International Economic Review*, June 1970, pp. 235–250.

‡ L. Taylor, 'The Existence of Optimal Distributed Lags', *Review of Economic Studies*, January 1970, pp. 95–106.

$$\frac{N(L)}{D(L)} = \frac{n_0}{1+d_1 L}.$$

The polynomial lag distribution is very convenient and tractable, but it serves more as a graduation formula than a process that is derived from theoretical economic analysis.

To summarize, in applied dynamic econometrics, expectations are widely represented by the use of lag distributions that attempt to portray the conditions of the economy at the time decisions are being made about significant economic variables. The use of lag distributions is growing rapidly and being extended to cover a wide variety of parametric specifications.

Direct measurement: An entirely different approach to the econometric treatment of expectations is taken in sample survey investigations. Instead of trying to infer people's expectations from lag variables, the survey researcher goes directly to the respondent and ascertains his expectations. For the United States, we have regular surveys of households, business firms, and other economic units. Expectations are ascertained by questionnaire on

- consumer buying plans
- consumer income, price, and financial expectations
- business capital expenditures
- business inventory, sales, and employment expectations
- area building plans.

The consumer surveys actually pose three kinds of questions:

1. buying plans for specific goods (or services); 2. expectations about incomes and market prices; 3. general attitudes towards the state of the economy and the state of personal economic situations. There is a dispute among economists on the comparative importance of specific buying plans against attitudes and expectations, but all three seem to be relevant in careful analysis.

These kinds of survey data are quite universal. Many countries have had long experience with surveys of investment plans, inventory expectations and sales expectations. Such data are used in several ways for econometric analysis. In single cross-section samples they may be used to determine effects of expectations or subjective variables generally on decisions together with more objectively measured variables on actual performance. For example consumer spending may depend on actual income and expected income levels as in

$$C_i = f_i(Y_i, Y_i^a) + e_i \qquad i = 1, 2, \ldots, N.$$

Price anticipations may be used to study both buying and portfolio decisions on the part of consumers or other economic units. This is of some interest because prices and other market variables are effectively held constant for a single cross section sample, but price expectations may vary widely across such a sample.

When direct questioning for expectation variables is done in sample surveys, these schemes often become regularized and a whole time series of expectations across successive survey samples may be constructed. Indices of attitudes, buying plans, and investment outlays are now available in the U.S. and elsewhere. These can be used as supplementary economic variables like other time series statistics in the estimation of econometric relationships. Instead of trying to represent expected prices and incomes by surrogates in the form of lag distributions, such variables may be directly represented by time series of sample indices. In a closely related way, realization relationships based on time series data can be estimated from variables that try to explain the discrepancy between actual and expected performance.

A principal problem with all these applications of directly estimated expectations, taken from sample surveys, is that they are primarily used only in a single direction, i.e. their effect on objective variables is studied. The missing link is an explanation of the generating processs of the expectations themselves. They were primarily introduced for predictive purposes and are constructed to have some lead time over actual economic performance. Much research has been devoted to using expectations indices as indicators of actual buying or actual economic activity in specific lines of endeavor. They are treated as *predetermined* variables to use the language of econometrics. A natural step to follow is to try to build an explanation of the generation of expectations, or to *endogenize* the subjective variables.

There are two noteworthy attempts to "explain" expectations. Jorgenson has hypothesized that expected investment, measured by sample survey intentions data, have the same explanation as observed investment, but the explanatory variables should simply be dated for earlier occurrence.* By this approach we would replace

$$I_t = \frac{N_1(L)}{D_1(L)} X_t + \frac{N_2(L)}{D_2(L)} K_t + e_t \tag{17}$$

---

* D. W. Jorgenson, 'Anticipations and Investment Behavior', *The Brookings Quarterly Econometric Model of the United States*, ed. by J. Duesenberry et al., Chicago, Rand McNally, 1965, pp. 33–92.

by

$$I_t^e = \frac{N_1(L)}{D_1(L)} X_{t-2} + \frac{N_2(L)}{D_2(L)} K_{t-2} + u_t \qquad (18)$$

where I_t^e are expectations of I_t, two periods (six months) in advance. A statistical procedure would be to estimate I_t^e from (18) and then phase I_t^e into I_t either by using (17) together with (18) or by establishing an empirical relationship between I_t and I_t^e of the sort that would be an implied specification of (17) and (18) together. The empirical relationship implied, in parametric form, between I_t and I_t^e is

$$I_t = \sum_i w_i I_{t-i}^e + v_t \qquad (19)$$

This is the kind of relationship estimated by Shirley Almon in her celebrated paper, except that she used capital *appropriations* instead of *expectations*.*

Yet another possibility is to use the approach of R. Eisner in developing capital realization equations that explain $(I_t - I_t^e)/I_t^e$ in terms of such variables as changes in sales, profits, orders and previous deviations between expected and actual investment.† All the effects of explanatory variables are estimated from lag distributions. A combination of equation types (18) with either (19) or realization equations estimated by Eisner seem to offer promise for future model building work.

Jorgenson's equation (18) provides a formal method for endogenizing expectations, but it may be less satisfying to research workers than a systematic empirical search guided by economic theory to the extent possible, for a good (best) statistical relationship between subjective expectations and objective economic variables. An attempt has been made by S. Hymans to derive a stable statistical relationship between the Survey Research Center's (University of Michigan) index of consumer attitudes and other macro variables of the economy that would be generated in a large scale model.‡ Hymans's study of consumer expenditures makes two significant contributions to the econometrics of expectations. Not only does he generate endogenously, but he also has an improved way of using expectations

---

* S. Almon, *op. cit.*

† R. Eisner, 'Realization of Investment Anticipations', *The Brookings Quarterly Econometric Model of the United States*, ed. by J. Duesenberry et al., Chicago, Rand McNally, 1965, pp. 93–128.

‡ S. Hymans, 'Consumer Durable Spending: Explanation and Predictions' *Brookings Papers on Economic Activity*, 2, 1970, pp. 173–206.

to predict consumer behavior. He "filters" expectations by requiring the index to change by a minimum amount or to change consecutively, in one direction for several periods before its value is counted as non-zero in affecting consumer expenditure decisions. In this way, small erratic movements that do not come up to threshold values are filtered out of the relationship. This seems to improve the predictive performance of the index. Other filtering devices may also be used. T. Juster recommends scaling of the intensity or probability of consumer buying plans in constructing an index of intentions.

The endogenous generation of expectations may be investigated empirically at the micro or macro level. At the level of individual decision-making such variables may be used in cross-section regression estimates, particularly to establish whether such variables are important or not.* Hymans, on the other hand, explains expenditures at the macro level in a way that is fully compatible with aggregative model structure.

There is a drawback, however, to Hymans's results in explaining an index of consumer sentiment, namely, that he makes use of stock market variables for part of his explanation. Econometricians, unsurprisingly, have been singularly weak in explaining stock market averages in macroeconometric models. Such variables probably have a large element of personal attitudes which is the thing to be explained. Results similar to Hymans's, from the point of view of degree of correlation, for explanation of consumer attitudes have also been obtained by Adams and Green, although they use mainly labor market variables in their statistical equations.†

A second issue that arises particularly in the case of consumer expectations is the mixture between attitudes and buying plans in an overall index. Economists at the Survey Research Center, led by G. Katona, claim that general consumer attitudes revealed by their subjective appraisals of national and personal economic conditions are more significant than specific buying plans in predicting actual consumer behavior. The empirical result is that buying plans correlate well with actual behavior in cross section samples but not in aggregative time series studies, unless possibly "filtered".‡

* See L. R. Klein and J. B. Lansing, 'Decisions to Purchase Consumer Durable Goods', *The Journal of Marketing*, October 1955, pp. 109–132.
† F. G. Adams and E. W. Green, 'Explaining and Predicting Aggregative Consumer Attitudes', *International Economic Review*, September 1965, pp. 275–293.
‡ See F. G. Adams, 'Consumer Attitudes, Buying Plans and Purchases of

The present *Index of Consumer Sentiment* has five component attitude measures of responses to questions on:

(i) Business conditions during the next 12 months.
(ii) Business conditions during the next 5 years.
(iii) Evaluation of present financial situation.
(iv) Expected personal financial situation during the next 12 months.
(v) Whether it is a good or bad time to buy consumer durables.

Formerly a scaling of buying plans was also included in the Index. Answers to other questions have been considered at one time or another. These are for price and income expectations. Stable, reliable results appear to come principally from the five-point Index.

To round out the presentation of materials on direct questioning of respondents on expectations, we have had some results with other variables or processes, such as sales, inventory, and employment expectations and forward commitment variables such as orders or building starts. The latter two serve the same role as expectations in providing short run predictions of behavior, but they are less subjective and derived from different kinds of samples. They are not obtained from depth interviews with persons as respondents. To a large extent, they are derived from regular records. The Munich business test data have been extensively analyzed by Theil for predictive content, and the U.S. series on inventories and sales do not have a long enough record to make a full assessment of their usefulness, but the prospects are not particularly bright.*

To what do these several investigations and results with the direct approach add in terms of future econometric model building? I have tried to formulate the Wharton Econometric Forecasting Model on a two-track system, one track with some equations entirely in objective form with the usual variables on income flows, stock levels, relative prices, etc. and the other track with these equations replaced by statistical equations that add expectations variables to all the others present.

The Index of Consumer Sentiment in consumption equations for cars and other durables.

* H. Theil, *Economic Forecasts and Policy*, Amsterdam, North-Holland Publishing Co. 1958.

Durable Goods: A Principal Components, Time Series Approach', *The Review of Economics and Statistics*, November 1964, pp. 347–355.

Investment intentions in the equations for capital formation.
Housing starts in the equations for residential construction.

The result is that short-run ex-post forecasts, within the sample period of fit, for the system as a whole perform better when the expectations track equations are included for one and two period forecasts than when they are excluded in favor of the other track.* This is only a preliminary result. It must be extended systematically to post-sample data; it must try equations on the expectations track one-at-a-time with the rest of the system; it must examine some forms of filtering. Yet it is quite suggestive. Careful direct measurement of expectations may help in prediction, and if Hymans's results can be extended they can be included on a self generating basis.

3. UNCERTAINTY IN ECONOMETRIC APPLICATION

A good deal of the work in applied econometrics is devoted to prediction—using estimated systems to extrapolate into the future. In this way expected magnitudes are estimated and then used in economic decision-making. The role of uncertainty in such applications has long been recognized and dealt with. Sampling error and estimated variance of random disturbances have been combined into a formula for standard error of forecast. The uncertainty surrounding econometric prediction has been recognized and dealt with through the construction of tolerance intervals associated with point forecasts. Although the relevant magnitudes are difficult to estimate in large econometric systems, the principles of their use in deriving appropriate forecast intervals or regions are well known. The calculus of uncertainty for this application is an established procedure drawn from statistical theory.

Another aspect of uncertainty in econometric applications is the uncertainty on the state of the world determining the exogenous inputs to a complete, estimated model. In the repeated (quarterly) forecast applications of the Wharton Model in the United States a set of practices has been developed for dealing with uncertainty. We have considered the range of plausible alternatives for exogenous variables and parameters. These may cover a range from bullishness

* See L. R. Klein, *An Essay on the Theory of Economic Prediction*, Chicago, Markham, 1971.

to bearishness; or from the assumption of occurrence of a labor disturbance to absence of such a disturbance, etc. Many alternatives are possible at any one time. Because the computerized models are so simple to recompute (solve again) and so quickly re-evaluated, uncertainty is handled by providing the economic decision-makers with separate calculations for each of the several exogenous readings.

Now, many of the large industrial companies and policy making public bodies make regular use of the Wharton Model or other econometric forecasting devices. For the future, this is the way that expectations are likely to be formed, whether they are for prices, incomes, sales or other economic variables. Expectations and forecasts will become synonymous, and such forecasts will be in an interval whose size is governed by uncertainty considerations.

The models, with internal dynamics, will be based on the translation of a theory of expectations into lag distributions as discussed above, and these estimated systems will then become the basis from which expectations will be formed for individual producer, consumer, or public authority decision-making in economics. At this time, the Wharton Model serves as a forecasting device for more than one hundred users, whose economic activities are carried out on a large scale. Econometrics and the analysis of expectations are, therefore, necessarily closely allied.

A complication is due to arise on the issue of self fulfilling (or defeating) expectations. If the larger corporations whose decisions are of predominant importance for the functioning of the American Economy, act on the econometric results of a given model, the model is likely to have a great bearing on the outcome of the economy's performance. This bearing would be predictable if we could estimate the "feedback" effects of a model solution on business or public behavior. Econometricians took the view for a long time that their work was largely experimental and would not be used for direct action by economic decision-makers. With the large development and improvement of econometric model building in recent years, it is no longer correct to regard econometric forecasts as purely experimental; they are seriously used for determining expected future values on a large scale. It is now necessary to turn attention to the feedback problem to try to estimate relationships that explicitly show the effects of econometric predictions on economic behavior. It is logically possible to close the system this way; econometricians simply have not tried extensively.

Information and Profit

D. M. LAMBERTON
Case Western Reserve University

A half century ago Knight wrote of "the most thoroughgoing methods of dealing with uncertainty; i.e., by securing better knowledge of and control over the future" (21, p. 260). Control of the future and increased power of prediction are, he added, "closely interrelated, since the chief practical significance of knowledge is control, and both are closely identified with the general progress of civilization, the improvement of technology and the increase of knowledge" (21, p. 239). "Information" was "one of the principal commodities" supplied by the economic organization (21, p. 261). The information industry included market associations, trade journals, statistical bureaus, advertising, and a "veritable swarming of experts and consultants in nearly every department of industrial life" (21, p. 262). But unfortunately Knight dismissed these methods of dealing with uncertainty because they represented "merely the objective of all rational conduct" (21, p. 260).

More recently Shackle has argued that "the pursuit of profit has become the pursuit of knowledge" (40, p. 12). Trends in non-price competition, the impact of science and technology, and the complex process of social change so inadequately labelled economic development all give meaning to this valuable insight shared by Knight and Shackle. Upon it can be built some important revisions of the theory of profit. In broad terms this involves not only recognition that inquiring, communicating, and deciding are necessarily complementary activities in the decision process but also the substitution, in the conceptualization of that process, of an active business policy for the passivity customarily implied when reference is made to "the inevitable connection between profit and uncertainty". As Shackle has remarked, "Uncertainty is freedom, freedom for the imagination, freedom to hope" (36, p. 172). But first the matter must be put into historical perspective.

I. AN HISTORICAL PERSPECTIVE

Profit has been described as "the central concept of the capitalistic economy" (45, p. 1262). Two corollaries might be noted: first, "few if any fields in economics can disclaim concern with profit. As the assumed objective of business behaviour, as a source of income, and as a dominant element in the supply of capital, a profit variable finds its place in most micro- and macroeconomic models. Policy questions such as the fostering of growth and stability, taxation, and the control of monopoly, reveal the same preoccupation with profit" (23, p. 1). If the direct nature of the link between information and profit be accepted for the moment, the pervasiveness of the profit influence is suggested by the comment that "the essence of conflict is the suspension of communication" (31, p. 283), for surely the reconciliation of conflicting private interests was and remains a prime concern of economics.*

Second, the significance of profit becomes shadowy if it be removed from the context of "the capitalistic system".† Yet modern economics, under the influence of positivism, has striven to perfect mechanistic techniques of model building with less and less consideration of people and institutions.‡ This trend in theoretical work is not new: as Georgescu-Roegen points out it was Pareto who asserted that "the individual may disappear" once his income was known and "a photograph of his tastes" had been obtained, because "The logic is perfect: man is not an economic agent simply because there is no economic process" (12, p. 104). There are important implica-

* Cf. Hahn: "The most intellectually exciting question of our subject remains: is it true that the pursuit of private interests produces not chaos but coherence, and if so, how is it done?" (14, p. 12).

† This is not to deny the meaningfulness of "profit" in other systems but the concepts of profit differ. One is reminded of Shackle's regret that "The confrontation of Eastern and Western conceptions of the meaning, genesis and role of prices is a subject to occupy ten years of conferences. Investment policy in West and East offers themes for another twenty" (37, pp. 402–3).

‡ G. L. S. Shackle and N. Georgescu-Roegen must be noted as major economic theorists opposed to this development.

tions for the theory of profit. Profit accrues to firms that are presided over by entrepreneurs, yet both firms and entrepreneurs are nebulous, even non-existent. As Shubik remarked recently, "as soon as our study becomes 'advanced', we do not bother to differentiate between General Motors and the local candy store" (41, p. 413). The Marshallian entrepreneur finds no place in advanced theory because "There is only a jigsaw puzzle of fitting given means to given ends, which requires a computer not an agent" (12, p. 104). As a consequence empirical testing has been hampered by inability to identify the "firm" of theoretical work and the theory of the firm is restricted to "optimality analysis of well-defined problems" (1, p. 67). "Conventional economics is not about choice, but about acting according to necessity" (39, p. 272).

A general defence of the conventional theoretical approach has been that the firm, presumably incorporating a given unit of entrepreneurial capacity, was merely a primitive unit in an analysis of *industry* behaviour. Such a defence was perhaps adequate in relation to the impersonal state of perfect competition but it becomes hopelessly inadequate in relation to a world of monopoly and oligopoly where the firm is obliged to make unique and crucial decisions, to optimize and to innovate. The making of such decisions puts a premium on information: its acquisition, storage and utilization become a major business activity. Shackle has noted some general implications:

There is a sense in which [the years 1926–1939] saw not only the eclipse of value theory by new branches of economics, but its veritable destruction. For value theory as an account of the mode of allocation of scarce resources in the *perfect knowledge* economy, is the theory of a *perfectly competitive* economy. The abandonment of the perfectly competitive assumption is part of the abandonment of the perfect knowledge assumption, and its consequences were enormously more far reaching than its authors seemed to have dreamed at the outset (38, p. 10).*

The real world in which policies are formed and decisions made is pervaded by uncertainty; the knowledge used to cope with that un-

* That Malchup perhaps misses the point of the protest by those who seek greater realism is indicated by his subtitle: "Realistic Models of the Firm *under Competition*" (28, p. 12; italics added). While he is fully aware that "To explain and predict price reactions under monopoly and oligopoly we need more than a profit-maximizing reactor" (28, p. 11), he does not seem to appreciate that these are the very reactions, along with non-price dimensions of business behaviour, to which the new developments in "the theory of the firm" are directed.

certainty is never adequate. "The paradox of business, in its modern evolution, is the conflict between our assumption that we know enough for our logic to bite on, and our *essential*, prime dependence on achieving *novelty*, the novelty which by its nature and meaning in some degree discredits what has passed for knowledge" (40, p. 155). Small wonder then that analysis that has excluded the decision-maker, both consumer and entrepreneur, has never adequately explained profit but has tended to rehash old theories.

Having suggested that the source of difficulty has been over-abstraction with neglect of the firm, its nature, policy criteria and even its activities,* it may be helpful to give an historical illustration of the intractable nature of this central problem of the theory of profit. Consider some of the early nineteenth century, non-Ricardian contributions.† William Ellis (1826) tangled with the problem of separating profit from interest and viewed profit as a return to risk-taking and management:

Where an individual employs his own savings productively, in the profit which he obtains is included, after deducting an adequate allowance for the risk to which his capital may have been exposed in his particular business, the remuneration for his time and skill, which remuneration may be called agency for superintendence; and the remuneration for the productive employment of his savings, which is called interest. The whole of this remuneration we may call gross profit. Where an individual employs the savings of another he obtains, after deducting the same allowance, the agency only. Where an individual lends his savings to another, what he obtains is interest. This interest may, without impropriety, for our present purposes, be designated as neat profits.‡

And G. P. Scrope (1831) listed the components of the "profit of stock":

what is thus vulgarly called profits, or living profits, comprehends much more besides the strict current profit on stock.... If we analyse the surplus produce defined above, which corresponds to the vulgar notion of

---

* See 23 for a fuller development of this view. If as author I be permitted to respond to a thoughtful and helpful review of *The Theory of Profit* after some years, I confess to real concern over my failure to convey to Edith Penrose my awareness of the vital difference between realism in the sense of preserving the infinite variety amongst firms and realism in the other sense of perceiving the significant characteristics of firms as a class (see 33).

† The following quotations from William Ellis and G. P. Scrope are drawn from the valuable paper by Gordon (13).

‡ *Westminster Review* (5 January 1826): 106 as quoted in 13, p. 383.

the living profits of capital employed in an active business by the owner and which the economists universally speak of as the "profits of stock", we shall find them in all cases to be made up of, 1. Interest of capital, or what can be got for its use without personal labour or risk; 2. Insurance against the risks incident to the particular business in which the stock is employed; 3. Wages of labour for the personal superintendence, skill, or talent of the capitalist; 4. Monopoly gains, arising from the possession of exclusive advantages, such as secret or patented processes or instruments, superior connexions, facilities of local position, of soil mines collieries, etc. Of these elements, the last comprehends rent itself, or that portion of it at least, to which as we shall shortly see, the economists have confined the term and which solely arises from monopoly.*

A glance at a well-known contemporary textbook (34) reveals that "what is ordinarily called profit" includes implicit returns or "the earnings of self-used factors" (p. 594), temporary earnings of successful innovators (p. 595), compensation for aversion to risk (p. 596), and monopoly profit (p. 599). The conceptual progress is not impressive.

The modern multiplicity of theories and definitions is readily apparent in such surveys as 20, 23, and 46. In this context, however, it is more useful to draw upon the classificatory scheme presented by Shackle who attempted to separate the meanings of profit by setting down a list of questions (39, pp. 252–3):

1. Does profit belong to a future or a past time interval?
2. Is profit something of specified amount looked forward to with a feeling of certainty?
3. Or is it a set of hypotheses to which are assigned various degrees of plausibility?
4. Is profit measurable absolutely or does it arise only from the comparison of two courses of action or two situations?
5. Can profit be imputed to a factor of production through the marginal productivity of that factor, or is it a residual?
6. Is profit something which is sought to be maximised, and does it thus play a part in allocating resources?
7. Or is it something ascribed to pure luck and uncontrollable circumstances?
8. Is profit something that has arisen, in an interval already past, in a manner and degree which were expected, or is it on the contrary something that has arisen and was not expected? Is it the difference between something that was expected and the corresponding thing that has been realised?

* *Quarterly Review* 44 (January 1831): 18 as quoted in 13, p. 384.

9. Is profit a prize, something hoped for by many though only able to go to a few?
10. Or are we to think of it as a reward already in the hands of those who have in some way deserved it?
11. Is profit the prize, or the reward, of uncertainty-bearing?
12. Or of decision-making?
13. Or of exceptional knowledge or of skill in forecasting?
14. Or is profit the spoils of monopoly power or of special bargaining power?
15. Is profit something implicit in the nature of a person's "structure of expectations" or "expectational vista", so that profit necessarily exists for any person who entertains plural hypotheses about the future course of events or about the consequence of each of several rival courses of action which are open to him, or is profit something which only arises as a consequence of the failure of experienced actuality to conform to what had been expected?

Shackle expressed the belief that there is a "unified conception or scheme of thought in which all necessary meanings and aspects of 'profit' can find a place": "that such a scheme can be built upon a foundation which has existed for many years, if we can adapt that foundation, as so much of economic theory needs to be adapted, to assume uncertainty instead of undoubtedly correct foresight" (39, p. 252).* He sought this unified conception with reference to "the capitalistic economy". Not only does production, consumption, and investment occur with a system of prices, but these result from the policies of decision-makers in a modern business economy based on private property (40, pp. 154–5). No longer is the economic problem the solution of a jigsaw puzzle: human affairs now require that the future be invented (11).

II. POLICY, PROFIT AND DECISION

Profit in Shackle's treatment is "a system of concepts" (40, p. 152).†
To summarise, *policy* is "the generic name of any formulation, simple

* This analysis of notions of profit had been presented in a lecture in Sweden and published in *Ekonomisk Tidskrift* in 1955. A starting point for Shackle's thought was E. Lindahl, "The Concept of Income", *Economic Essays in Honour of Gustav Cassel* (London: Allen & Unwin, 1933), pp. 399–407, reprinted in R. H. Parker and G. C. Harcourt, *Readings in the Concept and Measurement of Income* (Cambridge at the University Press), pp. 54–62).
† See 39, Chs. XXVIII, XXX and 40, Ch. 7.

or complex, vague or exact, general or special, discretionary or detailed, of guidance for action in face of circumstances which, lying necessarily in the future, can be approached only by conjecture and imagination" (39, p. ix). *Decision* is "the abandonment of an old policy and the adoption of a new one" (39, p. ix): the "invention of new policies, even policies that were beyond the mind's reach, that were logically non-existent, with the knowledge formerly possessed" (40, p. 149). *Profit* is "the instigator of radical re-thinking and reform of policy" (39, p. ix): positive or negative, it "measures the extent to which expectation has proved fallible" (39, p. ix). Actuality may elude policy. "There can and will be surprises, counter-expected and un-expected developments for which the policy does not provide" (39, p. 296). Such surprising consequences have power to induce a transformation of policy.

The distinction between counter-expected and unexpected events is important. "A hypothetical event or class of events can have been envisaged and excluded, can have been dismissed in the sense of being assigned a high degree of potential surprise. The actual occurrence of such an event would then occasion great surprise, and ought to be the signal for reconsideration of the whole system of assumptions on which high potential surprise had been assigned to it. But the over-turn of assumptions and beliefs would be greater still, if the actual event were of a character which had in no way entered into any reckoning or been even remotely imagined. The former class we may call counter-expected events, and the latter class unexpected events" (40, p. 151).

Expected events then are to be contrasted with others that are either counter-expected or unexpected. The dichotomy bears resemblance to many attempts to distinguish polar cases either in terms of decision problems or decision systems: e.g., mechanistic vs. organic (3, pp. 119–22), administrative vs. strategic (4, Chs. 2–3), systems vs. sequential (10, pp. 344–9), standardised vs. complex (5, pp. 327–8), programmed vs. non-programmed (42, pp. 49–58), and optimization vs. innovation (7). Similarly attempts have been made to set up simple classifications of investment decisions: voluntary vs. forced, habitual vs. genuine, earnings-justified vs. policy, etc. (23, pp. 118–19). All appear to be attempts to cope with the contrast between routine and the response to proven fallibility. Each may have merits for particular purposes but the Shackle scheme of thought has advantages for the theory of profit.

Unexpected events cannot, in this scheme of thought, be planned for but counter-expected events will, to the extent that the decision-maker has behaved and does behave in a rational manner, prompt the invention of new policy. The concept of elasticity of surprise provides a measure of the power to induce a transformation of policy. Consider the case of an investment project.

Typically a large outlay on an item or system of durable equipment will be envisaged for the near future, with other subsequent outlays at a lesser time-rate on services to operate this equipment and produce a stream of saleable goods. In each unit interval (quarter-year, or month) of the supposed useful life of the equipment, it will yield some quantum of sale-proceeds of product and absorb some quantum of operating expenses. The conjectural excess of the one over the other, in some named interval, we may call the trading revenue of that interval. This instalment is to be discounted at the market interest rate for loans of that term, which prevails when the decision is being made whether to order the equipment or not, and the sum is to be taken of all such discounted values of trading revenue, plus any scrap-value assigned to the plant after it ceases to be operated, to find a demand-price for this equipment for comparison with the initial construction cost or supply-price of the equipment. The decision to invest or not will depend on whether or not the demand-price exceeds the supply-price, and perhaps on the size of this (conjectural, ex ante) *investment-gain*.

The investment-project well illustrates some of those features of the concept of policy which we have tried to define. The trading revenue of any named future interval is a variable for which a wide range of rival hypotheses can be entertained. As the decision-maker considers larger and larger such values, he will come to those which begin to seem doubtfully possible, and this doubt will become stronger with each further increase of hypothetical size of revenue until he must regard any still greater values with complete disbelief. Somewhere within the range of increasing doubt the power of some hypothesis to arrest his attention and command his interest will be greater, at a point where marginal size and marginal doubt just balance each other, than that of any neighbouring hypothesis whether of greater or smaller profit, and this hypothesis, possessing maximum *ascendancy*, is what we mean by a focus hypothesis, in this case the *upper focus hypothesis of trading revenue*. In the other direction, hypotheses of smaller and smaller trading revenue, or numerically larger and larger trading loss, will similarly at first seem perfectly possible, then increasingly difficult to accept as able to come true, and at last quite unbelievable. Again, in this range of worsening hypotheses, there will be an hypothesis exerting greatest ascendency, the *lower focus hypothesis of trading revenue*. We should take note that a hypothetical investment gain being the excess of the discounted

Information and Profit 199

values in total of an entire series of hypothetical trading revenues covering the whole supposed life of a projected plant, over the supply price of the plant, will only be non-negative provided those hypothetical trading revenues are themselves mostly greater than zero. Lastly, in the midst of the range of no surprise, the decision-maker can perhaps settle upon a neutral trading revenue which, if it were to be realised, would strike him as suggesting neither a positive nor a negative ultimate, ex post, investment gain. Neutrality of a trading revenue hypothesis might be given other meanings, but that of compatibility with a zero investment gain seems to serve well as a basis for the concepts we wish to propose.

Let us write g for the excess of the upper focus hypothesis of trading revenue of some interval named or labelled m, over the neutral hypothesis for that interval. And let Δg stand for the excess, if any, of the recorded trading revenue of interval m over the upper focus hypothesis which has been entertained for interval m while it was still in the future. If the recorded, ex post, trading revenue of an interval does thus fall in the range of greater than zero surprise, and especially if it proves to be greater than the focus hypothesis, the decision-maker will have ground to revise upwards his previous assessments of investment gain for the plant. Suppose the effect is to raise the focus investment gain from j to $j+\Delta j$. Then we may speak of the ratio $\Delta j/j : \Delta g/g$ as the *valuation elasticity of surprise for gain of trading revenue*. This change in his assessment of his existing plant may induce a change in his intentions for further investment in plant. If his intended investment in the impending interval is raised from I_n to $I_n+\Delta I_n$, we may refer to the ratio $\Delta I_n/I_n : \Delta j/j$ as the *investment elasticity of surprise for gain of valuation*, and to the ratio $\Delta I_n/I_n : \Delta g/g$ as the *investment elasticity of surprise for gain of trading revenue*, both of these referring to the effect of an excess of realised, recorded, ex post trading revenue of some named interval over the upper focus hypothesis which had been entertained in respect of that interval. If the trading out-turn of the interval is lower than the lower focus value, we can define a *valuation elasticity of surprise for loss* in a manner corresponding to that for gain. We may remind ourselves that the lower focus value for trading revenue may represent a *positive* trading revenue, but one which is smaller than the minimum required to sustain a non-negative investment gain. Further we can evidently speak of the investment elasticity of surprise for loss of valuation, say $\Delta I_n/I_n : \Delta l/l$, and of the investment elasticity of surprise for loss of trading revenue, say $\Delta I_n/I_n : \Delta h/h$. We have now to consider the relation of some of these concepts to each other and in particular whether we need further concepts deriving the effect of a surprisingly high trading revenue recorded for one period on the plant valuation, from the revision it may compel of both upper and lower focus values of trading revenue for periods still to come (39, pp. 286–9).

It is not intended here to explore fully the wide range of meanings of profit, both *ex ante* and *ex post*, which are exposed through this presentation.* But it is useful to show Shackle's classification and to note some of those meanings. The basic dichotomy is between *ex ante* and *ex post*, expected and recorded quantities but under each symbols have been used to indicate groupings of definitions which form alternative answers (39, pp. 254–5):

Ex Ante	A
Unique hypothesis alone carrying potential surprise less than the absolute maximum, $y < \bar{y}$	k
Many hypotheses carrying $y < \bar{y}$, from which focus values are selected	λ
Excess over an absolute zero gain	I
Excess over the gain ascribed to a rival policy	II
Imputed to a factor of production through marginal productivity	(i)
Residual expected to remain after imputed income shares have beeen allowed for	(ii)
A simple maximand	1
The aim of a maximax strategy	2
The aim of a minimax strategy	3
The aim of a strategy seeking the highest attainable gambler indifference curve	4
Something about whose size no definite hypotheses are examined, the source of it being thought of as pure luck and uncontrollable circumstance	5
The prize of uncertainty-bearing	a
The prize of decision-making	b
The prize of exceptional knowledge or of skill in forecasting	c
The spoils of monopoly	d
Something implicit in the person's expectations existing at a single location of his viewpoint	E
Something arising from a comparison of his expectational vista existing at one viewpoint with that existing at another	G
Ex Post	B
Unique, actual and recorded result	μ
Many hypotheses carrying $y < \bar{y}$	λ
Excess over absolute zero gain	I
Excess of an actual outcome over what might have been achieved by a different policy	II
Imputed to a factor of production through marginal productivity	(i)

* See 23, pp. 69–75 and 39, Ch. XXVIII.

Residual actually remaining after payment of income shares imputed through marginal productivity	(ii)
Something which has emerged and is ascribed to pure luck	5
The reward of having borne uncertainty	a
The reward of having made decisions	b
The reward of having applied exceptional knowledge or skill in forecasting	c
The spoils of monopoly	d
Something arising from the passage of the viewpoint through some time interval	G

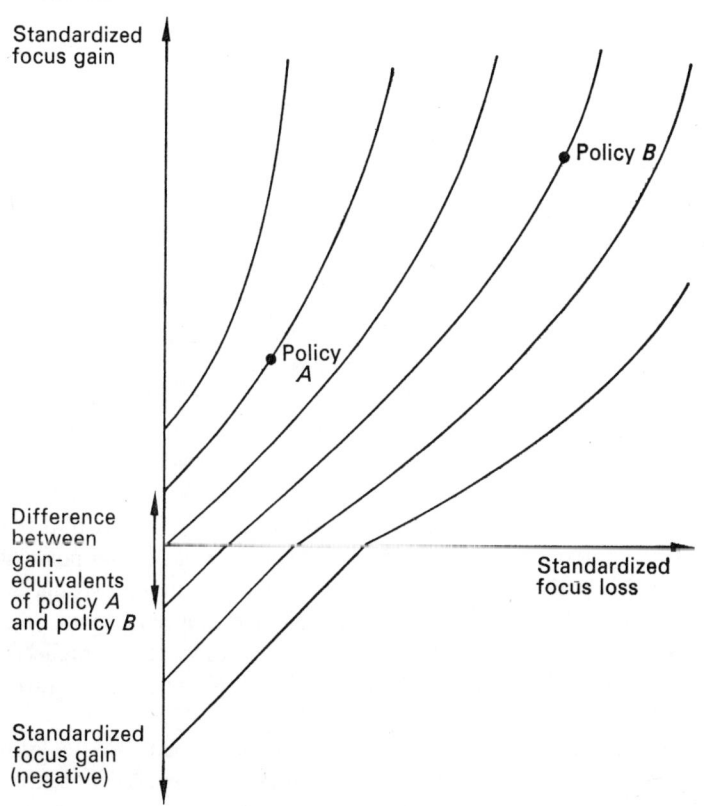

Some of the meanings of profit can be distinguished by means of the gambler indifference map. The absolute profit of a policy could be its standardized focus gain (classified A, λ, I, *, 1, *, E in Shackle's scheme, where * indicates no classification); or such an absolute profit could be the gain equivalent measured on the gain axis

(A, λ, I, *, 4, *, E). The corresponding differential profits when policies are compared would be A, λ, II, *, 1, *, E and A, λ, II, *, 4, *, E respectively. A further important meaning of profit would be the difference between the earlier and later gain equivalents of different policies amongst which the decision-maker still feels free to choose. This difference Shackle calls "dynamic increment of gain equivalent" (39, p. 265) and classifies as A, λ, I, *, 4, a and b, G.

What then are the events that impinge upon valuation and the decision-making process? Shackle notes as factors affecting expectations:

(i) "information ... of a great variety of events which will have occurred in the interval and of new aspects of events which were already past at the earlier location of his viewpoint" (39, p. 264);

(ii) "the interest rate" (39, p. 289);

(iii) "his own trading revenue" (39, p. 289);

(iv) "the news" (39, p. 293);

(v) "elections" (39, p. 215);

(vi) "personal fortuitous experience" (40, p. 153);

(vii) "systematic study of things" (40, p. 153).

In a fundamental way Shackle's scheme of thought is relevant to the modern business system and it makes provision for people to be decision-makers, to learn and be creative. "To forget that the business of living, and within that larger whole, the business of producing and exchanging goods, essentially and inescapably involves and requires the continuous and endless gaining of knowledge, is to divorce our theories from half their subject matter. To say that there is always potential new knowledge to be gained is to say that possessed knowledge is always incomplete, unsure and potentially wrong. Part of the state of adjustment to circumstances as they are known, which constitutes equilibrium, ought therefore to be a moral and intellectual readiness to adjust the knowledge itself according to the out-turn of seeking to apply it. All is experiment" (40, p. 148).

This theoretical framework is a major achievement but the knowledge theme can be developed further with advantage. As one searches out the factors affecting expectations that were mentioned by Shackle they seem to take on a "learning-by-doing" form (cf. 23, p. 74). Elections, the news, interest rates, and events generally are beyond the entrepreneur's control and information about them, to the extent recorded and analysed, probably will be readily available at low cost. But the entrepreneur's "systematic study of things" will absorb resources and may well be very costly. These activities, e.g., market research, R & D, general education, could, within the framework of Shackle's analysis, be treated as separate investment decisions. One would then be obliged to stress externalities. But perhaps it is more meaningful to emphasize the degree of complementarity, the inter-temporal character of these activities and to abandon the old taxonomy of factor inputs and attempt to treat information and knowledge as a factor deserving separate analysis and perhaps giving rise to a separate category in income distribution.

III. INFORMATION AND BUSINESS STRATEGY

Shackle's thesis about the pursuit of knowledge argues eloquently for an economics of information and knowledge. The information and knowledge revolution has far-reaching economic, social, and political consequences. There have been suggestions that land, buildings, and machinery are no longer the most important forms of capital: information and knowledge may now be taking precedence. This is not a new suggestion, for Alfred Marshall argued that "Ideas, whether those of art or science, or those embodied in practical appliances, are the most 'real' of the gifts that each generation receives from its predecessors. The world's material wealth would be replaced quickly if it were destroyed, but the ideas by which it was made retained. If however the ideas were lost, but not the material wealth, then that would dwindle and the world would go back to poverty" (29, p. 780).

But this theme has become more insistent as the producer and consumer has become more dependent upon the communication system. These developments, evidenced in a broad sense by the statistic that a quarter of U.S. gross national product is accounted for for by knowledge production and distribution (27), is clearly at variance with the assumption in traditional economics that rich and sure information is available to decision-makers. An economics of information and knowledge would explore the consequences of relaxing this assumption about information. A general recasting of much of economics may be needed because the other key assumptions of modern economics, rationality and the theory of competition, themselves rest upon implicit assumptions about information.

Before going on to consider the firm's information system and its role in business strategy, it will be helpful to relate the approach suggested here, i.e., the analysis of information activities and their costs, to the concepts of satisficing behaviour and threshold sensitivity. The former, as illustrated in the case of satisfactory or reasonable profit, is sub-optimization with respect to profit (23, pp. 89–91), but it does not imply a preference for a lesser profit or even indifference between greater and lesser profit. The sub-optimization results from a failure of perception but is itself subject to limitation: beyond some level it will stimulate a revision of policy aimed at securing greater profit through cost reduction, price increase, or sales expansion. While the satisfactory or reasonable profit might be regarded as determined primarily by long-run considerations it "would seem to be open to a wide variety of influences and might also be subject to sudden changes. Changing relations with customers, suppliers, labour, and competitors could call for revision; aspiration levels should adjust to past performance; economic policy decisions on such matters as taxes and tariffs could have their impact; the general climate of opinion can change; certainly finance requirements for expansion plans and the satisfaction of existing and potential shareholders will vary. In view of all these considerations, it would be surprising if the satisfactory level displayed stability" (23, p. 91). Now it has been argued that satisficing and optimizing tended "to converge when costs and difficulties of acquiring information about future parameters and outcomes were sufficiently great".* The important point is that such convergence implies that the concept of optimization ignores these "costs and difficulties of acquiring information".

Threshold sensitivity introduces the proposition "that a positive range, however small or large, exists for every chooser such that the difference between any two alternatives confronting him represents so small a stimulus as to be unable to induce consistent response or preference" (8, p. 164). This can lead to a failure to respond to a stimulus and it can also imply intransitivity of preferences. One might be content merely to acknowledge that decision-makers are threshold sensitive, or one might seek to show how information costs determine the threshold. But these two approaches can be viewed as complementary: "If threshold sensitivity can be taken to refer to the inability of individuals to perceive small differences—due to lack of information or sufficient stimulus, so that the expected utilities of

---

* Discussion remark by Haynes reported in 2, p. 7.

alternative actions could remain equal—the two models are different sides of the same coin" (8, p. 168).

It is clear that profit, in the meanings outlined in Part II of this essay, in the satisficing approach, and in the optimization of customary marginal analysis, requires some assumptions about information. Any assumption may be translated into a statement about the nature and functioning of the firm's information system.

The nature of a management information system is by no means a matter of general agreement although a measure of consensus emerges in the following statements:

Co-operation between the several members of a concern is achieved by organization. In setting up an organization, the concern confers and defines, for each member, certain rights to control the activity of others (and of himself) and to receive information, and certain obligations to accept control and transmit information. The way in which a concern confers and defines rights and obligations of this kind constitutes the management system (3, p. 97).

The analytical model of a system demands that we treat the phenomena and the concepts for organising the phenomena as if there existed organisation, interaction, interdependency, and integration of parts and elements. System analysis assumes structure and stability within some arbitrarily sliced and frozen time period (6, p. 17).

An organisation can be defined as an assemblage of materials, machines, technical and scientific facilities, and personnel geared to task accomplishment through a series of interactions and integrated into a total social system (19, p. 308).

A management information system is a system of reports specially designed to provide the necessary intelligence on a timely basis to help management plan, execute and control (22, p. 173).

The firm can be looked on as a system—something with explicit overall objectives, its parts meshing together with functional fitness to achieve the results. The parts, the subsystems, do not, however, contribute their bit to the overall objective of the system with simple machine-like automation (4, p. 4).

Some few of the myriad possibilities have been described and charted in the literature now referred to as management and information science. Here it will suffice to attempt a general classification of the firm's information requirements:

Category 1: Information on current activities covered by present policy, e.g., costs, sales trends, actual and potential competition, organizational conflicts, managerial preferences, government policies, technological change, scientific advances, international affairs.

Category 2: Information on contemplated activities covered by existing policy. This would cover a range of matters similar to those included in Category 1.

Category 3: Information on unidentified developments that may impinge upon either or both existing and contemplated activities. As one industrial research practitioner observed: "Like science-fiction writers, I and my colleagues must be curious about events ten, twenty, and thirty years ahead, and project the effects of living closer together, of medical advances, and of politics. Science is not enough, and sociology of a new kind is needed" (7, p. 578). These activities cannot be regarded as lying wholly outside the scope of present policy but they create a gap in any formal definition of the system that means it must be viewed as an open system.

The provision of information necessary to permit inquiry, communication, and decision and the operation of control in respect of such varied activities could and probably does absorb a great deal of resources, even if neither private nor social accounting is designed to reveal the extent of that allocation. Despite the proliferation of literature in management and information science, little appears to be known about the costs and productivity of information activities. Is sub-optimization in the operation of the firm's information system likely? The technical problems of a balanced contribution to activities that are complementary in either a functional or divisional sense are great. These are accentuated by the intertemporal nature of many activities. No accurate assessment of the revenue attributable to information outlays can be made. And to the extent that the system is an open one, creating its own ends, an objective measure of contribution may be impossible to devise.* And, given the importance of externalities with respect to information, if reorganization of the structure and grouping of decision-making units, e.g., the firms of an industry, is contemplated, an even wider range of possibilities is revealed. Disequilibria, whether they be those of short-

---

* Cf. Georgescu-Roegen: "Social production and its corollary, social organization, require a specific category of services without which they cannot possibly function. This category comprises the services of supervisors, coordinators, decision-makers, legislators, preachers, teachers, newsmen, and so on. What distinguishes these services from those of a bricklayer, a weaver, or a mailman is that they do not possess an objective measure as the latter do" (12, p. 100).

run fluctuations or those incidental to the broad process of economic and social change, must accentuate both the practical decision problems and the difficulties of defining an optimum allocation of resources to the operation of the firm's information system.

If it can be assumed that information activities absorb a significant share of resources and that the allocation of resources to those activities can be non-optimal—subject to the reservations mentioned above about the meaning of optimality—some interesting conclusions arise:

1. The efficiency of the information system will determine the classification of events as counter-expected and unexpected, the *ex ante* profit of those events, and the elasticities of surprise. Where the planning horizons are long changing information flows can impart the truly dynamic character to Shackle's "dynamic increment of gain equivalent". This in turn has implications for those attempts to take account of the lack of information by building flexibility into decision models. As one moves closer from the long-run, perfect knowledge situation towards the present creating more and more flexibility, predictive value declines: the turnpike becomes a misty, mountain road without direction signs.

2. Competitive relationships, and changes in them over time, will depend upon the firm's information systems. For example, if the firms in an oligopoly situation are within "a stability zone" (16, pp. 80–1), the information systems may have been one of the attributes creating and maintaining such a situation. It should not be a radical suggestion to argue that the study of oligopoly behaviour might conceivably benefit from an approach emphasizing information systems, more especially if the oligopoly problem is seen to call for "an essentially non-equilibrium treatment" (37, p. 403). Latterly it has been accepted that whether a firm will find it profitable to reduce price or increase advertising expenditure is an empirical question (44). Perhaps the same might be said about decisions involving, for example, the reactions of rival firms and the development of new technology.*

3. Generally the efficiency of the information system will be a factor to be taken into account in explaining productivity differences, including the diffusion of technological change. To what extent do

---

* For a discussion of some aspects of the theoretical problems in a treatment of information agreements and the policy implications of such agreements see 17 and 30.

economies of scale arise from information activities?* In similar fashion the concept of X-efficiency (cf. 26) might be clarified by focussing attention on the firms' information systems.

IV. CONCLUDING NOTE

Perhaps the simplest way to sum-up the theme of this essay is to recall Harrod's statement: "It has been much debated to what extent equilibrium theorists should assume knowledge on the part of the individual. In some cases the matter is easily settled. Many future developments, e.g., technological changes, are in principle unforeseeable, and in those cases the correct assumption is ignorance. The theory of profit rests essentially on this assumption" (15, p. 153). Technological forecasting may not have achieved sound professional standing but "the pursuit of knowledge" in the evolutionary process of social and economic change calls for decisions "taken in the consciousness that they are part of a developing chain".† The real problem lies in the nature of equilibrium economics: "The dominance of the equilibrium idea, in one or other of its many forms, goes very deep in economics. Is it beneath the dignity of humans to recognise the human predicament of uncertain expectation?" (38, p. 270).

The other matter deserving mention here is the theory of income distribution. As Weintraub rightly suggested (45, pp. 1262-3), the theory of profit should illumine factor shares. Shackle holds that "The orthodox theory of income shares belongs in origin and in its essential nature to a static, timeless economics where the distinction between past and future has no place or meaning" (39, p. 268). Nevertheless, the distribution categories customarily employed derive from "English classical economics, which developed in response to the early stages of the industrial revolution, when a sharp distinction between capital goods and raw labour power made more sense than it does under modern industrial conditions, and when moreover the distinction between wages, profit and rent corresponded to a meaningful division of society into politico-economic

---

* See 32 *passim*. Raymond Vernon has recently presented some interesting evidence on organization as a scale factor in the growth of firms in J. W. Markham and G. F. Papanek (eds), *Industrial Organisation and Economic Development* in Honor of E. S. Mason (New York: Houghton Mifflin, 1970).

† Discussion remark by Hart reported in 2, p. 6.

classes. With the progress of technology, the replacement of brute human strength by mechanical power, and the increasing importance of skill and scientific knowledge on the part of the labour force, the traditional distinction between labour as an original factor and capital as a produced factor has become increasingly unrealistic, while these developments together with the declining importance of rent consequent upon technical progress in agriculture and the alteration of the relationship of property ownership to economic control consequent on the development of corporate enterprise have increasingly deprived the functional distribution of income of sociopolitical content" (18, pp. 221–2). If in the contemporary world information "inputs" are the most important requirement for economic growth (9, 27, 43), the analysis of income shares ought to reflect this state of affairs.

REFERENCES

1. W. J. Baumol, "Entrepreneurship in Economic Theory", *American Economic Review*, 58, 2, May 1968, pp. 64–71.
2. M. J. Bowman (ed.) *Expectations, Uncertainty, and Business Behavior*, New York: Social Science Research Council, 1958.
3. Tom Burns and G. M. Stalker, *The Management of Innovation*, 2nd ed. London: Social Science Paperbacks, 1966.
4. N. W. Chamberlain, *Enterprise and Environment: The Firm in Time and Place*, New York: McGraw-Hill, 1968.
5. P. W. Cherington, "The Interaction of Government and Contractor Organisations in Weapons Acquisition", in R. A. Tybout (ed.), *Economics of Research and Development*, Ohio State University Press, 1965.
6. Robert Chin, "The Utility of System Models and Developmental Models for Practitioners", in P. P. Schoderbek (ed.), *Management Systems*, New York: Wiley, 1967, pp. 16–26.
7. D. Davies, "A Scarce Resource called Curiosity", *The Listener*, LXXVII, no. 1988, May 4, 1967, pp. 577–9 reprinted in D. M. Lamberton (ed.), *Economics of Information and Knowledge*, Penguin Modern Economics, 1971, pp. 315–322.
8. N. E. Devletoglou, "Thresholds and Transactions Costs",

Quarterly Journal of Economics, LXXXV, February 1971, pp. 163–70.

9. E. F. Denison assisted by Jean-Pierre Poullier, *Why Growth Rates Differ: Postwar Experience in Nine Western Countries*, Washington, D.C.: The Brookings Institution, 1967.

10. J. S. Dupré, "Comment on Part V Papers", in R. A. Tybout (ed.), *Economics of Research and Development*, Ohio State University Press, 1965.

11. Dennis Gabor, *Inventing the Future*, Penguin Books, 1963.

12. Nicholas Georgescu-Roegen, *Analytical Economics: Issues and Problems*, Cambridge, Mass.: Harvard University Press, 1966.

13. Barry Gordon, "Criticism of Ricardian Views on Value and Distribution in the British Periodicals, 1820–1850", *History of Political Economy*, 1, Fall 1969, pp. 370–87.

14. F. H. Hahn, "Some Adjustment Problems", *Econometrica*, 38, January 1970, pp. 1–17.

15. R. F. Harrod, *Economic Essays*, London: Macmillan, 1952.

16. R. B. Heflebower, "Stability in Oligopoly", *Manchester School*, XXIX, January 1961, pp. 79–93.

17. John Jewkes, "The Industrial Policy Group—An Experiment in Communication", *National Westminster Bank Quarterly Review*, November 1970, pp. 19–28.

18. H. G. Johnson, "Towards a Generalized Capital Accumulation Approach to Economic Development", in *The Residual Factor and Economic Growth*, Paris: O.E.C.D., 1964, pp. 219–25 reprinted in M. Blaug (ed.), *Economics of Education 1*, Penguin Modern Economics, 1968, pp. 33–44.

19. F. E. Kast and J. E. Rosenzweig (eds.), *Science, Technology, and Management*, New York: McGraw-Hill, 1963.

20. B. S. Keirstead, "Profit", *International Encyclopedia of Social Sciences*.

21. F. H. Knight, *Risk, Uncertainty and Profit*, New York: Houghton Mifflin, 1921.

22. J. W. Konvalinka and H. G. Trentin, "Management Information Systems", in P. P. Schoderbek (ed.), *Management Systems*, New York: Wiley, 1967, pp. 170–82.

23. D. M. Lamberton, *The Theory of Profit*, Oxford: Blackwell, 1965.
24. D. M. Lamberton, "Design Aids: Documentation", Proceedings of Le Conseil International du Bâtiment pour la recherche, l'étude et le documentation 5th World Congress, Versailles, 1971.
25. D. M. Lamberton (ed.), *Economics of Information and Knowledge*, Penguin Modern Economics, 1971.
26. H. M. Leibenstein, "Allocative Efficiency vs. X-Efficiency", *American Economic Review*, 56, June 1966, pp. 329–415.
27. Fritz Machlup, *The Production and Distribution of Knowledge*, Princeton, N.J.: Princeton University Press, 1962.
28. Fritz Machlup, "Theories of the Firm: Marginalist, Behavioral, Managerial", *American Economic Review*, 57, March 1967, pp. 1–33.
29. Alfred Marshall, *Principles of Economics*, 8th ed., London: Macmillan, 1925.
30. D. P. O'Brien and D. Swann, *Information Agreements, Competition and Efficiency*, London: Macmillan, 1968.
31. J. Pen, *Harmony and Conflict in Modern Society*, trans. by T. S. Preston, London: McGraw-Hill, 1966.
32. E. T. Penrose, *The Theory of Growth of the Firm*, Oxford: Blackwell, 1959.
33. E. T. Penrose, "Review of Lamberton, *The Theory of Profit*", *Economic Journal*, LXXVI, September 1966, pp. 623–5.
34. P. A. Samuelson, *Economics*, 8th ed., New York: McGraw-Hill, 1970.
35. P. P. Schoderbek (ed.) *Management Systems*, New York: Wiley, 1967.
36. G. L. S. Shackle, "Review of Egerton, *Investment Decisions under Uncertainty*", *Economic Journal*, LXXIV, March 1964, pp. 172–4.
37. G. L. S. Shackle, "Review of D. C. Hague (ed.), *Price Formation in Various Economies*", *Economic Journal*, LXXVIII, June 1968, pp. 401–3.
38. G. L. S. Shackle, *The Years of High Theory: Invention and Tradition in Economic Thought 1926–1939*, Cambridge at the University Press, 1967.

39. G. L. S. Shackle, *Decision, Order and Time in Human Affairs*, 2nd ed., Cambridge at the University Press, 1969.
40. G. L. S. Shackle, *Expectation, Enterprise and Profit*, London: Allen & Unwin, 1970.
41. Martin Shubik, "A Curmudgeon's Guide to Microeconomics", *Journal of Economic Literaure*, VIII, June 1970, pp. 405–34.
42. H. A. Simon, "The role of Expectations in an Adaptive or Behavioristic Model", in M. J. Bowman (ed.), *Expectations, Uncertainty, and Business Behavior*, New York: Social Science Research Council, 1958.
43. H. A. Simon, "Decision Making as an Economic Resource", in L. H. Seltzer (ed.), *New Horizons of Economic Progress*, Detroit: Wayne State University Press, 1964, pp. 85–94.
44. G. J. Stigler, "Price and Non-Price Competition", *Journal of Political Economy*, LXXII, February 1968, pp. 149–54, reprinted in Stigler, *The Organisation of Industry*, Homewood, Illinois: Irwin, 1968.
45. Sidney Weintruab, "Review of Lamberton, *The Theory of Profit*", *American Economic Review*, 56, December 1966, pp. 1261–3.
46. J. F. Weston, "The Profit Concept and Theory: A Restatement", *Journal of Political Economy*, LXII, April 1954, pp. 152–70.
47. O. E. Williamson, *Corporate Control and Business Behavior: An Inquiry into the Effects of Organization Form on Enterprise Behavior*, Englewood Cliffs, N.J.: Prentice-Hall, 1970.

Potential Surprise in the Context of Inquiry

ISAAC LEVI

Columbia University

1. INTRODUCTION

G. L. S. Shackle introduced his measure of potential surprise as part of an account of decision-making applicable in particular to investment decisions. The role of potential surprise as a measure of uncertainty and the theory of decision-making in which it is incorporated remain subject to considerable controversy. I have argued elsewhere* that even for those who, like myself, are not prepared to endorse Shackle's account of decision-making, a closer examination of Shackle's notion of potential surprise remains worthwhile. In this paper, I intend to restate the reinterpretation of Shackle's ideas that I have already proposed and to elaborate further on the significance of potential surprise so reconstructed.

2. ON CORRECTION

In "On the Sources of Knowledge and Ignorance", Karl Popper observes that the question about the sources of our knowledge

... has always been asked in the spirit of: "What are the best sources of our knowledge—the most reliable ones, those which will not lead us into error, and those to which we can and must turn, in case of doubt, as the last court of appeal?" I propose to assume, instead, that no such ideal sources exist... and that *all* 'sources' are liable to lead us into error at

* I. Levi, *Gambling with Truth*, New York; Knopf (1967), pp. 135–138 and "On Potential Surprise", *Ratio* VIII (1966), pp. 107–129.

times. And I propose to replace, therefore, the question of the sources of our knowledge by the entirely different question: '*How can we hope to detect and eliminate error?*' (p. 25).*

Thus, Popper turns his back on the classical quest for an incorrigibly and infallibly secured foundation for human knowledge and, following a path already trod by C. S. Peirce and John Dewey, shifts the focus of epistemological concern from the "foundations" of human knowledge to an examination of procedures whereby human knowledge may be corrected. Popper's own account of the "growth" of knowledge is itself open to criticism and it is perfectly possible to follow him in abandoning classical epistemological concerns without endorsing the details of his own proposals. The reconstruction of Shackle's view which I consider here is embedded in an alternative approach. In what follows, I shall first outline some aspects of such an alternative address to the problem of the growth of human knowledge in order to clarify both the interpretation and the importance of Shackle's notion of potential surprise.

Whether one is engaged in practical deliberation aimed at the resolution of some moral, political, economic or other practical problem or one is engaged in scientific inquiry aimed at criticizing or expanding our knowledge, appeal is made to assumptions in designing experiments and justifying decisions and conclusions reached. This need to appeal to premises has traditionally led epistemologists to seek authoritative first premises functioning as infallibly secure basis for our conclusions. In rejecting this approach, Popper concludes that all of our knowledge is tentative and open to criticism. In one important respect Popper's conclusion is misleading; for the assumptions of a given inquiry or practical deliberation are, at least in the context of that inquiry or deliberation, quite certain in the sense that such assumptions serve to distinguish relevant possibilities from impossibilities. To regard H as certain is to discount the risk of error in acting on the truth of H. In this sense, H bears a fair betting quotient probability of 1. It is, in Dewey's words, a "resource for inquiry".

Even Popper acknowledges that hypotheses are tested relative to a background which includes not only observation reports but general laws, statistical claims and theories. Such background

* K. R. Popper, *Conjectures and Refutations*, New York: Basic Books (1962), p. 25.

assumptions function in the context of tests and inquiry as certainties in the sense just indicated. As long as they continue to function as settled assumptions in this way, they are to be distinguished from hypotheses and from "tentative" assumptions which function as assumptions only hypothetically. They are qua settled assumptions immune to testing and criticism; for should they stand in need of criticism they could no longer function as settled resources for inquiry, i.e., if we are to avoid begging questions.

To distinguish between settled assumptions which are certain and hypotheses and tentatively held assumptions which merit criticism is not to maintain that settled assumptions are infallibly secured and are forever immune to criticism. They are immune from criticism only within the contexts of inquiries in which they function as settled assumptions. They remain, however, potentially, if not actually, in need of criticism. Moreover, the very fact that they lack infallible security suggests the desirability of fostering an intellectual climate where efforts at trouble making designed to unsettle settled assumptions are protected from suppression.

Trouble making, however, is no easy matter. One cannot undermine the claims of quantum theory merely by registering dissent. One's dissent counts as grounds for removing these claims from the status of settled assumptions and regarding them as hypotheses in need of testing only if serious difficulties are shown to obtain in the continued use of these claims as settled assumptions. Thus, one can agree with Popper that all claims, including settled assumptions, merit efforts at trouble making while denying that settled assumptions are in need of testing—at least as long as efforts at trouble making fail.

On the view taken here, one of the central challenges to epistemology is to provide some sort of account of the conditions of successful trouble making which unsettles settled assumptions and renders them open, in Peirce's words, to "real and living doubt". I do not intend here to consider the complications involved in providing an account which escapes the psychologistic overtones of Peirce's formula. For our purposes, it suffices to note that successful trouble making involves removing erstwhile settled assumptions from the "evidence" and converting them into hypotheses eligible for testing. Such removal entails a contraction of the set of settled assumptions and a consequent weakening of the evidence which can serve as resources for inquiry and deliberation.

Some authors seem to hold that a necessary condition for successful trouble making for a hypothesis H is the availability of some alternative. The availability of rival alternatives is undoubtedly relevant in many contexts. Whether such availability is necessary, however, is a matter for controversy into which we need not enter here. We should keep in mind only that should a rival G to H be available, this does not imply that G replaces H as a settled assumption. At best, it means that H loses its status as a settled assumption and that both H and G are to be regarded as hypotheses eligible for admission into evidence subsequent to further inquiry—inquiry which may result in the devising of still further rival hypotheses before a decision is made how to replace the loss of information resulting from the removal of H from the stock of settled assumptions.

The fact that trouble making results in the loss of information from the corpus of settled assumptions indicates that successful trouble making breeds a demand for new information to replace the old. It occasions inquiry to provide answers to unanswered questions.

Such inquiry aiming at the expansion of our knowledge stems not only from loss of information due to successful trouble making. We seek to reduce our ignorance even in the absence of such a loss. Indeed, intellectual curiosity and inquiries occasioned by it often constitute the most effective means for detecting errors in old settled assumptions.

Thus, an adequate account of the growth of knowledge should include not only a treatment of the contraction of settled assumptions resulting from successful trouble making but a treatment of the expansion of settled assumptions stemming from efforts to answer questions raised in specific inquiries. I shall no more attempt a full account of expansion of our knowledge than of contraction. However, some tentative outline of the various stages of inquiry aiming to answer questions will prove useful in locating the relevance of Shackle's measure of potential surprise to a systematic account of the manner in which our knowledge is revised and corrected.

3. EVIDENCE AND PROBABILITY

Notice has already been taken of the fact that taking h as a settled assumption or as evidence involves a commitment to discounting any risk or error in acting on the truth of h. h is "certain" in the sense that it bears probability 1. Moreover, ruling out as impossible the truth of $-h$, involves a commitment to counting any logical consequence of h or of h together with other settled assumptions as also settled and certain.

Thus, the set of assumptions which an investigator is committed to regarding as settled at a given time is deductively closed. In imposing this commitment, we are not condemning a person to irrationality if he should not consciously count as settled all the consequences of explicitly settled assumptions. To do so would be to impose an excessively high standard of rationality; for he may not be able to decide whether a claim g is deductively implied by his evidential assumptions or, even if he has this ability, he may not have consciously exercised it. All we can require is that the agent count g as settled should he recognize it to be a deductive consequence of his settled assumptions.

In a similar spirit, the settled assumptions endorsed by an agent ought to be consistent in the sense that should the agent detect an inconsistency in such assumptions he should take steps to eliminate the inconsistency by deleting items from his assumptions so as to remove the trouble.

Consistency is a desideratum because among the functions of a corpus of settled assumptions is the specification of a theory of truth both for settled assumptions and for hypotheses. Assuming (as we shall do) that settled assumptions incorporate ordinary laws of logic and a Tarski-like theory of truth both for settled assumptions and hypotheses, the presence of a contradiction implies that at least one settled assumption is false and it does so as a settled assumption. Given that we wish to restrict settled assumptions to true statements, consistency is clearly desirable.

Not only do agents lack the ability to identify explicitly the set of deductive consequences of the evidential assumptions they explicitly identify, they also lack the ability to consider explicitly a set of assumptions such that the deductive consequences of these assumptions constitute the totality of the settled assumptions to which the agents are committed. Thus, should we represent the settled assumptions of a given agent as a suitably characterized deductively closed set of sentences E, we need not be implying that this set includes all his settled assumptions; for there may be some assumptions tacitly held which are not members of E. Hence, in characterizing an agent's evidential assumptions by means of a set E, a rider should be attached to our characterization providing for its modification due to subsequent explicit identification of erstwhile tacitly held assumptions.

With this caveat, we may regard the set of evidential or settled assumptions endorsed by an agent at a given time as a deductively closed and consistent (pending correction) set of assumptions E. The settled assumptions in E will typically include truths of logic, principles of mathematics, scientific theories, universal laws and reports of observations. In addition, E will contain statistical assertions and other claims which support constraints on fair betting quotient probabilities which may be assigned to hypotheses.

Writers who have interpreted probability assignments to sentences (or propositions) as specifications of fair betting quotients have tended to agree that the injunction to avoid dutch book provides a weighty argument in favor of requiring that fair betting quotient probabilities conform to the conditions of the calculus of probabilities. Many writers despair, however, of imposing further "objective" constraints upon such determinations.

Yet, there are many situations in which such objective constraints do seem appropriate. For example, if one knows that a ball is to be drawn from an urn thoroughly mixed before drawing which contains 50 black balls and 50 white, one should assign a fair betting quotient of .5 to the hypothesis that the ball drawn will be black.

Sometimes, of course, the constraints are not so sharp. Thus, if one knew not that the urn contained exactly 50 black balls out of 100 but that it contained anywhere from 45 to 55 black balls, one would be free to assign a fair betting quotient bearing any real value between .45 and .55.

In the first case, we may view the corpus of settled assumptions E as including an "objective" probability judgment assigning the hypothesis that the ball drawn will be black an objective probability of .5. In the second case, E includes a probability judgment assigning an interval valued probability of (.45, .55).

In the two examples just cited, the evidential assumptions are more or less adequately captured by statements about the urn, its contents and the manner in which draws from the urn are to be made. In other situations such as tosses with coins or spinnings of roulette wheels, the evidential assumptions are quite different. I wish to suggest that even in cases where no appeal to random devices can be made, we may still be in a position to make objective probability judgments assigning interval valued probabilities to hypotheses. Thus, interval valued probabilities of this kind may be assigned not only to predictions about the outcomes of trials on chance devices but to theories, laws, statistical hypotheses, etc. For example, in the case where the urn may contain anywhere from 45 to 55 black balls out of 100, one might assign to each hypothesis of the form "The urn contains i black balls out of 100" an interval of probability equal to (.09, .11) where i bears all integral values from 45 to 55. Such a system of interval assignments are to be considered as settled assumptions which are, at least in principle, as open to correction and revision as any other factual assumptions.

Notice that objective interval-valued probability judgments acquire the features of mathematical truth only in cases where the interval assigned to a hypothesis is (0, 1).

The view of objective probability all too briefly sketched here agrees with frequentist interpretation in regarding probability judgments as factual claims, it agrees with both frequentist and logical interpretations in regarding probability judgments as objectively grounded and writers as varied in outlook as Keynes, Koopman, and Kyburg in considering such objective judgments as interval valued.* Finally, it concedes to personalists that fair betting quotient cannot in general be uniquely constrained by evidential or settled assumptions.

Thus, we shall regard the set of evidential assumptions E as including interval valued probability (including conditional probability) judgments assigning values to sentences or propositions—which are hypotheses (and which therefore are not in E) as well as to evidential assumptions (which must receive definite probabilities of 1).

4. ABDUCTION

Given a system E of settled assumptions including probability judgments, investigators often engage in inquiries aiming at enlarging

---

* The upper and lower bounds of my interval valued probabilities may be regarded as having the properties of I. J. Good's upper and lower probabilities. (I. J. Good, "Subjective Probability as the Measure of a Non-measurable Set", *Logic, Methodology and Philosophy of Science* ed. by E. Nagel, P. Suppes and A. Tarski, Stanford: Stanford U. Press (1962), pp. 319–329). However, my interpretation of the formal machinery differs from any of those listed by Good on pp. 319–320.

or strengthening E by adding new information. Such inquiries do not seek any information that comes along. They are directed by the questions which are regarded as meriting serious investigations. These questions control what are to count as potential answers. Thus, predictions do not count as potential answers to questions which request explanations and questions about the molecular structure of DNA do not permit hypotheses about the influence of a sales tax on consumption of goods and services as potential answers.

The identification of potential answers is, as has been pointed out ad nauseam, a creative affair for which no algorithm is available. Nonetheless, once a hypothesis has been proposed as a potential answer to a question, it becomes arguable whether it is indeed a potential answer. Thus, one might seek to devise a "logic" of abduction which formulates general conditions which hypotheses must meet to be potential answers to questions in large categories of cases. Peirce's pragmatic criterion was intended to be a principle of abduction distinguishing potential answers from other hypotheses. Popper's demarcation principle may be construed in a similar vein.

Our chief concerns here do not require that we devote much attention to the logic of abduction. Some method is needed, however, for representing a set of potential answers devised at the abductive stage for the purpose of answering a given question Q relative to settled assumptions E.

Strictly speaking, a potential answer is not simply a case of (tentatively) adding a single sentence or proposition to E. Rather it is a commitment to add that sentence or proposition to E together with all deductive consequences of such an addition. If this is well understood, however, there is no harm in representing a potential answer by a sentence or proposition H—namely, an H such that the potential answer is the set of deductive consequences of H together with E. We shall say that H is a "strongest" sentence (or proposition) added to E.

Thus, if H is a strongest sentence added to E, HvG is also to be added to E. On the other hand, if HvG is a strongest sentence added to E, H is not to be added to E. Taking HvG as strongest is tantamount to suspending judgment between H and G.

Note that if E logically implies S, regarding S as a strongest sentence added to E is, in effect, to refuse to make any addition at all. Such an "answer" is tantamount to total suspension of judgment. At the other extreme, if E logically implies $-C$, adding C to E is to contradict oneself and to commit oneself to adding all sentences to E.

Sometimes all the essentially distinct potential answers to a given question are finite in number. (Two potential answers represented by H and G are essentially the same if adding H to E and adding G to E yield the same set of sentences.) In such cases, the potential answers can be represented by sentences belonging to a finite set M generated from another finite set U as follows:

I: U is a finite set $H_1, \ldots, H_n$ of sentences such that E implies that at least and at most one H_i is true and such that E is consistent with each H_i.

U shall be called an "ultimate partition".

II: Let the members of U be arranged in some suitable alphabetical order.

The sentence S which is a disjunction in which each member of U appears once and only once and in alphabetical order is a member of M.

The sentences which are disjunctions of i ($1 \leqslant i < n$) members of U occurring once and only once and in alphabetical order are members of M.

The sentence C which is a conjunction in which each member of U appears once and only once and in alphabetical order is a member of M.

Each potential answer to a given question may be regarded as a case of taking a member G of a suitable set M as being a strongest sentence added to E. Alternatively, each potential answer may be regarded as a case of rejecting a subset of the members of U and adding the disjunction of the surviving members of U as a strongest sentence added to E.

Example 1: Let an investigator be concerned to devise theory in order to systemize a given subject matter. At the abductive stage he has formulated two theoretical hypotheses T_1 and T_2 which are mutually incompatible given his "background" E and which are both consistent with E. Since these two theories do not exhaust the possibilities, U will consist of T_1, T_2 and a "residual hypothesis" R which asserts that both T_1 and T_2 are false. M will consist of taking one of the following 8 sentences as the strongest sentence to be added to E: $S = T_1 v T_2 v R$, $C = T_1 \& T_2 \& R$, $T_1 v T_2$, $T_1 v R$, $T_2 v R$, T_1, T_2, R.

Example 2: Suppose the aim is to predict the frequency of heads of n tosses of a coin where E implies that on each toss the coin will land either heads or tails. U consists of the $n+1$ possible predictions of the exact value of r and M includes 2^{n+1} sentences.

Example 3: Suppose the aim is to estimate the value of the p determining the binomial distribution of tosses of the coin in example 2. More specifically, the aim is to determine whether the true value of p falls in one of the following $\frac{e}{2}+1$ intervals: $(0, 1/e)$, $(e, 3/e), \ldots, ((2i-1)/e, (2i+1)/e), \ldots, ((e-1)/e, 1)$ where e is even and i ranges from 1 to $(e-2)/2$. Here U has $e/2+1$ members. $e/2-1$ members of U are interval estimates where the interval is of length $2/e$ and 2 members of U (the extreme estimates) are in intervals of length $\frac{1}{e}$.

In many situations, finite U's and M's seem adequate to represent potential answers. However, the somewhat strained description of example 3 suggests the desirability of being able to consider cases where the set of potential answers may be noncountably infinite as well. Thus, in estimating the value of p, it seems plausible to allow as a potential answer any interval estimate (including "degenerate" point estimates) of p, disjunctions (including "countable" disjunctions) of such estimates and denials of these. I shall not attempt to provide a general account of potential answers to accommodate all cases where infinite lists of potential answers might be required. However, we may come to terms with illustrations of the sort just mentioned as follows:

If U consists of the set of all point estimates of a parameter k of the form "$k = x$" where x may take any real value on some segment X of the real line, the set M consists of all sentences of the form "k is a member of A" where A is a Borel set in X.

Example 4: If the aim is to estimate the value of p determining the binomial distribution of the coin in example 2, without the restrictions imposed in example 3, M contains all statements of the form "the value of p is a member of A" where A is a Borel set of points on the unit real line. The U which generates M is the range of values of p.

5. EVIDENCE COLLECTION AND INDUCTION

Given a list of potential answers represented by a set M generated by an ultimate partition U and a background of settled assumptions E, an investigator may wish to evaluate the potential answers devised at the abduction stage in the light of E and the demands of his question Q. Such evaluation involves determining which potential answer he would add to E were he to stop inquiry at that point. The conclusion thereby reached is by no means decisive; for the investigator may have good reason not to terminate inquiry. Nonetheless, as we shall see, for purposes of analysis, it is often helpful to determine hypothetically what conclusion one would reach relative to settled assumptions E, question Q and potential answers M. Determination of such "hypothetical" or "tentative" conclusions occurs at what I shall call the "inductive" stage of inquiry. The reason for calling this stage "inductive" is that the "conclusion" "accepted" typically involves claims which are not logically implied by the evidence.

In addition to the abductive and inductive stages of inquiry, mention should be made of a data collecting stage where experiments are designed and conducted or observations made. Given a set of background assumptions E and question Q, one may view the conduct of inquiry, for purposes of analysis, as follows:

(1) At an abductive stage a list of potential answers is devised.

(2) New data are collected at a data collecting stage.

(3) Given the new data and the background E, an induction is performed to determine which potential answer to "accept" in the tentative or hypothetical vein mentioned before.

(4) An appraisal of the conclusion reached at stage (4) together with an examination of the tentative conclusions of other inquiries in progress and a judgment as to the costs of further investigation is then used as the basis for deciding whether to return to stage (1) or stage (2), to regard the background E as in trouble and to undertake contraction of E before repeating the process or, finally, to regard the conclusion reached at stage (3) as so satisfactory as to warrant cutting off inquiry and adding that conclusion to the settled assumptions.

The preceding list of "stages" of inquiry aiming at the expansion of a set of settled assumptions is no more than a first approximation to an analytical table of contents for a program aimed at providing a systematic account of expansionist inquiry. It is no substitute for such an account. Its main value is that it provides a means for locating the relevance of special questions and topics to a general discussion of evidence expansion.

In particular, the list of stages can be used to indicate the role of Shackle's measure of potential surprise in the context of inquiry. Such a measure can be used to represent the conclusions reached in an inductive stage of inquiry in a manner which focuses on considerations which are relevant to determining whether inquiry ought to continue or to be terminated. Substantiation of this claim requires taking a somewhat closer look at the inductive stage of inquiry and at criteria for determining what are to count as legitimate conclusions reachable via induction at that stage.

6. TRUTH AND INFORMATION

As has been noted previously, a potential answer may be represented in one of two ways: (a) as taking some member of M, adding it to E and taking the deductive consequences as the new system of settled assumptions. (b) as rejecting some subset of U and taking the logical consequences of E and these rejections as the new set of settled assumptions.

Since a potential answer is, strictly speaking, a commitment to regarding a set of claims as settled assumptions, such an answer counts as erroneous or false if and only if at least one of the sentences in the set is false. The potential answer is correct if no sentence in the set is false. Given the status of the members of E and their deductive consequences as settled assumptions, they automatically count as true. Hence, if G is a member of M, a necessary and sufficient condition for the potential answer corresponding to M being correct (erroneous) is that G be true (false).

In seeking to expand the set E by answering a given question, it seems reasonable to suppose that correct answers are to be preferred to erroneous ones. Such preference seems part of the commitment entailed by the view that in scientific inquiry men seek truth.

Note, however, that given the truth of the members of E, only one potential answer is secure against error—namely, complete suspension of judgment as represented by the sentence S. If truth alone were the desideratum, no expansion of evidence would ever be justified. But clearly we do wish to expand our evidence, i.e., to make E more informative.

Thus, even though we favor correct answers over erroneous ones, we also favor more informative answers over less informative ones. As Popper has put it, we seek not only truth but interesting truth.

In order to indicate more precisely how the two desiderata of truth and information function in determining what is the best of the potential answers to a given question, I have suggested elsewhere that "epistemic" utility functions be constructed representing the goal of seeking the truth without regard for information and the goal of seeking information without regard for truth and that the goal of seeking true and informative answers be represented by a utility function which is a linear function of these two separate utility functions.

My reasons for using linear functions have been elaborated elsewhere and shall not be repeated here.* Given, therefore, a utility function $T(H, x)$ which represents the truth utility of adding H to E and taking the deductive consequences when H bears the truth value x (where x may be t or f for true or false), and a utility function $C(H, x)$ representing the informational value of accepting H when H has the truth value x, the utility function $V(H, x) = aT(H, x) + (1-a)C(H, x)$ represents the value of adding H to E when seeking true information ($a<1$).

How are the T and C-functions to be constructed? Without repeating arguments offered elsewhere,† I suggest the following definitions:

Def. 1: $T(H,t) = 1$
$T(H,f) = 0$
for all H in M.

Def. 2: Let $m(H, E)$ be a suitable probability measure defined for all H in M.
$C(H, t) = C(H, f) = 1 - m(H, E)$

Given these definitions, we have the following definition for $V(H, x)$.

Def. 3: $V(H,t) = a + (1-a)(1-m(H,E))$
$V(H,f) = \quad (1-a)(1-m(H,E))$

Definition 2 requires that informational utility increase with a

---

* I. Levi, *Gambling with Truth*, Ch. III and "Information and Inference" *Synthese* 17 (1969), pp. 373–381.

† I. Levi, *Gambling with Truth*, Ch. III and "Information and Inference", pp. 381–384.

decrease in probability. This condition conforms well with views of Popper and others who have stressed information measures as relevant to the appraisal of scientific hypotheses. Unlike Popper and others, however, the probability function in terms of which utility of information is determined is not to be identified with any other type of probability. It is not a "logical" probability in either Popper's or Carnap's sense. It is not an objective probability in any sense in which such probabilities constrain fair betting quotient assignments. Nor is it a fair betting quotient probability.

Thus, in any specific context where potential answers are being appraised at an inductive stage, two types of probability are relevant: (a) objective probabilities $P(H, E)$ (which may be interval valued) of the sort discussed earlier and (b) informational probabilities $m(H, E)$ which determine informational utilities as represented by the C-function. Although in some circumstances $m(H, E)$ may equal $P(H, E)$, in general this will not be the case.

Because the m-function is used to represent the informational utility of potential answers to a given question, the definition of the m-function depends critically upon the demands of the specific question. Aside from the fact that the m-function is a probability measure defined on a boolean or σ-algebra of propositions M, no strong constraints may be imposed upon it applicable to all questions and all inquiries. The best one may hope to do for the purposes of systematic study is to classify various types of problems in terms of the m-functions appropriate to potential answers to such problems. Consideration of the four examples will illustrate the point.

Example 1: In this case, the demand of the problem is to add to E a theory which will systematize some subject matter. Granting that both T_1 and T_2 are potentially serviceable for this purpose, the residual hypothesis R remains deficient in this respect; for R is, after all, not a theory. Hence, the informational utility assigned R ought to be much lower than that assigned the other members of U. Consequently, T_1 and T_2 ought to bear much lower m-values than R.

Examples 2: The aim is here to predict which of the $n+1$ possible frequencies of heads in n trials will occur. Each such prediction is as satisfactory in meeting the demands of the question as any other and so each element of U ought to be counted as informative as any other. Hence, each element of U may plausibly be accorded an m-value of $1/(n+1)$.

Example 4: In this case, the aim is to determine which value of the parameter p is the true value. This suggests that the informational value of one point estimate ought to be the same as any other. The only way, however, this condition might be satisfied is by assigning each point estimate informational probability 0.

This condition is not, however, fully satisfactory; for it is compatible with regarding different interval estimates where the intervals are of the same length as possessing different informational value. Intuitively, the demand that each point estimate is as valuable from the point of view of information as any other requires that the informational utility of an interval estimate be inversely proportional to the length of the interval. Thus, we define a continuous informational probability density $d(p, E)$ which is uniform when $d(p, E) = 1$ for all values of p. The m-value of the interval estimate that p falls in the interval between a and b becomes $\int_a^b d(p, E)\,dp = b - a$. By this method, it becomes possible to assign an m-value to every member of M.

Example 3: This case is, perhaps, more equivocal than the others in that it is not clear whether all elements of U are to be regarded as equally informative or whether the two extreme interval estimates $(0, 1/e)$ and $(1-1/e, 1)$ are to be regarded as twice as informative as the other interval estimates of U owing to the fact that the lengths of the intervals involved are half those of the intervals involved in the other estimates.

7. DEGREE OF CAUTION

The weight a occurring in the definition of the V-function represents the relative importance attached to the demand for truth as compared to the demand for information. In order to insure, on the one hand, that both truth and information are taken seriously, a must be positive and less than 1. If, moreover, errors are never to be preferred to correct answers so that $V(H,f)$ is never greater than $V(G,t)$ for H and G in M, a must be greater than or equal to one half.

If we form the ratio $(1-a)/a = q$, the conditions just laid down imply that q must bear a positive value less than or equal to 1. A person who uses a q-value of 1 is maximally bold or minimally cautious in the sense that he is prepared to take a considerable risk of error in order to obtain informative answers. As q goes to 0, more caution and less boldness are operative.

8. AN ACCEPTANCE RULE

Suppose a definite objective probability function could be specified relative to E for all elements of M. In the first three examples where M and U are finite, such a function would accord non-negative probabilities to all members of U in a manner such that these probabilities add up to unity. In example 4, a probability density $f(p, E)$ defined for all values of p on the unit line is appropriate.

Given a suitable probability function, one can now define an expected utility function for all potential answers in M where utility is defined in terms of the V-function.

Def. 4: $EV(H, E) = aP(H, E) + (1-a)C(H, E)$
$= aP(H, E) + (1-a)(1 - M(H, E))$.

Because evaluations of expected utility are unique only up to a linear transformation, the Ev-function will assign a maximum value to H in M if and only if the following function also assigns a maximum value.

Def. 5: $EU(H, E) = P(H, E) - qM(H, E)$.

It can also be proven that if a given set of elements of M bear maximum EU-values, their disjunction also does. Hence, we can propose breaking ties for optimality by recommending acceptance of the weakest conclusion bearing maximum EU-value.

In the case where U (and, hence, M) is finite, the recommendation to accept such an optimal conclusion (in the tentative sense indicated earlier), is tantamount to the following rejection rule:

A: Reject all elements of h_i of U such that $P(h_i, E) < q(h_i, E)$ and take the deductive consequences of these rejections and E.

Example 2: Suppose that the true value of p is known so that the objective probability distribution over the $n+1$ frequencies is for each frequency r equal to

$$\binom{n}{r} p^r (1-p)^{n-r}.$$

For a given value of the index of caution q, rule A recommends rejecting an element e_r of U asserting that r of the n trials show heads if and only if

$$\binom{n}{r} p^r (1-p)^{n-r} \frac{q}{n+1}.$$

Potential Surprise in the Context of Inquiry 229

When n is very large, this rule recommends predicting that the relative frequency r/n falls within a small interval around the true value of p. This is, of course, what presystematic intuition requires.

Example 3: Suppose that relative to background information E and prior to sampling, the unknown value of the parameter p bears an objective probability density $f(p, E) = 1$. After observing n trials and noting that r times out of n the coin lands heads (e_r), the posterior density of p, $f(p, E)$ is the Beta density

$$\frac{(n+1)!}{r!(n-r)!} p^r(1-p)^{n-r} \, dp.$$

The objective probability that p falls in in the interval (a, b) where a and b may take on the values specified for this example will equal, therefore,

$$\frac{(n+1)!}{r!(n-r)!} \int_a^b p^r(1-p)^{n-r} \, dp.$$

The informational probability equals $b - a$. Hence rule A recommends rejecting an element of U if and only if

$$\frac{(n+1)!}{r!(n-r)!} \int_a^b p^r(1-p)^{n-r} \, dp < q(b-a).$$

When n is very large, the conclusion recommended will be the element of U which contains the value of p equal to the observed value of r/n.

As it stands, rule A is applicable in cases where U and M are finite. In cases like example 4, the injunction to pick the weakest optimal potential answer remains in force; but rule A clearly cannot be used. The ultimate partition now consists of all point estimates. In typical cases, both the objective and informational probabilities assigned to such estimates will be 0. If rule A were used directly, no element of U would be rejected—even in cases where the objective probability assigned to some interval estimate in M is less than q times the informational probability of the same hypothesis.

In cases like example 4, however, where both objective and informational probabilities are determined by continuous densities it can be shown that the weakest optimal answer where optimality is measured by the EV function yields the following rule:

B: Reject an element of U if and only if the objective density of p,

$f(p)$ is less than the informational density of p, $d(p)$ times the caution index q.*

Applying this procedure to example 4, one obtains the recommendation to reject a point estimate of p if and only if

$$\frac{(n+1)!}{r!(m-r)!} p^r(1-p)^{n-r} < q.$$

Note, however, that a value of p will be rejected if and only if the likelihood of p on the data that r/n trials of landed heads is less than $q/n+1$. That is to say, the value of p is rejected if and only if, on the assumption that p is the true value, the prediction that r out of n trials will show heads would be rejected.

The results obtained in examples 3 and 4 presuppose that the investigator has sharp objective prior probabilities for the values of p. This assumption is normally unrealistic. To handle cases where vague objective probabilities are involved, rule A and B may be modified by permitting rejections of elements of U if and only if these elements of U are elements of U that would be rejected no matter what betting quotient probability permitted by the objective probability judgments was used in applying rules A and B.

Thus, if in example 4, our objective judgment was that for all p between 0 and 1 the prior density $f(p)$ falls in an interval between $1+e$ and $1-d$ (e and d nonnegative), the posterior density would have to be less than

$$\frac{(n+1)!}{r!(n-r)!} p^r(1-p)^{n-r} \cdot (1+e)/(1-d).$$

If this value is less than q, the hypothesis that the true value of p is less than q must be rejected, according to rule B, no matter what permitted betting quotient probability is used.

Note that in this case also we can rely on likelihoods to determine rejection. A value of p will be rejected if and only if

$$\binom{n}{r} p^r(1-p)^{n-r} < \frac{q(1-d)}{(n+1)(1+e)}.$$

---

* Proof of this claim requires minor additions to the rule for breaking ties mentioned earlier.

9. ON FACTORS INDUCING INQUIRY

Rules A and B and the considerations on which they are based are designed to provide criteria for determining conclusions which ought to be reached relative to given settled assumptions E, question Q and potential answers M to Q on the hypothetical and often counterfactual assumption that inquiry is to be terminated and the conclusions reached are to be incorporated into the settled assumptions.

The advantage of making such tentative inferences is that features of the conclusions drawn can be exploited relevantly in deciding whether inquiry ought to be terminated or continued and, if it is to be continued, in what direction it ought to turn.

Clearly one factor which determines whether inquiry ought to continue is the costs of such inquiry. We shall ignore cost considerations here save for one short comment. Should further inquiry be too expensive to undertake, inquiry will perforce terminate; but the conclusion reached tentatively at the inductive stage will not necessarily be added to the settled assumptions. Even though a conclusion stronger than total suspension of judgment may have been tentatively reached, judgment may remain suspended precisely because the tentative conclusion is somehow deficient in a manner which suggests that were further inquiry feasible it ought to be undertaken. In the absence of sufficient evidence, regardless of how difficult sufficient evidence might be to obtain, the appropriate posture is refusal to adopt tentative conclusions as settled.

Thus, in our subsequent discussion, attention will be restricted to features of tentative conclusions reached at the inductive stage which recommend the continuation of inquiry ignoring the problem of costs.

One such factor is conflict between the conclusions reached in the context of inquiry into one question with conclusions reached in the context of other inquiries. The demands of truth require that the system of settled assumptions be consistent. Hence, conflict of the sort just described is sufficient grounds for suspecting that inquiry ought to continue into all of the questions involved until consistency can be obtained. No more shall be said about the matter of the "foreign relations" between inquiries here.

Another factor is the definiteness of the answer reached at the inductive stage. In example 3, where the ultimate partition U is finite, it is clear that should the conclusion reached be one of the eleven interval estimates of p in U (i.e., should all but one of the members of U be rejected), one would have obtained a maximally informative consistent answer in the sense that no other consistent potential answer in M logically implies given E the conclusion reached. As far as considerations of specificity matter, there would be no further need for inquiry.

On the other hand, should the conclusion reached be suspension of judgment between two or more of the 12 interval estimates, further inquiry would be in order so that a more definite answer is obtained.

In some situations, however, obtaining a maximally specific answer is not sufficient to satisfy the demand for definiteness. Thus, in example 1, the residual hypothesis R is a member of U and is, therefore, maximally specific. But it is plainly not a theory. The demand of the question is for a theory which will systematize the subject matter involved. Should R be accepted and T_1 and T_2 rejected, the demand for definiteness would not have been met even though T is maximally specific. In this case, a return to the abductive stage is appropriate.

In still other situations, obtaining a maximally specific answer need not be sufficient. Thus, in example 4, a point estimate for p would be maximally specific. Yet, the demand for definiteness might be satisfactorily met by an interval estimate of length smaller than or equal to some specific length.

Notice that when the demand for definiteness fails to be satisfied and inquiry ought to continue, it may still be appropriate to incorporate the insufficiently definite conclusion reached into the settled assumptions. Thus, in example 1, the theories T_1 and T_2 may be so decisively rejected as to warrant admitting as a settled assumption that R is true. That would strengthen the corpus of settled assumptions while still requiring that further inquiry be undertaken.

Aside from consideration of foreign relations between inquiries and definiteness, decisiveness is a critical factor in deciding whether a tentative conclusion ought to be made final or inquiry continued.

Note that both rules A and B require for their application the adoption of a value of the index of caution q. We have not legislated a definite value for q save for requiring that it be positive and no greater than 1. Yet, if a conclusion reached tentatively is to be made settled, it must be acceptable to everyone who is prepared to take moderate risk of error for information. In this sense, it must be decisive for all save the extremely cautious.

Potential Surprise in the Context of Inquiry 233

Thus, it is possible that a conclusion is reached which is definite enough but only when fairly high q-values close to 1 are used. Such a conclusion will not be decisive. Further inquiry will be desirable until a definite conclusion is reached which is decisive as well, i.e., which is acceptable at a suitably low q-level.

One way in which to represent conclusions reached at the inductive stage so as to test for decisiveness is to fix upon a suitable value for q as the standard for sufficient decisiveness and only report conclusions reached relative to that standard.

It is often desirable, however, to have information regarding the behavior of rules A and B for a broad range of values of q-values and to provide for the representation of inductive conclusions that would be reached relative to all values of q in the range.

One way of obtaining such a representation is by introducing the measure $Q(H, E)$ defined for all H in M and relative to the total "evidence" or settled assumptions E which represents the maximum value of q less than or equal to 1 such that H goes unrejected when that value of q is used. In the case of the contradictory C and other sentences which are rejected for all positive values of q, the Q-value is set at 0.

Notice that the value of $Q(H, E)$ decreases as the decisiveness with which H is rejected increases. To obtain a measure which increases with decisiveness of rejection, we introduce the function $Y(H, E) = 1 - Q(H, E)$. Thus, a contradictory answer has a maximum Y-value.

The Q-function and Y-function directly represent decisiveness of rejection. We may define a function which represents decisiveness of acceptance, since H in M is accepted at a given q-level if and only if the contradictory given E of H in M is rejected.

$$B(H, E) = Y(-H, E) = 1 - Q(-H, E).$$

Notice that use of any one of these three functions provides information about any potential answer pertaining to decisiveness. The Q-value and the Y-value for H in M determine the range of q-values for which it is rejected and another range for which it escapes rejection. The B-value determines a range of q-values for which H is accepted and a range for which it is not accepted. When one is concerned, therefore, to determine a standard for sufficient decisiveness, one can do so by specifying a Q-value, Y-value or B-value as standard.

Thus, one might insist that a decisively rejected H is one whose Q-value is .3, whose Y value is .7 or such that the B-value for $-H$ is .7. Each of these equivalent conditions is tantamount to specifying a q-level of .3. The advantage of the representation in terms of functions is that one might then be able to reach conclusions at the inductive stage without having fixed beforehand on a definite q-level.

10. POTENTIAL SURPRISE

Professor Shackle has always insisted that his measure of potential surprise is a rival to probability as a measure of uncertainty to be used in making risky decisions. In this paper, I have assumed, without argument, that some form of probability measure is an appropriate measure of uncertainty. Nonetheless, I continue to regard Shackle's notion of potential surprise to be of considerable importance. The difference between us concerns the locus of its importance. I claim that the Y-measure defined previously constitutes an adequate explication of Shackle's measure in the sense that it captures the salient formal features of Shackle's measure. I would also suggest that it captures much of the presystematic intuition underlying Shackle's measure.

On the other hand, the Y-measure, as I construe it, is clearly not a rival to objective or fair betting quotient probability as a measure of uncertainty. Indeed, the definition I have proposed itself presupposes probabilistic ideas. Whereas objective probability judgments determine fair betting quotient determinations appropriate for risky decision making, potential surprise serves as a means for representing the decisiveness with which a potential answer is to be tentatively rejected in an inquiry aimed at adding new information to a set of settled assumptions.*

Whether rejection of a potential answer will be legitimately counted as settled depends, as has already been stated, on several considerations. A necessary condition, however, is that it be rejected with sufficient decisiveness, i.e., that the evidence warrants regarding its truth as highly surprising. If the surprise is insufficient, this may

* *In Gambling with Truth*, Ch. X, I suggested that potential surprise is a good index of what Keynes calls "weight of arguments". In *A Treatise on Probability*, London: Macmillan (1921), pp. 74–75, he contends that probable error is not a good index of weight of arguments. His objection does not, in my opinion, apply to potential surprise.

Potential Surprise in the Context of Inquiry

constitute good reason to continue collecting new data (if such be otherwise cheap and feasible).

I have shown elsewhere that Shackle's measure of potential surprise shares the formal properties of the Y-measure. I shall only repeat the argument in the case of the most striking features of Shackle's measure—namely, the claim that the degree of surprise accorded HvG is the least degree of surprise accorded the two disjuncts.

Let HvG be in M. HvG will be rejected if and only if both H and G are rejected. But both H and G will be rejected for all q-values greater than $\max(Q(H), Q(G))$. Hence, $Q(HvG) = \max(Q(H), Q(G))$. Given this equation and the definition of the Y-function, it is easy to see that $Y(HvG) = \min(Y(H), Y(G))$ as Shackle's theory requires.

The following results can also be established in a similar manner.

$Y(S, E) = 0$

$Y(C, E) = 1$

If $H_1, H_2, \ldots, H_n$ are exhaustive given E, for at least one i, $Y(H_i, E) = 0$ and more than one H_i may bear 0 Y-value.

Shackle has often intimated that potential surprise captures some presystematic ideas concerning degrees of disbelief and has also used potential surprise to define a measure of degree of belief resembling fairly closely the measure represented by the B-function. Many Bayesians have contended, to the contrary, that fair betting quotient probability or some other notion of subjective probability serves the purpose.

Although the Bayesians, in my view, do indeed capture some of our presystematic ideas regarding the relations between belief and action, they fail abysmally to do justice to other presystematic ideas which Shackle's proposal handles better.

Note at the outset that in ordinary language, degrees of belief are not measured along a single scale. We consider rather two scales: one measuring degrees of belief and one measuring degrees of disbelief. According to probability representations of degree of belief, any hypothesis bearing positive probability receives a positive degree of belief. This, however, is absurd in ordinary usage; for a hypothesis bearing a low probability would ordinarily fail to be believed at all and, hence, would fail to receive a positive degree of belief. Indeed, such a hypothesis might receive a positive degree of disbelief.

Both Shackle's notions and my Y and B measures conform to these intuitions very well. Indeed, they conform to the further requirement that the degree of belief in H be equal to the degree of disbelief in $-H$.

Advocates of probabilistic representations of degrees of belief are likely to reply that they have resources for accommodating these intuitions. The probability line can be divided into three parts: a domain of positive disbelief from 0 to e (less than .5), a domain of positive belief from $1-e$ to 1 and a domain of 0 belief and disbelief from e to $1-e$.

This retort, however, faces considerable difficulty; for it has the following strongly counterintuitive consequence. The degree of belief in $H\&G$ should in general be less than the degrees of belief accorded H and accorded G separately. Indeed, it is possible for both H and G to be positively believed and for $H\&G$ to be accorded 0 degree of belief. Yet, ordinary logic would seem to recommend believing a conjunction when the conjuncts are believed.

The B-measure, however, is so defined that $B(H\&G)$ equals $\min(B(H), B(G))$ and thereby avoids the objection. This property of the B-function derives from the fact that $Y(HvG) = \min(Y(H), Y(G))$—the feature of potential surprise upon which Shackle has placed so much emphasis.

The appeal to ordinary language, however, is far from decisive especially in situations where claims can be made that conflicting analyses capture different features of presystematic discourse. It is obviously pointless to argue that probability or surprise provides a correct reading of "degree of belief". The far more fruitful way to proceed is to indicate how surprise and probability function in the context of practical deliberation and inquiry aimed at adding to our settled information. The claims of probability on this score are all too familiar. These claims, together with Shackle's own insistence that surprise is a rival to probability have, perhaps, tended to obscure the significance of potential surprise in the context of inquiry. Far from being a rival to probability, surprise performs different services. These services are worth attending to. Anyone seriously interested in the systematic study of the growth of knowledge should find Shackle's contribution to be of lasting importance.

Uncertainty and Crisis Behaviour:
An Illustration of Conflict and Peace Research

MICHAEL NICHOLSON

Richardson Institute for Conflict and Peace Research

1. INTRODUCTION

Traditionally the analysis of peace and war has been left to the historian, the area specialist and, for some rather technical purposes, the lawyer. It has been seen as the domain of the humanities to be analysed by such mixtures of "insight" and "judgement" (and in the words of the more confident practitioners, "wisdom") as might seem appropriate. More recently, and primarily during the last two decades, the analysis of the causes of war and the conditions for peace has been regarded as something which is suitable for the social scientist, employing the type of analytical tools which have been used in economics, particularly in micro-economics and organization theory. The attempts to do this have gone back some time, but intensive work has only gone on relatively recently.

In this paper I shall give some broad outline of this development as a lead-in to a particular piece of analysis on international crises and the concept of deterrence, which will hopefully serve the dual purpose of being an example of the genre of analysis which is most likely to appeal to economists and also being a modest contribution to the discipline.

2. THE NATURE OF THE FIELD

The analysis of war and peace is, even within the newer frameworks, approached in many different ways. It is perhaps easiest to describe it in terms of the four neighbouring and overlapping fields of "Conflict Analysis", "Strategic Studies", "Peace Research", and "International Relations". They are distinguished partly by the phenomena they study and partly by the political values implicit in them.

The most general of the fields is Conflict Analysis (used nearly synonymously with Conflict Research and Conflict Studies). Its name is self-descriptive. It is the study of how people behave in conflict situations, how conflicts start, develop and end.* This, of course, could be regarded as covering the whole of social science, which could be described as the study of the problems of conflict and co-operation. However, the prime interest of theorists in this area is in conflicts where violence is an actual or potential element, leaving other social conflicts to the appropriate disciplines. Clearly, there are some sorts of problems which can be viewed generally in a number of disciplines, for example, bargaining theory. However, the existence of a general bargaining theory which has, for example, applications in economics does not mean that economics is not a useful subdivision of social activity. In the same way, conflict analysis can be viewed primarily as the study of violent conflict without it reflecting adversely on the usefulness of theories which apply to any sort of social situation in which there is conflict. The restriction of the field to violent or potentially violent conflict between social groups comes from the co-incidence of two criteria. First, it is likely that the introduction of violence adds a new dimension which makes violent conflict rather different from other forms of conflict. The effects of non-rational factors may well be more significant in cases where there is violence. This is not proven so far, and further analysis might blur the distinction, but on the basis of present knowledge it is a reasonable view. Secondly, the field is defined by reference to ethical factors. Most social scientists at some level or other want to reform the world. This does not in itself affect the objectivity of the science they do, but (as is now a platitude) it does affect the sorts of problem they decide to probe into. Given a desire to reduce violence whether it is the threat of nuclear war, or of large scale (or even small scale)

---

* Two books which originally set the scene and which are still relevant reading are T. C. Schelling, *The Strategy of Conflict*, Cambridge, Mass., Harvard University Press, 1960 and K. Boulding, *Conflict and Defense*, New York, Harper and Row, 1962. Other books giving general pictures are Anatol Rapoport, *Fights, Games and Debates*, Ann Arbor, University of Michigan Press, 1960 and Michael Nicholson, *Conflict Analysis*, London, English Universities Press, 1971.

conventional wars, a field is determined which is relevant to this aim. These two criteria only accidentally coincide but together they at least indicate areas of emphasis. Few definitions of academic disciplines do much more.

In principle, at least, conflict analysis is a social science in the sense of being a positive analysis of conduct in conflict situations and is not normative, despite of course forming the basis of normative analysis at later stages. Hence the theoretical framework is that of an operational (that is, testable) deductive theory, and the propositions are about classes of events and not specific events. The aim is to build up some sort of body of testable theory analogous to economic theory, tested by a variety of familiar means including the statistical testing of hypotheses (becoming to be known as "interpolimetrics"!). However, not a great deal of progress has been made so far. This is an aspirant rather than an existing science.

There is within the field the inevitable debate over the use of mathematics and statistical methods. The debate is almost exactly the same as that which was carried on about the usefulness of mathematical methods in economics. There is little point in describing again a familiar battle-field.

International Relations is a narrower field, being essentially that part of political science which deals with the relations between states. Like the rest of political science there is a running battle between the "traditionalists" who see international relations as the study of contemporary political events (along with international history) and political philosophy, and the "behaviouralists", a most unfortunately and rather misleadingly named group of scholars who argue that international relations, at least in its non-normative aspects, can be analysed as a social science.* This then overlaps very considerably with conflict studies, differing only in being narrower and concerned with one form of conflict. Viewed as a social science, international relations is a large sub-set of conflict studies. In principle this again is a positive and not a normative study.

The normative studies are Peace Research and Strategic Studies. These are explicitly policy studies using the knowledge of conflict behaviour from the other disciplines as the bases of their analysis.

* For a survey of "behavioural" International Relations see Karl Deutsch, *The Analysis of International Relations*, Englewood Cliffs, Prentice Hall, and James N. Rosenau (ed.), *International Politics and Foreign Policy*, Toronto, Free Press, 1969 (revised edition).

Strategic Studies, in its extreme form, is the study of how to preserve the national interests of the actors—namely the nation states. This is readily extendable to alliances. Peace Research, also in its extreme form, has as its goal the study of how to reduce or eliminate violence while hopefully making it possible for social change to come about and without being particularly concerned with the interests of any special nation state. The term "Peace Research" carries with it in Britain (though less in the United States) the connotation of woolly-minded lefties whose soft hearts have led them to have soft heads. This might be true of some of the work, but it is unfair on much of it including, it is to be hoped, the present paper.

Both disciplines are concerned with the problems of peace and war and differ in the emphasis on various goals. However, there is not a dichotomy of goals but a spectrum, so there is a body of material in the middle which could well be classified as either. In any case, the avoidance of such events as a nuclear war would be widely agreed to be in the national interest of most countries, no matter how narrowly the national interest were defined, so this, if nothing else, would be common ground for peace researchers and students of strategy. Both disciplines are the result of a greater sophistication of various political goals, given the realization that social science is relevant to social ends.

A knowledge of social behaviour is helpful no matter what the social goals, and if the common social goals concern conflict then the same social behaviour is relevant to any form of social engineering. However, this does make it hard to differentiate too clearly peace research from strategic studies, at least in their more sophisticated versions. Perhaps the most satisfactory guide is to suggest that they represent the left wing and the right wing social engineering versions of a common body of knowledge about social behaviour, along with the recognition that left wing and right wing are not two neatly defined, dichotomous categories.

3. THE DEVELOPMENT OF THE DISCIPLINE

The analytical study of war and peace is primarily a post-war phenomenon and did not begin on any significant scale until about the mid 1950s. An identifiable discipline of conflict research could be said to have emerged by 1957, when the *Journal for Conflict*

Resolution first appeared from the University of Michigan. Journals define a field in simple pragmatic ways perhaps better than anything else, and this particular journal can be quoted without embarrassment or even apology for the intellectual level of its content.

However, there were founding fathers of the field. Notable on the Peace Research side was Lewis Fry Richardson, who throughout the inter-war period had done a lot of work, both on the statistical analysis of conflict behaviour, and in the formation of deductive theory of arms races. His work was published in various journals in the inter-war period, but it was only with some difficulty that it was finally published in book form. Two volumes appeared posthumously in 1960—*Arms and Insecurity*, which was an analysis of arms races, and *Statistics of Deadly Quarrels*.* The theory of arms races is rather reminiscent in general style of some theories of the trade cycle (even though the subject matter is rather different). However, for the physicist turned meteorologist (and becoming a Fellow of the Royal Society because of his contributions to the discipline), a dynamic model was interpreted in terms of differential equations, whereas the economists were turning more instinctively to difference equations.

The statistical study of conflict behaviour consisted partly of a very detailed collection of the various wars fought in the nineteenth and twentieth centuries, and partly of an elaborate testing by statistical means of a whole variety of hypotheses about the causes of conflict. So far as I know, Richardson was not aware of the work which was going on in the development of econometrics at roughly the same time. This is a pity, for he was working in almost complete intellectual isolation from the one other academic group which was trying, in some rigorous sense, to test statistically hypotheses about social behaviour. Richardson's work is impressive by any standards, but given that it was a one-man show, regarded at the time as very odd, it was a remarkable intellectual achievement.

More or less simultaneously with Richardson's isolated study, a group of scholars at the University of Chicago was working on the general problems of war and peace which resulted in 1942 in an enormous, two-volume work called *A Study of War* by Quincy Wright.† Though less rigorous than Richardson's work, it was another major step in the direction of the analytical study of war as a social phenomenon.

* Pittsburgh, The Boxwood Press, 1960.
† Chicago, University of Chicago Press, 1942.

While scientific approaches on the strategic side were latent in the various "War Games" which became widely used in the nineteenth century and had particular vogue amongst the German general staff, the forerunner of a truly scientific approach to strategic questions is the engineer Lanchester who worked on some problems of fire-power during the First World War, which, needless to say, were ignored by the military at the time.* Perhaps it would be fairer to regard Lanchester as the forerunner of military operational research rather than of strategy proper. Military operational research was much more respectable in the Second World War under the impact of people like Professor P. M. S. Blackett and was then taken seriously.

The grander problems of world strategy were not treated seriously in a scientific manner until the post-war period. In this period organizations such as the RAND Corporation, the think tank of the U.S. Air Force, have done a great deal of work on strategic problems where, as its sponsorship would indicate, the values involved in the work imply the pursuit of the national interest.

In the early 1960s the discipline became more clearly defined with Schelling's *The Strategy of Conflict* (1960) and Boulding's *Conflict and Defense* (1962). Schelling's book applied concepts derived from the Theory of Games (though not the Theory of Games itself) to the problem of Grand Strategy, while Boulding's was a more general attempt to apply economic style models to problems of war and peace. Both Schelling and Boulding were economists, though I do not think it is merely disciplinary loyalty which leads me to ascribe to them importance in establishing the field as legitimate for social scientists. Economists have played a significant role just as they have in parallel developments affecting other aspects of political science where deductive models have been applied. Conspicuous here is the theory of voting where the economists Arrow and Black have played important parts.† This is natural as the development of deductive theory in the study of war and peace is just one aspect of the development of deductive theory in all branches of human behaviour. As economics was by far the most developed of the social sciences as far as deductive theory was concerned, it was natural that economists,

* F. W. Lanchester, *Aircraft in Warfare*, London, Constable, 1916.
† Kenneth Arrow, *Social Choice and Individual Values*, New York, Wiley, 1951; Duncan Black, *The Theory of Committees and Elections*, Cambridge, Cambridge University Press, 1958.

full of missionary zeal, should turn their attention to neighbouring areas of social behaviour.

This account of the development of the discipline in which the economist is regarded as the dominant source of deductive theory might not be viewed with enthusiasm by adherents of disciplines who have not been lucky enough to have had an economic training. However, while admitting that an economic training might have biased me towards finding certain types of analysis more attractive than others, I think that the case that the economic style of deductive theory has been important in the development of conflict studies would be hard to dispute.

It is within this tradition that the rest of this paper falls. I want to present a model of an international crisis in the hypothetical-deductive mode and which is a simplified picture of reality. Because of its simplified structure it is not really subject to falsification in the strict Popperian sense but is still at the stage which Papandreou alleges that most economic theory is—namely it is possible to verify but not, except in a rather naive sense, to refute, for a refutation may just be a confirmation of its undue simplicity.* Thus it is not really a theory of the process of a crisis so much as a theory of a non-existent simpler process which is of interest inasmuch as it paves the way for a more realistic theory of crises.

4. INTERNATIONAL CRISES

One of the problems on which some work has been done in conflict analysis has been that of international crises.† These are usually defined as situations where there is a short period of tension between a number of countries and for a brief period there is a considerably larger probability of war than is usual. The Cuba Missiles Crisis of 1962 is often quoted as the classic example of a crisis, along with the crisis of 1914 which immediately preceded the First World War. However, one can easily make a list of many more.

* Andreas Papandreou, *Economics as a Science*, Chicago, 1958.
† For example: R. C. North, O. R. Holsti, M. G. Zaninovitch and D. A. Zinnes, *Content Analysis: A Handbook with Applications for the Study of International Crises*, Northwestern University Press, 1963; Charles Hermann, *Crisis in Foreign Policy: A Simulation Analysis*, New York, The Bobbs-Merrill Co. Inc., 1969; Oran Young, *The Politics of Force: Bargaining During International Crises*, Princeton University Press, 1968.

The short period crisis is usually distinguished from the larger period of tension between two countries which in some respects seems, at least superficially, to have different characteristics. There seem good reasons for considering the short period crisis as a somewhat distinct phenomenon. It is a period where the decision-making capacity of the relevant bodies is severely taxed. A lot of very important decisions are having to be taken in a hurry, where the alternatives before the decision-makers are relatively new and may have not been considered until the crisis got under way. Thus the more thorough analysis of problems which is possible in the long period situation where the careful evaluation of alternatives can take place is not a possibility when decisions have to be made quickly.

A crisis can be defined by three characteristics. First, it is a period of great uncertainty, where the gap between the best outcome and the worst outcome of the situation is very large in comparison with normal. In the sort of situations we are considering the worst outcome is war (or at least defeat in war) while the best outcome is the status quo or some modification of the status quo which in probability language can be described as a situation where the probability of an adverse outcome is high compared with normal. In terms of potential surprise, it is a situation where the severely adverse outcome of war, which normally has a positive degree of potential surprise associated with it, has a zero degree of potential surprise. The second characteristic is that the crisis takes place over a short period of time (which justifies the use of the word "abnormal" to describe it). The third characteristic is that the problems which occasion the crisis are unexpected to at least one of the parties involved.

Following from these defining characteristics, we have a situation where a decision-making group is considering essentially a new problem, and is involved in much more intensive work than normal. This creates different patterns of decision-taking (with effects on the decisions taken) from the normal. There arise the problems of decision-taking under stress, which have their own characteristics. However, that is a question which to a certain extent we wish to underplay in this paper. Instead we want to present a model of crisis decision-making which is at least closely related to a rational decision model. It might be useful to elaborate and modify this model to incorporate factors specifically connected with stress, but it is convenient to use a rational model as a starting point.

The interesting things to ask about crises are why some of them result in war, while others result in a return to the status quo (more or less), but in a way which is not easily predictable by observers at the time, or even, if published records are to be believed, by the participants. It is, of course, possible that crises exist where the doubt about the outcome exists in the mind of only one party and whether the war breaks out or not depends entirely on whether one or both sides wish it to do so. An analysis on these lines would make some sense but the degree of unpredictability still seems surprising. Consequently, a further analysis of the problems seems justified.

We have a system which is obviously close to some critical boundary where, beyond it, it becomes unstable whereas for presumably relatively small changes in the parameters involved a stable system results. This sort of situation is one which is common to a number of both social and political systems and it is tempting, on grounds of intellectual curiosity alone, to investigate this particular system.

However, there are grounds other than intellectual curiosity for regarding international crises as important topics to investigate. First, simply because the proximate antecedents of wars are normally crises, they are at the heart of the subject matter of conflict studies. Evaluated by some criterion of social importance they come out as very significant. Secondly, of all the phenomena within the discipline, they are perhaps the most amenable, or potentially amenable, to analysis by the existing techniques of the social sciences. Because it is a short period phenomenon, the number of factors which are variables is smaller than in most problems which are relevant in this discipline, so that, on the whole, the problems are likely to be less complex. This may turn out to be an illusion, but at least it is a plausible intuition. Thus we have the coincidence that this is a problem which is both important and probably tractable.

However, despite the interest in international crises as a social phenomenon, there is no existing deductive theory of the process. Nevertheless it seems on the face of it to be a process which would lend itself to just this sort of theorizing. A stumbling block, mentioned already, is the unusual degree of stress which might make the normal decision-making rules of the organization falter. However, this does not rule out the possibility of some sort of micro-analysis particularly of the form which abandons simple optimizing models. What may be of interest is the sort of decision-making rule which is in fact adopted in crisis situations irrespective of whether it is different or not from the rules applicable to normal times. However, despite this, it is convenient to fit the analysis into an optimizing model as a base and modify this if and when it appears to be necessary.

The studies which have been done on international crises fall under two heads. First, the analysis of the change in the actual decision-making structure in response to a crisis situation, and secondly the analysis of the ways in which the perceptions of the decision-makers of other countries (particularly opponents) alter. A very crude summary of the state of knowledge at the moment is that it is common, though not universal, for the decision-making group to contract very markedly in size. Thus decisions tend to be taken by one or two very senior members of the government along with some particularly relevant members of the foreign office (or equivalent department) and perhaps of the armed forces. It is common for the whole process of decision-making to involve only some half a dozen people and to short-circuit the complex process of administrative decision. There are counter-examples—notably the United States decision-making group during the Cuba Missiles Crisis—but this seems to have been a quite self-conscious departure from the norm, initiated by the late President Kennedy on the grounds that in the past (notably in 1914) crisis decision-making had not been conspicuously skilful and had led to results which at least some members of neither side had wished.

As far as the question of perception is concerned, there seems to be a tendency towards a growth of rather stereotyped political thinking, particularly as far as the opponent is concerned. However, apart from very intuitive studies, our knowledge of this is based almost entirely on the very intensive study of the 1914 crisis done at Stanford University.

5. CRISIS THEORY AND DETERRENCE

Threats are a conspicuous feature of international crises, and threats are deterrents. A deterrent involves the implicit or explicit statements of the form "if you do X to me (presumably something which harms me), then I shall do A to you (which harms you)". The operation of the deterrent may or may not benefit the user directly, though if it does then presumably it is more credible because of it. Obviously a crisis situation is one where the deterrent threat may or may not be used, but where there is some doubt about it.

One of the problems which, though vaguely recognized, is nevertheless not always clearly stated, is that deterrence as it is applied in International Relations is not exclusively a matter of nuclear deterrence. It is both obvious and understandable why nuclear deterrence has been the dominant element in the analysis of the concept, as after all a nuclear war would be catastrophic for all concerned and for a lot of people who would rather not have been concerned at all. However, we shall extend the analysis for whenever the threat of force is involved there is an issue of deterrence. While the possibility of a nuclear war makes other wars seem puny in comparison, there are and have been many extremely destructive wars since 1945 (and it looks as though there may continue to be), so we cannot dismiss the problem as a minor one; non-nuclear war is still an acutely important social problem. Similarly, while crises between the Soviet Union and the United States have nuclear overtones, crises between other countries, such as the Suez crisis or the various Middle Eastern crises, do not (or at least have not done so far).

One drawback of the consideration of deterrence largely in terms of nuclear deterrence is that this case has some special characteristics which are not always shared by other sorts of crises. In particular, war may not be quite the acutely feared problem that it is in the nuclear case. With nuclear deterrence, particularly since the advent of second strike capacity, a nuclear strike is like the bee's sting where the final result is just as harmful to the initiator as it is to the victim. There is no such thing as a "successful nuclear war" in which the attacker is in a better position after it than before it. However, in the case of at least some non-nuclear conflict between countries, there is a definite possibility that one country will feel itself better off by fighting (and winning) the war than it would have been if it had not fought it. A possible instance of this is Israel in 1967. The understandable emphasis on nuclear deterrence and nuclear war should not distract us too much from this other set of possibilities.

A final point on the relationship between deterrence and crisis is that the decisions which are taken where the deterrent threat is relevant are by and large taken in crisis situations. This should be borne in mind in any analysis of the concept. Inasmuch as in crisis situations people act emotionally, then arguments about deterrence which depend on rational behaviour become suspect. Analyses of deterrence need to bear in mind that critical decisions are typically taken in a very emotional atmosphere.

5. A MODEL OF THE CRISIS

Consider the question in the terms of an artificial model with two countries. Despite the prominence of the virtually two-party Cuba Missile Crisis in most people's minds, two party crises are rarities, but it helps us to get rid of the problems of more than two party conflicts, problems which are only two painfully familiar to students of oligopoly. The parties are assumed to be unitary decision-makers —there are no problems of internal dissensions. There are two alternatives available to each party; to initiate an attack or not to initiate one. The non-initiate strategy nevertheless involves the conditional choice of "respond if the other attacks". We can assume, not unrealistically, that these alternatives are known to each side. However, what neither side may know of its rival is the pay-off to it of the various courses of action.*

We can specify the alternatives and their consequences in the form of a pay-off matrix, when the pay-offs are the payments to A.

	B_1	B_2
A_1	α_{11}	α_{12}
A_2	α_{21}	α_{22}

A_1 is the act of "do not initiate hostilities but respond if the rival initiates". A_2 is the act "initiate hostilities". B_1 and B_2 are interpreted similarly. The pay-offs are then interpreted as follows: α_{11} is the consequence of neither side fighting; α_{21} is the consequence of A initiating an attack and having the attack responded to, α_{12} is the result of being attacked and then responding, while α_{22} is the result of both attacking simultaneously. The pay-offs must be expressed in utility terms (or national interest terms or whatever. It must be some form of weak cardinal measure, as in the standard utility measures.) However, these utility functions, though logically the same

* This problem was first discussed in rather intuitive terms by Schelling in the *Strategy of Conflict*. A more rigorous and elaborate extension of Schelling's model is discussed in economic terms by the present author in *Oligopoly and Conflict: A Dynamic Approach*, Liverpool University Press, 1972. The model presented in section 5 is essentially the same model, but adapted for our present needs.

as in economics, are more complex affairs. In economic problems, the ordering of alternatives is usually obvious even if the actual utility function is not. However, in a political context, even the ordering of the pay-offs in utility terms of an opponent may be very unclear even where the actual consequences in physical terms of a particular pair of acts may be relatively clear cut.

Let us suppose that A views his pay-offs as in fact ordered $\alpha_{11} > \alpha_{21} > \alpha_{22} > \alpha_{12}$. This is a plausible ordering implying the view that a war, even if initiated by A, is against A's interest. However, in many

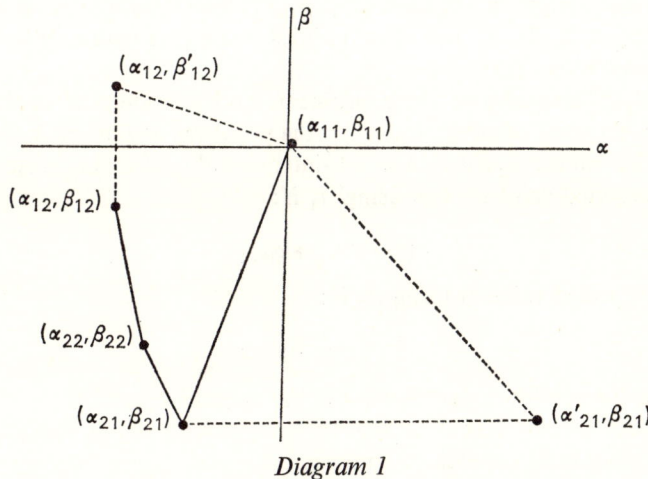

Diagram 1

cases B may not be confident of this, and consider the possibility that instead of α_{21}, α'_{21} is the case, where $\alpha'_{21} > \alpha_{11} > \alpha_{22} > \alpha_{12}$. If A's orderings had been in fact like this then A would attack B irrespective of B's behaviour.

Now consider the following problem: suppose B believes α'_{21} to be the case with probability p, and α_{21} with probability $(1-p)$, what are the conditions that B will attack A solely out of fear of A's attack (i.e. make a pre-emptive attack) when the situation is such that A has no direct interest in attacking? B's doubts whether α_{21} or α'_{21} is the case can be due either to a doubt about the physical consequence of the act, or a doubt about the utility valuation of some particular consequence (or, of course, both).

To round the model off, let us make parallel assumptions about

B's matrix, we shall assume B's utility orderings in fact to be $\beta_{11} > \beta_{12} > \beta_{22} > \beta_{21}$ (the first subscript describing A's act, the second B's). A believes this to be so with probability $(1-q)$, but that β_{12} is replaced by β'_{12} ($> \beta_{11}$) with probability of q. The overall situation then is that neither side would want to initiate a war but that nevertheless one might break out through the fear of the other side which we, as omniscient observers, know to be against everyone's interest. This is all illustrated in diagram 1. The points connected by the continuous lines represent the bargaining set as it really is. The other two points $(\alpha'_{21}, \beta_{21})$ and $(\alpha_{12}, \beta'_{12})$ represent the alternatives which each fears might be the case. $(\alpha_{11}, \beta_{11})$ is the status quo point, and defined as $(0, 0)$. All the other utilities (except, of course, α'_{21} and β'_{21}) are then negative.

Let us disaggregate these problems and consider the problem from A's point of view. Neglecting the problems of B using B_2 from fear, he will use B_2 from direct self-interest with probability q. Hence, the expected value to A of using A_1 is:

$$(1-q)\alpha_{11} + q\alpha_{12} \quad (1)$$

The expected value of using A_2 is:

$$(1-q)\alpha_{21} + q\alpha_{22} \quad (2)$$

Thus, the condition that A will use the aggressive strategy A_2 when $\alpha_{21} < \alpha_{11}$ out of fear of B's possible aggressive act is that (2) is greater than (1) or, with re-arrangement:

$$q(\alpha_{11} + \alpha_{22} - \alpha_{21} - \alpha_{12}) + (\alpha_{21} - \alpha_{11}) > 0 \quad (3)$$

Now this is not a probability statement but a simple numerical relationship which is either true or false depending on the numerical values involved. If we make the further rather strong assumption that B knows the numerical values, then it also knows whether the criterion holds or not and in consequence knows whether A will use strategy A_2 out of fear. In its turn this determines B's action and the process does not accumulate beyond this point.

The same argument applies to B and we deduce that the aggressive strategy will be used if the following inequality holds

$$p(\beta_{11} + \beta_{22} - \beta_{12} - \beta_{21}) + (\beta_{12} - \beta_{11}) > 0 \quad (4)$$

These relationships can easily be represented as a linear equation on a graph. Let us represent $V(A_2)$ as the expected value to A of playing A_2. We thus have:

$$V(A_2) = q(\alpha_{11}+\alpha_{22}-\alpha_{21}-\alpha_{12})+(\alpha_{21}-\alpha_{11}) \qquad (5)$$

From the ordering assumptions of the matrix, the coefficient of q is unambiguously positive while the expression in the second brackets is negative. As q is only defined for 0 and 1 and the values in between, the graph is as follows (diagram 2):

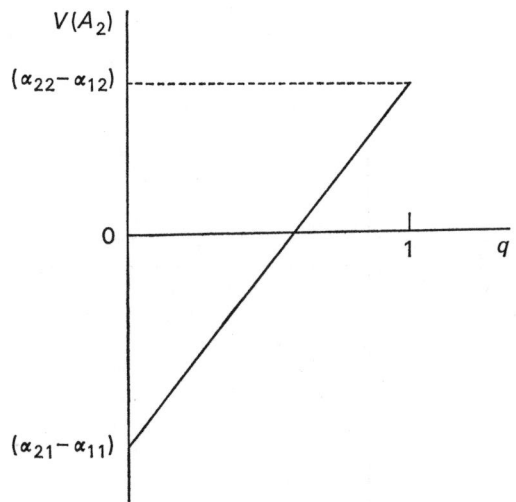

Diagram 2

The interpretation of (3) in this is direct. It simply indicates that the function is the positive quadrant. It is clearly arbitrary as to whether this analysis is done in terms of $V(A_1)$ or $V(A_2)$ as $V(A_1) = -V(A_2)$.

An exactly parallel argument can be carried out to derive $V(B_2)$ for B. $V(B_2)$ consists of the left hand side of inequality (4) and hence we derive the relation:

$$V(B_2) = p(\beta_{11}+\beta_{22}-\beta_{12}-\beta_{21})+(\beta_{12}-\beta_{11}) = -V(B_1) \qquad (6)$$

The graph of this is illustrated in Diagram 3.

Under these assumptions the problem is clear-cut. If either $V(A_2)$ or $V(B_2)$ is positive, both sides will attack, even though the ordering of the alternatives in each one's matrix means that they would both have been better off not attacking. The attack comes about purely through uncertainty. However, such an attack need not occur as there is nothing inherently odd about both $V(A)$ and $V(B)$ being negative. Thus, while uncertainty may produce an unnecessary attack, it need not do so.

This is, of course, an absurdly simple model and while it demonstrates the logical point that uncertainty does not necessarily bring about an attack irrespective of the pay-off motive and the probability of profitable attack, it does little else. However, one modification can bring it substantially closer to reality. A major implausibility is

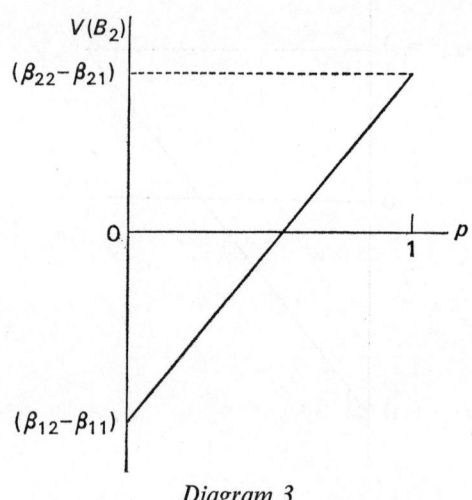

Diagram 3

that A knows for sure whether $V(B_2)$ is greater or less than zero and similarly B is unlikely to know with certainty the value of $V(A_2)$. Apart from any other considerations, the probabilities which enter into the determination of $V(B_2)$ and $V(A_2)$ are subjective, are unlikely to be articulated, and under no remotely realistic circumstances are likely to have been experimented on. Hence we suppose that A thinks there is a probability Q that B will attack out of fear of a pre-emptive attack by A itself as distinct from an attack out of simple self-interest. Hence the over-all probability held by A of an attack by B is $(q+Q-Qq)$. With this we can re-define equation (5) and introduce $V^*(A)$ where:

$$V^*(A_2) = (q+Q-qQ)\{\alpha_{11}+\alpha_{22}-\alpha_{21}-\alpha_{12}\} + \{\alpha_{21}-\alpha_{11}\} \qquad (7)$$

Q in this is interpreted as A's probability that B believes $V^*(A_2)>0$. In reasonably high states of information one would suppose that the value of Q is closely related to whether $V(A_2)$—the unstarred version—is in fact positive or negative.

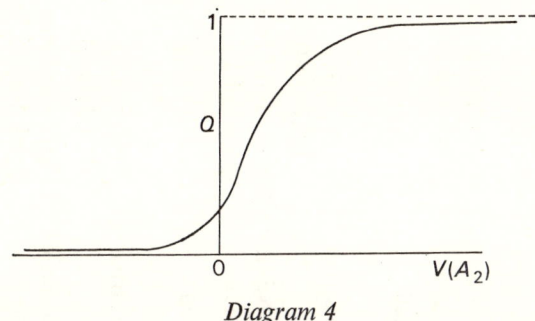

Diagram 4

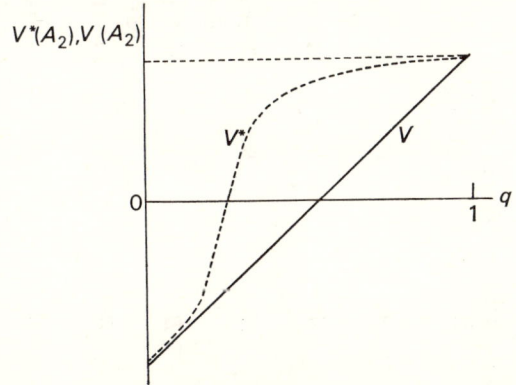

Diagram 5

If $V(A_2)$ is clearly negative then Q will be close to zero and $V^*(A_2) \simeq V(A_2)$. Similarly if $V(A_2)$ is clearly positive then Q will be close to unity and $V^*(A_2) \simeq (\alpha_{22} - \alpha_{12})$, though in this case it might well lie above $V(A_2)$. Let us suppose that the relationship between $V(A_2)$ and Q is that presented in Diagram 4. This will yield the relationship between $V(A_2)$ and $V^*(A_2)$ depicted in Diagram 5, where both are presented as functions of q.

Notice that there is a basic asymmetry in the argument which

THE TERMS

Degree of belief	Who believes it	About whose act	Nature of the act	State of variables believed in
q	A	B	Self-interested aggression	$(\beta_{11} < \beta_{12})$
Q	A	B	Pre-emptive strike	$(\beta_{11} > \beta_{12})$ $V^*(B_2) > 0$
$(q+Q-qQ)$	A	B	Over-all probability of aggression	Either above two conditions
P	B	A	Self-interested aggression	$(\alpha_{11} < \alpha_{21})$
P	B	A	Pre-emptive strike	$(\alpha_{11} > \alpha_{21})$ $V^*(A_2) > 0)$
$(p+P-pP)$	B	A	Over-all probability of aggression	Either above two conditions

makes $V^*(A_2) \geqslant V(A_2)$ deriving initially from the fact that $(q+q-qQ) \geqslant q$. This makes the situation more unstable. A belief by B that $V^*(A_2) \geqslant 0$ when in fact it is false creates an instability which is not balanced by some corresponding situation whereby B believes that $V^*(A_2) < 0$ when in fact the reverse is true. Any single condition for instability is sufficient but not necessary, whereas the conditions for stability are all necessary but not sufficient.

As, despite appearances, it is not our intention to be obscure, the meanings of the various probabilities can be listed in a table for reference. The critical thing to notice is that no one has a degree of belief (other than certainty) about his own actions, only about those of others.

While it is not a logical point, it seems plausible empirically that high values of $V^*(A_2)$ and high values of $V^*(B_2)$ will be associated and similarly for low values. Remember that Q is the degree of A's belief that B will carry out a pre-emptive attack. If Q is high this means that $V^*(A_2)$ is also high. However we would expect $V^*(A_2)$ to be positively associated with P, B's belief in A's pre-emptive strike and lead to a high value of $V^*(B_2)$. These propositions may not hold but they are certainly not absurd.

The introduction of $V^*(A_2)$, and a corresponding term $V^*(B_2)$, does not alter the basic working of the model. We have at this point a static model which gives the conditions under which offensive actions will be taken. The next step is less adequately to put some dynamic elements into it, as it is the movement of the situation through time which is a crucial factor in the analysis of crises.

6. THE PROCESS OF A CRISIS

Suppose a situation arises where a war might break out. In terms of the model this means that either $V^*(A_2)$ or $V^*(B_2)$ are close to being positive. In some cases the war does break out and in other cases it does not. To what extent can this be illuminated by the model?

The crisis situation is aggravated by uncertainty, but the uncertainty is created by the possibility that either α'_{11} is the case and hence $\alpha'_{21} > \alpha_{11}$ or β'_{12} is the case. Suppose that α'_{21} is in fact the case. The result of the crisis would then be war. If this were so one would expect A to attack as soon as possible which on the face of it would seem to be immediately. However, there would then never be such a thing as a crisis which lasted any length of time. Either it would profit A (or B) to attack in which case it would do so immediately without going through the preliminary of a crisis. Alternatively $\alpha_{11} > \alpha_{21}$ and this would be known with certainty by B from the failure of A to attack. Consequently, it has to be possible either for the relative values of the pay-off matrices to alter during a crisis, or for there still to be some use or need for A to delay an attack even though $\alpha'_{21} > \alpha_{11}$. We must examine these cases with care as, apart from being of interest in themselves, they are also of use in analysing crises where neither side really wants the war, whether or not they in fact get it.

The reasons can conveniently be classified into three heads even though there are many variants under each. First, an attack may take some time to prepare even if the forces are in basic readiness. Due to the emphasis on nuclear deterrence, where the relevant military equipment is at virtual instant readiness, this factor is sometimes overlooked. However, in situations where nuclear weapons are not available—which is still in the vast majority of cases—this is an important consideration and in such classic situations the deployment of forces and mobilization of reserves are as relevant as ever. It takes time for some armed forces to get into a favourable attack position and hence, even though $\alpha'_{21} > \alpha_{11}$ a delay might be expected.

The second factor is that the utility orderings of the country may themselves be in doubt even internally and during the course of the crisis the decision makers are trying to work out their relative valuation of α_{21} and α_{11}. They may not put it this way, but it can be described as such. This sort of problem is particularly acute in political affairs. The problems involved in establishing a preference ordering are sometimes overlooked, as in many economic contexts where formal preference theory has been mainly considered: the orderings as such are not at issue, particularly when the literal pay-offs are money. However, in situations where the arguments in the utility function are not to be ordered in a self-evident way, a number of problems arise. We draw attention to three of them. First, while it is convenient to assume that in the analysis of decision taking the utility function is given prior to the analysis and that the problem is started up from that point, this is convenient but no more. When a problem is one which is under review or at least likely to be, it is plausible to assume that the decision-makers have at least some general notion of their preference orderings and that the utility function is relatively clear cut. However, it is not plausible to assume that decision-makers have a clearly defined utility function over all possible states of the world, including those which are not likely to come into some current decision problem. Hence, when some new sets of situations arise the process of defining a utility function involves both time and decision-making resources.

This leads on to the second point which is that while again in standard treatments of decision-taking problems a utility function is assumed to be relatively stable through time or at least through the relevant period, it might in fact fluctuate and this is particularly true in situations where there is considerable tension. Even individuals, never mind groups, do not always have stable utility functions as even simple observations will confirm.

The final point is that the decision-takers concerned are groups (though a recognition of this is a temporary abandonment of one of our initial assumptions) of individuals and not single individuals. Thus the process of determining utility ordering involves discussion and possible internal bargaining. It is fair to surmise that even when the preferences of the individuals over the relevant alternatives are clear cut, the group will spend some time in determining its group preference ordering. This is at least a plausible interpretation of the delay involved in the entry of the Soviet Union into Czechoslovakia in 1968 which was in excess of the time required to make it militarily possible. Different groups and individuals in the Soviet Union probably had different preference orderings and the final group preference ordering only emerged after some delay and internal bargaining. This is probably usual, though sometimes also dominated by the other problem of the search for alternatives.

These three reasons, then, are *prima facie* grounds for not taking the utility function as necessarily stable throughout the crisis, though they indicate (but no more) that this might stabilize after a time.

The third class of factors which might delay an attack even though it were profitable is that a period of crisis often involves periods of negotiation around the status quo point. While we have represented $(\alpha_{11}, \beta_{11})$ as a single point, this is, in fact, an unrealistic portrayal of the situation. There is commonly a period of rather anguished bargaining which goes on during the period of the crisis which sets up a whole series of possible $(\alpha_{11}, \beta_{11})$'s, some of which are greater than the respective (but relatively fixed) α_{21} and β_{12} and some of which are not.

This can be represented on diagram 6. The line MN is a line on which some bargain might be struck. A problem during the course of the crisis is in trying to find some mutually acceptable point. The line drawn is $\alpha_{11}+\beta_{11}=0$ so it represents a zero sum boundary to the bargaining set (providing a bargain is reached—"the game" is not zero sum) though this is not required. If the bargain is struck on the segment of the line $M'N'$ then there is no point in either of the

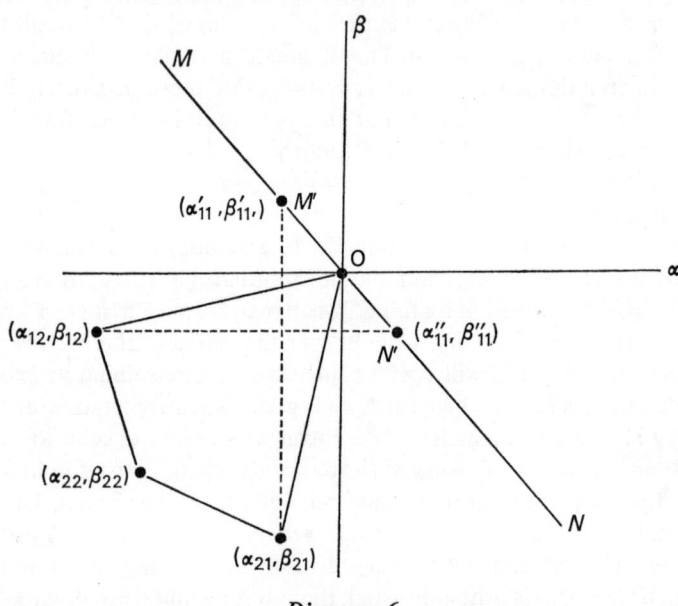

Diagram 6

parties going to war. However, if a bargain cannot be struck within this segment then war will be profitable for one or other party (but not both). During the course of negotiation there may be genuine doubt about whether some acceptable bargain can be struck and hence genuine doubt about the outcome of the crisis.

These three classes of consideration give some plausibility to the view that even if it is the case that a crisis ends in war because it was for the direct self-interest of the parties that the war might not break out immediately. In its turn this lends credence to the view that two parties might genuinely fear war for a period of time even if it turns out not to be to anyone's advantage. The non-declaration of war at the first sign of danger is not in itself conclusive evidence for thinking that it never will break out.

From this it is obvious that one outcome for a crisis is for there to be a war because it is in the interest of one of the parties after a delay caused by one of the above reasons. There is no particular problem here, nor is the result a particularly surprising one. Another alternative is that because of the results of the negotiations, or the variation in the utility function, peace is preserved because it is in no one's interest to go to war. This would seem to dispose of the problem. The outcome of the crisis can be explained in terms of the ambiguity of the relative values of α_{11} and α_{21}, similarly β_{11} and β_{12} and is determined once the ambiguity is resolved.

However this still leaves us with the problem of uncertainty which cannot be ignored as it adds another dimension to the problem. The valuations in the probability judgements of the various parties effect the result of the crisis just as much as the pay-off. This must now be examined in greater detail.

7. PROBABILITY, UNCERTAINTY AND THE DEVELOPMENT OF A CRISIS

In the earlier part of the analysis, the concept of probability has been used with little attempt at justification. This is not really the place to enter into a discussion of subjective probability and potential surprise as the battle lines are more-or-less clearly marked out. In order to classify this part of the analysis, the concept is used as a subjective probability of the form clearly expressed by L. J. Savage in *The Foundations of Statistics*.* The general position on the potential surprise and subjective probability debate has been gone into elsewhere so here we shall content ourselves with using the concept of subjective probability without further argument while acknowledging the problems to be controversial.

The various probabilities which appear in the equations and inequalities earlier in the analysis are all obviously subjective probabilities in the sense that there exist no obvious and "objective" rules for determining what such probabilities are as is the case where there are repeated instances of "similar" events or when some appeal can be made to symmetry (such as with dice). Thus, while some prob-

* New York, Wiley, 1954.

ability judgements can be regarded as eccentric, it is difficult to regard them as incorrect for to do so would imply that there is some rule which can be applied and will then generate some "correct" probability. A number of different probabilities can be easily justified as being reasonable and the one which is picked out is to some extent arbitrary. Thus a probability estimate can change not only in response to evidence but also in response to a change in a state of mind.

A brief elaboration of the determination of a subjective probability is in order. Suppose at time $(t-1)$ a decision-maker is forming some probability, $P_t(E)$ that some event E will take place at time t. There are only two alternatives: either that it will take place, or that it will not; there are no degrees of this. The decision-maker forms some estimate of this probability and the relevant considerations are various characteristics of the world both in period $(t-1)$ and probably some preceding periods as well. Hence, a function which gives the probability might be of the form

$$P_t(E) = f(x_1(t-1), x_2(t-1)\ldots, x_1(t-2), x_2(t-2)\ldots) \qquad (8)$$

where the arguments represent various events in the world at various times. The precise status of this function has to be considered with care, for while it is a characteristic of the individual making the probability judgement it is not simply a matter of idiosyncratic preference on the part of the decision-maker. Hence, while it might be a question of individual characteristics what the weight of an argument is in the probability function, whether the argument should or should not appear should be a question of broad agreement (we stay clear of the term "objective" so as to avoid some temporarily unnecessary philosophical disputes). Furthermore, some characteristics of the direction of a change in one of the arguments on the value of probability should also be the subject of widespread agreement. Hence supposing that $x(t-1)$ is a continuous variable, whether $[\partial P_t(E)]/[\partial x_2(t-1)]$ is greater or less then zero should be the subject of widespread agreement even if the functional forms, much less the numerical values, are not agreed to by different observers.

The reasons for expecting agreement between different observers is that they would be expected to share common theories, at least at an informal level, about the behaviour of the world which are relevant to the occurrence of the event E. In all social questions, the determinants of E are probabilistic, first, because the theories are likely to be commonly informal and not fully tested and secondly, whether some of the antecedent conditions take on the values supposed is itself often a probability question. However, while there is clearly a lot of play in the situation, the general outline of the theoretical structure in which the probability statement is made should involve some measure of agreement. In fact people do have a very high degree of agreement of the outline structures of their theories of the world—social life and communication would be totally impossible without it.

Unfortunately this is not a complete picture of the determination of the value of the probability. If explicitly asked what factors affect the probability of some event, then the person or group whose subjective probability we are interested in would specify the set of variables in equation (8), and for many problems we would expect widespread agreement. However, we must explore further those factors which determine what the functional will be. There are two classes of variables involved in this which do not appear in equation (8), the first sort I shall call *circumstantial variables* and the second sort *personal state variables*.

By circumstantial variables I mean those characteristics of the situation such as the amount of time the individual has for reaching his judgements. If someone has to make up his mind very quickly about something then it is quite possible that his judgement will be different from the one arrived at with more time for reflection. Such factors must enter into an analysis of actual decision-making if it is to provide an accurate description of people's behaviour.

By personal state variables I mean such things as degree of anxiety stress and so on experienced by the decision-maker at the time of making his judgement. Given adequate theories of the factors which cause anxiety and their effect on conduct one could reduce these variables to circumstantial variables. Thus, anxiety might be related to short decision-making time and lack of sleep, but it is worth while pointing out that some circumstantial variables operate directly, and some via the emotional states of the actors. Such variables are not usually considered in orthodox decision theory, but they can be important for an analysis of certain types of decision situation (of which the international crisis is a conspicuous example.)

Now let us state the probability function in a concise way which takes into account these different variables:

$$P_t(E) = \phi(X(t-i), C(t-1), S(t-1)) \quad \text{for } i = 1 \text{ to } n \quad (9)$$

This represents the determination of the probability held at time $(t-1)$ of the event E happening at time t. $X(t-i)$ is a summary of the variables involved in equation (8) which for convenience we can call the *general state variables*, $C(t-1)$ represent the circumstantial variables at time $(t-1)$ while $S(t-1)$ represent the personal state variables at time $(t-1)$.

This poses the categories in which the problem can be analysed. All that is now needed are some hypotheses. Of these we are not short, though of soundly tested ones we are; thus all we can provide at the moment is a rather speculative analysis, to indicate the issues involved.

Now in terms of the earlier part of the analysis the probability we are interested in is q, or, as now we are admitting the possibility that this will be different at different points in time we have the equation:

$$q(t) = \phi(X(t-i), C(t-1), S(t-1)) \quad \text{for } i = 1 \text{ to } n \qquad (10)$$

For simplicity let us assume that the circumstantial variables $C(t)$ remain the same in each period of the crisis. For example, in each period there may be a shortage of time, but if this is the same in each period we can assume that its effect on the evaluation of the probabilities is also the same (which assumes there is no cumulative effect: but this is a refinement we shall not consider).

In each new period there is a flow of information coming in under the heading $X(t-i)$, so the set of information which is relevant to the decision is constantly expanding, for it is unrealistic over the short periods involved to assume that there is any sort of forgetting process in operation which would eliminate old information. Initially, for the purposes of argument, let us assume that this information is neutral as far as the probability of war is concerned neither increasing nor decreasing it. However, we must qualify this in one important respect; namely, after some period of time if the war has not occurred the probability that there is going to be one will also decrease. All the arguments for why there might be a delay in attacking if a war was profitable are ones which apply to a short delay, except for the argument concerning bargaining. Thus it takes time to prepare to attack but if no attack takes place after there has been ample opportunity to prepare, then the failure to attack is evidence that it is not in the interests of the other side to do so.

Hence, $q(t)$, defined as the probability of attack in period t, providing there has not so far been an attack, is going to be constant for a while, after which it will decline, if one assumes that all the other variables remain constant. Thus, it will look roughly as illustrated in diagram 7. The evidence from the various empirical studies* which have been done suggest some general lines for the effect of changes in $S(t-1)$ on $q(t)$. As tense situations proceed, hostile images get stereotyped, suspicion of a potential enemy grows, and there is a general pessimism about the goodness of his intentions. While it does not follow logically, nevertheless it seems a plausible hypothesis that this results in increases in $q(t)$.

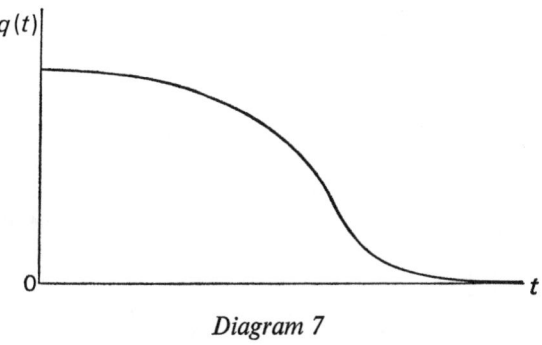

Diagram 7

This is strengthened when we consider the relation of the personal state variables to the general state variables. If one country does not want to go to war out of self-interest but is nevertheless fearful of war, then it is going to prepare to fight one nonetheless. Thus military preparations will take place, some of which, at least, will be known to the other side. However, it is difficult if not impossible to distinguish those military preparations which are genuinely defensive from those military preparations which are offensive. Viewed from a sufficiently detached point of view it would seem that the fact that a country in crisis was carrying out military preparations was evidence neither of its desire for war nor of its innocence. Such facts should not alter the probability that the country will attack in the eyes of its potential rival. Nevertheless, if the hypothesis stated earlier is correct, the military events will in fact be interpreted as hostile, and will therefore increase the subjective probability in the eyes of one party of the other's aggressive intentions. Hence, as far as A is concerned, q will increase.

* North, op. cit.

We have thus got two factors operating on the probability. The first one suggests that the probability of war will be constant but after a while decline, while the other suggests that the probability of the other's aggressive action will increase with time, though given the tentative way in which the hypotheses are held in any case, it would be most unreasonable to assume that we could say anything very much about the nature of the increase.

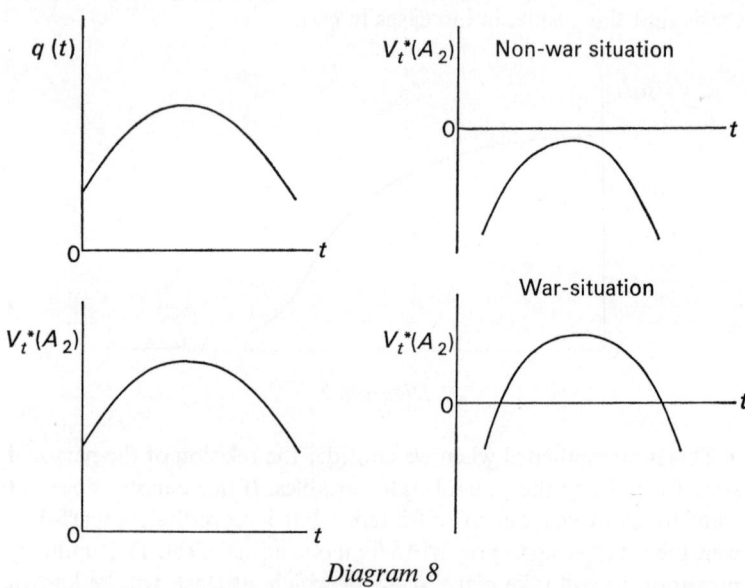

Diagram 8

Combining the hypotheses we get that $q(t)$ increases initially. However, after some time there will be factors which will either slow down the increase and perhaps bring about a decrease, though there are no *a priori* grounds for saying which of the two possibilities is the more likely. Suppose, for the sake of argument that $q(t)$ increases and then decreases, it follows from equation (7) that $V_t^*(A_2)$ also increases and then decreases. The issue then boils down to whether $V_t^*(A_2)$ goes above zero at any point during the course of the crisis, or not. If it does, then the result will be war (no matter what the values in the pay-off matrix are except inasmuch as they determine the value of $V_t^*(A_2)$), whereas if it does not, then there will not be. This is illustrated in diagram 8.

8. CONCLUSION

This model of the crisis process has some of the characteristics which are required in such a model. It describes a system which can totter along on a path which might move in one of two directions for relatively small variations in the variables involved. Clearly one cannot claim that this is more than a preliminary theory of a crisis process. There is nothing inherently very implausible about any of the stages but they rest on some still thin empirical findings. There are alternative possibilities which are also not implausible and not so far ruled out by empirical investigations. No doubt further empirical and theoretical studies will either confirm or reject this particular approach.

This genre of analysis is growing in the study of international conflict and for that matter in political science as a whole. Hopefully adequate theories of crisis processes will lead on to policy suggestions about how to control them instead of having to rely on hopeful intuitions which, for the most part, is all that we have at the moment.

Risk as a Dimension in Measuring Level of Service*

CARL S. SHOUP

Columbia University

The task of measuring or ranking the level of a governmental service, difficult enough in any case, is more so when the actual output from any given input is uncertain. This uncertainty is indicated by the fact that output will vary from period to period while input remains constant, as when the crime rate fluctuates against the background of an unchanged police force. In addition, any one individual's experience may vary from period to period even when output in the aggregate is stable. The number of crimes striking a given individual will normally vary even if the crime rate for the community as a whole remains unchanged. Under these circumstances, the value that any particular recipient of the services places on the input may be presumed to depend in part on the expected value of the output going to him and partly on the degree of dispersion of the possible outputs about the expected value.†

Thus an increment of policemen, patrol cars and other associated equipment might be estimated to reduce crime by a certain expected amount. But the recipients of this service, that is, the potential victims of crime, who are going to have to pay for this increment of

---

* I am indebted to Marion Hamilton Gillim, Ruth P. Mack, and Rudolph G. Penner for comments on an earlier draft of this paper. I am also indebted to B. W. Lindgren for a reply to an inquiry of mine. But none of these colleagues has seen this much-altered final draft.

† My attention was called to the possible significance of variance in ranking the level of a government service by Douglas Dosser, in his "Notes on Carl S. Shoup's 'Standards for Distributing a Free Governmental Service: Crime Prevention' ", *Public Finance*, Vol. XIX, No. 4, 1964, pp. 400–401. In my article (*Public Finance*, same issue, pp. 383–394) I had used only the actual crime rate, or at most the expected value, for ranking outputs.

police input by an increase in taxation, may also want to be given some idea of the dispersion of the new crime rate about its expected new, low, value. Let this dispersion be high; then an increment of police input will have a good chance of proving much more effective than the expected value would indicate, but also will quite possibly leave the crime rate virtually unchanged. The voter might consider such an increment of police input not worth while, at the same time being ready to vote for an input increment of the same amount but of a different mix that would almost certainly yield a reduction in crime within a narrow range above and below the expected value of the reduction. Perhaps, instead, the voter would react in the opposite manner, or, conceivably, he would be indifferent as to the degree of dispersion.

Dispersion is here equated with risk; high risk means a high degree of dispersion of the possible outputs from a given input. But no implication is intended that the kinds of uncertainty discussed here can be analyzed in the objective terms of a coin-tossing experiment, even though it will be convenient to discuss some of the problems as though they could be so treated.

The kinds of service that are characterized by appreciable dispersion of possible outputs from a given input include virtually all those services that are designed to prevent something undesirable from happening, at least when that something seems to be the result of numerous and obscure causes. These are preventive services, in contrast to creative services. An example of a creative service is the removal of garbage or other refuse by the city's sanitation department, or the production of an automobile by a manufacturer. Preventive services are those that prevent crime, illness, accidents, and the like.

It might be argued that garbage removal is a preventive service, since it prevents garbage from accumulating. But, as just suggested, the essence of a preventive service is that the thing to be prevented is the resultant of many causes that are only dimly perceived or not understood at all. Predictability of what will happen, with or without an increment of input, is low. In contrast, it is not too difficult to foresee the consequences of not collecting the garbage: the garbage would not be collected.

"Prevention" is of course not taken here in its literal sense, but as a proxy for "reduction in the amount." Crimes, fires, illnesses and accidents will never be reduced to zero. What is prevented is the amount of crime, of fire, and the like that would occur in the absence of a specified increment of input.

Although the analysis might readily be extended to preventive goods and services supplied by the private sector, examples being warning systems, vitamin pills, and automobile driving lessons, it is here confined to services supplied by governments. A large part, if not the greater part, of the preventive services consumed even in private-enterprise economies is supplied by government. Perhaps it is more difficult for a private firm to induce purchase of a service or a good that prevents something disagreeable from happening than it is to sell something enjoyable in itself. But this question need not be considered, for the purposes of the present paper. Governments do supply preventive services, among other things, and the conceptual task of measuring or ranking the level of service from a given input is in these instances complicated by the presence of uncertainty.

The uncertainty discussed here does not rest on the difficulty, admittedly severe, of obtaining agreement on how to weight various sub-types of the service so that a total amount of output can be computed. Crimes of different types, for example, must be given different weights, if a concept of "crime rate", and hence "reduction in crime rate" is to be employed. It remains true that, for any given set of weights, the total output for any one period of time from a given input is uncertain.

Variation in the crime rate from period to period, it may be argued, can represent not a change in the level of the service, protection against crime, but merely a change in the environment over which the dispensers of the service have no control. Thus a fluctuation in the crime rate, by this reasoning, would not necessarily denote any uncertainty in the linkage of input with output, if the same number of policemen are patrolling the same streets at the same times, in the two periods.

To accept this reasoning, however, we should have to depart from the analysis used in describing output sold for a price. If commuter service is on the average slower and also more erratic in winter than in summer, do we consider that a winter's output of that service is on the same level as a summer's output? Evidently we do not even though commuters are not asked to pay more in summer. If unusual weather reduces the number of bushels of wheat harvested below some expected level, is the output of wheat deemed not to have fallen? Evidently not.

At this point it is helpful, for purposes of exposition, to employ the language of simple probability analysis, even though the probabilities cannot be understood in the objective sense, and reflect essentially qualitative differences based on subjective appraisals.

With this proviso, let us consider alternative courses of action—alternative patterns of input—that yield the same expected value of output but different variances of output. For example, let certain different patterns of deployment of a fixed amount of police input yield the same expected crime rate per capita in a given community over a given period of time but let them differ in degree of dispersion of possible outcomes about this mean. The expected crime rate may be thought of as the mean crime rate in the population of time periods for an unchanging group of persons in an unchanging environment, deduced from a sample of crime rates experienced over past periods, or in cross-section. Indeed, the policy-maker will tend to think of the expected crime rate as some sort of average of rates for recent periods, modified by an intuitive forecast. The degree of dispersion of crime rates can be thought of, similarly, as the variance in that population of time periods. This dispersion may be termed community variance, to be distinguished from variance for any given individual in the group, now to be explained.

Let us further assume that there are a number of different deployments (by area, and time of day) that will yield not only the same mean but also the same community variance, but that will differ in their implications for any particular person in the community with respect to variance, though again not with respect to the mean. That is, for any one person, the expected number of crimes to strike him in any one period is the same under any one of this sub-set of deployments, but the variance differs from one deployment to another. The individual cannot be presumed to view these different deployments as yielding to him the same output; the results are not to be presumed to be equally valuable to him.

The two varieties of variance just noted merge, of course, into one, for any one individual. He faces a single probability-weighted distribution of number of crimes to strike him during a given period of time. From that distribution a mean and variance can in principle be computed.

The question now arises, whether policy-makers can in fact manipulate input patterns to alter the variance in the manner just suggested. The apparent lack of any discussion of this problem in the literature on crime prevention perhaps indicates how difficult it must be to implement any given policy of variance. Yet surely the possibilities are there, even if somewhat remote. A fanciful example may indicate the nature of those possibilities for choice in policy-making.

Let us imagine a community subject to occasional pillage by a band of marauders who roam across the country in a random manner. The perimeter of the community is to be guarded by an armed force of a fixed amount, say 100,000 man-days a year. The community faces a choice between (1) deploying this force along the perimeter in a manner that does not change from month to month, and (2) deploying it in amounts that vary randomly from one month to the next. Under deployment (2) the community takes a chance that the marauders will strike during a month when the perimeter is lightly guarded, compared with the steady state of guarding afforded by deployment (1). As compensation for taking this chance, it can expect to keep the damage at a much lower level than under deployment (1) if the attackers happen to strike when the perimeter is heavily defended. The variance of the crime rate in a sample of periods will be higher under deployment (2), even if the expected rate is the same.

Another choice is between (A) spreading the defending force uniformly along the perimeter (whether or not the total force changes from month to month) and (B) always deploying the force in an uneven spatial pattern so that one section of the perimeter in any one period is more heavily guarded than is another section, while this unevenness is rotated so that over the full year, on the average, all sections of the perimeter obtain the same input for protection. Under option (B) the residents of any given section are faced with a wider dispersion of outcomes than under (A), even though the expected outcome may be the same as under (A). If option (B) is coupled with deployment (2), the residents of any one section are afforded a large amount of protection input in some months and small amounts in others. At the opposite extreme, under a combination of (1) and (A), residents of any section are assured of an in-between but steady level of input for protection throughout the year.

Whether most recipients of a service like crime protection prefer a larger or a smaller variance (with a given mean) is not known. No data on such preferences appear to have been gathered. Indeed, the question itself has probably not been posed generally, in the terms outlined above. Once the issue is raised, most of the recipients of the service will probably not be found indifferent, even if they view risk (dispersion) in terms of focus-gains and focus-losses as developed by Professor Shackle—a point to be taken up below.

Meanwhile, therefore, one has only introspection and general observation to appeal to. The case for assuming that the smaller variance would be preferred is based on an analogy with the standard reasoning explaining risk aversion when the outcomes are all favorable events (the fact that some of the outcomes do not bring in enough to cover the investment does not make them unfavorable in themselves). In the preventive-service case, we are counting in terms of events that are disagreeable: crimes, fires, accidents, and the like. The marginal disutility of these events, for any one person over any given period of time, may increase with the number of events, as the marginal utility of an enjoyable good like money decreases as its amount increases. If this is so, choice of the distribution with the larger variance is not sensible, at least over the long run of choices. Just how an individual would react if he had only one choice (suppose he had only one more period to go before he was to move to another city) may be more difficult to infer.

To be more specific, let us consider a case where one of the police deployments will result in the individual's being subject, with equal probability, either to zero crimes or to 3 crimes, while an alternative deployment presents him with equal probabilities of 1 crime or 2 crimes. It might be that the possibility of experiencing any crimes at all, even just one, will seem so disagreeable to him that the disutility from one crime will be larger than the increase of disutility from 1 crime to 2 crimes, although, from 1 crime on, the increase in disutility continually increases. The expected disutility of the zero-crimes 3-crimes distribution could then be less than that of the 1-crime 2-crimes distribution. As a numerical example, the disutility of experiencing zero crimes being zero, let that of experiencing 1 crime be 10, of 2 crimes be 11, of 3 crimes be 13.

If the zero-crimes possibility is deemed so remote as to be negligible, the traditional analysis may be more surely applicable.

It may turn out that those who dislike variance need only to rank alternative police deployments, or other similar actions, according to the expected value. This will be so if the distribution facing the individual is well described by the Poisson formula.* In the Poisson distribution, the variance always equals the mean. There can then be no change in deployment, or other action, that keeps the mean unchanged while changing the variance. A course of action that increases the expected number of crimes to strike the individual will also increase the variance, and this action is bound to rank lower in the preference scale of the individual who dislikes dispersion of possible outcomes. Those, on the other hand, who seek dispersion will have to weigh the disagreeable aspect of this action (the increase in expected crime) against its favorable aspect (increase in variance).

The Poisson distribution has been found useful in describing events distributed randomly over time or space: for example, number of telephone calls arriving at a switchboard during one minute, or the number of flaws in a length of electric cable. That distribution would therefore seem applicable to the events that preventive services are concerned with.†

---

* For an analysis of the Poisson distribution produced "directly from a simple and popular model of stochastic behavior dealing with events distributed randomly over time or space", and not "merely as an approximation to the binomial distribution", see Harold Freeman, *Introduction to Statistical Inference*, Reading, Mass.: Addison-Wesley, 1963, Ch. 11, pp. 105–112 (quotation from p. 108), and, in the same vein, B. W. Lindgren and G. W. McElrath, *Introduction to Probability and Statistics*, New York: Macmillan, 1969, 3rd ed., pp. 66–71. See also M. J. Moroney, *Facts from Figures*, Harmondsworth, Middlesex: Penguin Books, 1962, 3rd ed., Ch. 8, pp. 96–107; Paul G. Hoel and Raymond J. Jessen, *Basic Statistics for Business and Economics*, New York: John Wiley & Sons, 1971, pp. 118–119; Paul G. Hoel, *Introduction to Mathematical Statistics*, New York: John Wiley & Sons, 1962, 3rd ed., pp. 89–94. This model represents "an area of great and expanding interest in modern probability", Freeman, *op. cit.*, p. 108. Among the applied fields, that of the analysis of preventive services may prove to be one that makes extensive use of this distribution.

† The Poisson distribution obtains when the following postulates hold:

"(a) The numbers of events in nonoverlapping regions are independent.

"(b) The probability of an event in a region of size h is approximately proportional to h for small h, independent of the location of the region.

"(c) The probability of more than one event in a region of size h is negligible in comparison with the probability of one event, for small h" (Lindgren and McElrath, *op. cit.*, p. 68).

Correspondingly, in the present analysis, we assume, with an interval (time period) of width h of one day, that

(a) the number of crimes impacting on a given individual in any one day, week, or year or decade, is independent (in the probability sense) of the number of crimes impacting on him in any other day, week, year, or decade, respectively;

(b) the probability that just one crime will strike him in one day is half as great as the probability that just one crime will strike him in a period of two days, twice as great as the probability that one crime will strike him in half a day, and so on;

Risk in Measuring Level of Service

Another possibility is that the individual regards his prospects for escaping crime, or experiencing it to various degrees, in terms of focus-outcomes. He will then disregard all but two potential outcomes from any given amount and mix of input ("mix" includes any particular deployment of a given police force). One of these outcomes will be a loss, in not being worth the money spent to achieve it, the other, a gain. Reduced to standardized focus-outcomes, they give rise to a point on a gambler indifference map that shows indifference curves with standardized focus-loss measured or ranked on the x-axis, and standardized focus-gain on the y-axis.

An alternative mix (alternative deployment of police, for example) gives rise to another point. The point lying on the higher indifference curve represents the preferred course of action.

(c) the probability that more than one crime will strike him in one day is negligible, compared with the probability that just one crime will strike him in one day.

We seek the probability that zero, 1, 2, 3, 4 ... crimes (n crimes) will strike the given individual in an interval much larger than h, say a year. This large interval we denote by t. The probability distribution is given by

$$p(n) = e^{-\lambda t}\left(\frac{(\lambda t)^n}{n!}\right)$$

where λt is the average or expected number of changes in an interval of length t.

Suppose that the record of the past shows that the individual (or any other one in a like environment) has been the victim of a crime on the average once every 2,000 days. What is the probability that over a 500-day period no more than one crime will strike the individual?

The value of λt is first noted. If the unit for measuring t is 2,000 days, t is 1, and λt is 1 (since just one crime struck the individual, on the average, in a 2,000-day period).

For the 500-day period, therefore, λt is 1/4, since for such a period, (1/4) t expresses the length of a 500-day period.

Using the Poisson distribution, with $\lambda t = 1/4$, we find
P (no more than one crime in 500 days) =
P (no crimes in 500 days) + P (one crime in 500 days) =

$$e^{-\frac{1}{4}}\left[\frac{(\frac{1}{4})^0}{0!}\right] + e^{-\frac{1}{4}}\left[\frac{(\frac{1}{4})^1}{1!}\right] \doteq .97$$

The probability that the individual will be struck by no crimes over a 4,000-day period is given by an expression where $\lambda t = 2$ crimes on this individual over a period of 4,000 days (from the fact that the average number of crimes on this individual in 2,000 days has been 1):

P (zero crimes on this individual in 4,000 days) =

$$e^{-2}\left(\frac{(2)^0}{0!}\right) \doteq .135$$

Let us say, by analogy with probability reckoning, that two points with the same algebraic sum of the two distances from the origin (the distance along the x-axis counting as negative) have in some sense the same "mean". Then we can compare two points that are alike in this respect. The shape of the indifference curves as given by Shackle implies that a greater dispersion between focus-loss and focus-gain lands the individual on a lower indifference curve, since the positively sloped curves bend upward. This interpretation almost surely infers more than Shackle's analysis permits, especially in the measurement aspects, but the reason that Shackle gives for the way the indifference curves change slope does seem to be applicable to the analysis above, and hence to imply risk-aversion, or something very much like it.* Of course the degree of dispersion of all outcomes except the two that give rise to the focus-gain and the focus-loss does not influence the individual's attitude toward the input amount and mix in question; all those other outcomes do not count. In this important sense the Shackle analysis disregards variance as an explanation of behavior. If we accept the Shackle analysis as the one that best describes the individual's choices among alternative patterns of a fixed total input, we should probably abstain from attempting to measure a role attributable to something called dispersion, considered by itself.†

The present discussion of dispersion of outcomes of a preventive service has not specified the techniques by which such dispersion can be increased or decreased. The case of the marauders and the perimeter is of course not representative of the problems faced by the police in today's cities. The techniques for influencing dispersion (while keeping the expected value unchanged) can be found only by working with officials in the several services. Initial research might

---

* "Now this origin indifference-curve [which indicates 'those combinations of focus-gain and focus-loss' that 'are no more nor less attractive' than 'a high degree of confidence that he will experience neither gain nor loss'] is likely to slope upwards to the right with increasing steepness; for a focus-loss equal to the whole of one's capital would in the minds of most people need a focus-gain many times as large as itself to compensate it ... while a focus-loss which is a hardly noticeable proportion of one's capital can perhaps be offset by a focus-gain equal to itself...." G. L. S. Shackle, *Expectation in Economics*, Cambridge, The University Press, 1952, p. 84.

† For a hypothetical illustration of a government service (separation of road and rail, at a grade crossing) analyzed in terms of the Shackle focus-gain and focus-loss, see Carl S. Shoup, "Some Implications for Public Finance in Shackle's Expectation Analysis", *Metroeconomica*, Vol. XI, No. III, Sept. 1959, pp. 96–103.

well be devoted simply to estimating how the variance does, incidentally, differ among alternative input mixes that are being compared for quite other reasons. Cross-sectional studies of input mixes might yield some clues. Spatial distribution of fire stations, amounts and kinds of equipment at each station, and spatial and time patterns of station staffing suggest input patterns that could be compared. Rules for activation of snow removal staff and equipment (start at the first hint of snow, or wait until a storm is well under way?) and for spatial allocation of the men and equipment almost surely influence the variance of possible results for any given period of time for any given area.* Similar varieties of input mixes for other preventive services can be suggested.

It is possible that one outcome of preliminary research would be that differences in variance are not very important, or, if important, cannot be controlled appreciably. But for the present writer, at least, such a finding is associated with a high degree of potential surprise.

* The snow removal case lies near the borderline between preventive services and creative services. If no effort were made to anticipate a snow storm, and the task were considered merely one of removing the snow after the storm was over, there would be little uncertainty as to the outcome of any given input amount and input mix. The service would not be a preventive one. But reference here is to measures of anticipation. One such measure is early activation so that if the storm does develop the equipment can keep up with it. This action may, however, turn out to be unprofitable, since the storm may in fact not develop.

The Political Economy of the Environment: Problems of Method*

PAUL STREETEN

Queen Elizabeth House, University of Oxford

A colleague of mine has a name for those whose heads are as soft as their hearts. He calls them goody-woollies. These goody-woollies have their fashions, and preserving the environment is currently a strong candidate for the top goody-woolly cause of the decade. As a reviewer of one of the flood of books on the subject pointed out, it has many of the ingredients beloved of women's magazines—animals, a strong medical interest and a readily identifiable villain. It performs the difficult feat of appealing to the most advanced sociologists and to those who detest change in any form, to old women of both sexes and to the revolutionaries of unidentifiable sex, to the silent majority and the screaming minority, to the young swingers and the old danglers.

Economists have not been slow to jump on to the bandwagon. The smoke and sparks emitted by a factory chimney, which had been a curiosity in Pigou's *Economics of Welfare* now pervaded the atmosphere and set alight social cost–benefit analysis, which swept like a wildfire through articles, books, commissions and reports. Ministries in particular welcomed the opportunity to shift the burden of political choice on to a set of mathematical formulae. Peter Self, Professor of Public Administration at the University of London, has borrowed Bentham's description of natural rights and applied it to some of the products of the growth industry of cost–benefit analysis: nonsense on stilts.

* I am grateful to Diane Elson and Nicolas Lethbridge for help in the preparation of this paper, and to Wilfred Beckerman for stimulating discussions.

THE PROBLEM

'Cost–benefit analysis is a practical way of assessing the desirability of projects, where it is important to take a long view (in the sense of looking at repercussions in the further, as well as the nearer, future) and a wide view (in the sense of allowing for side-effects of many kinds on many persons, industries, regions, etc.) i.e. it implies the enumeration and evaluation of all the relevant costs and benefits.'*
A stream of future social benefits and of future social costs, properly adjusted for uncertainties, are discounted by a social rate of time preference and then compared.

Applied to the environment in underdeveloped countries, the problem is how to strike a balance between the benefits of raising the level of living of the mass of the people in poor countries, and its costs in terms of the deterioration of the environment. The basic criterion for deciding how much to spend on reducing the deterioration of the environment, e.g. by choosing a more costly site for a dam, can be stated as follows. The deterioration should be reduced to the point where the costs of doing so are covered by the benefits from this reduction.† This formal statement—being a tautology—is immensely easier than its practical application. Two points of elaboration are in order. First, there are many aspects of a deteriorating environment, and these are spread over time. It is therefore important not to apply the analysis to one aspect in isolation. Intertemporal and interspatial interdependence must be allowed for, so that, for example, a programme designed to bring water does not later lead to excessive salination, or a programme to increase electricity supply to the excessive spread of schistosomiasis, or chemical pest control to the excessive killing of the destroyers of the pest. Second, priorities relating to the desirable objectives must be supplemented and modified by consideration of costs. Thus a high priority objective of environmental improvement which is very costly may have to give way to a lower priority one which imposes lower costs.

Applied to, say, river development projects, the need is to identify

---

* A. R. Prest and R. Turvey, 'Cost–Benefit Analysis: A Survey', *Surveys of Economic Theory*, vol. III, Macmillan, 1966, p. 155.
† First Report of the Royal Commission on Environmental Pollution, Cmnd. 4585 HMSO 1971, paragraph 20, p. 6.

options and to estimate the benefits and costs in the light of social priorities. Environmental safeguards, such as the preservation of fishing facilities, of farming land for existing tribes, the avoidance of canal-borne diseases, of aquatic weeds or of secondary poisoning of the killers of pests, are costly. These additional costs are acceptable if, but only if, the added benefits exceed them.

Plainly, planning the environment and balancing control of the environment against other objectives of policy, require a comprehensive analysis and calculation of the costs and benefits involved. After a brief discussion of 'growth *versus* environment', the rest of this paper, except for the last two sections, is devoted to showing some of the limits and dangers of such calculations, particularly when applied to underdeveloped countries.

GROWTH *V*. ENVIRONMENT

Some writers have presented to us a choice between preserving the environment and promoting economic growth. Growth, the argument goes, pollutes. As normally calculated, the growth of GNP does not allow for these social costs of growth. A more welfare-orientated policy would decelerate growth—some even argue for zero GNP growth—in order to preserve or restore a purer environment.

Many things are wrong with this argument. Perhaps the most basic objection to it is that growth, *properly composed and properly weighted*, can be complementary with environmental protection. Industrial anti-pollution devices and the technology that produces them are part of the GNP. And faster growth renders obsolescent more rapidly such polluting agents as the motor car. It is true that both pollution and the reduction of pollution are a function of the level of 'income'. The argument presented here depends upon the condition that the proportion of income devoted to anti-pollution devices or pollution-free innovations exceeds the proportion of income adding to pollution. If the appropriate social weights are attached to the components of income, measured 'income growth' will show up as genuine growth only if the condition laid down in the previous sentence is met.

On the other hand, there is almost certainly some trade-off between environmental objectives and growth in the short- and medium-long-run. The following diagrams illustrate possible temporal growth paths of GNP and of something to be measured by an index of the preservation of the environment (or of reduced pollution). *H* is the high growth path, *L* the low growth path. Until time *T* the high growth strategy sacrifices the environment. But at *T* and forever after, high growth promotes a purer environment.* Which path is chosen will depend upon the rate of time discount for environmental purity, compared with that for GNP. Since the marginal utility of consumption declines with rising income, whereas the relative value attached to reducing pollution increases with rising income, the rate of time discount for the environment is likely to be

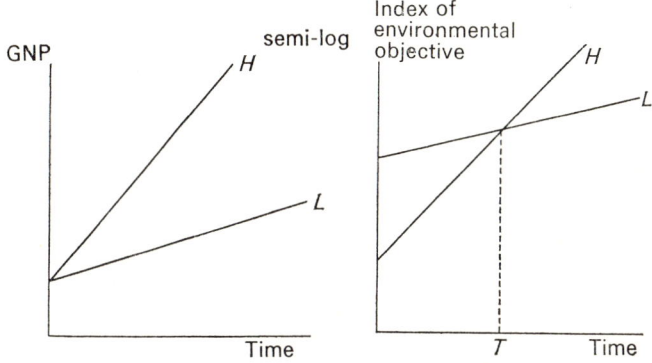

lower than that for GNP. If this is so, those who lay much store by the environment ought to advocate a *higher*, not a lower, growth strategy than that dictated by optimising consumption over time. Only then can devices to protect the environment (a new growth industry) and the technology that evolves anti-pollution techniques, processes and products develop sufficiently rapidly.

Even this way of posing the problem greatly oversimplifies it. In fact, depending upon the relation between production and pollution and upon citizens' preferences, four choices are open. First we may abstain from producing as much as we otherwise would in order to reduce pollution. Second, we may devote resources that might have produced goods to produce products that combat pollution. Whether this means stepping up national product, slowing it down or changing its composition depends on conventions of national income account-

---

* The argument is adapted from an article by Frances Stewart and Paul Streeten, 'Conflicts between Output and Employment Objectives' in *Oxford Economic Papers*, July 1971.

ing. Third, we may step up the production of ordinary goods, notwithstanding the fact that they aggravate pollution, to a degree that compensates for the growth of pollution. Finally, we might produce different products, not as attractive as those that would have been produced without regard to pollution, but with the compensating merit that they carry with them less pollution.

THE USE OF MATHEMATICS

All cost–benefit analyses must use mathematics. Its scope and limitations depend on the problems treated. It is sometimes said that mathematics permits rigour, though possibly at the expense of relevance. In fact, much mathematical economics is vague, but for quite different reasons than those that give rise to vagueness in literary treatments. This is so because it is not made clear what real entities the mathematical symbols stand for, or, if it is made clear, the assumptions about the symbols do not apply to the concrete entities. While a, b and c lend themselves to rigorous manipulations, the identifications of a with an individual, b with a farm household and c with a firm constitute large logical jumps. Rigour is lacking because the symbols are not identified or are ill-defined.

One danger of the use of mathematics is that it lulls its practitioners into a false sense of certainty. The temptation for the mathematical economist, and even more his mediocre disciple, is to mistake logic for economics or validity for truth, i.e. the correct deduction of logical conclusions for the discovery of facts about the real world. For a minimax player it may be professionally comforting that the damage done by the computer in economics is less than in defence analysis. In both it can lead to disastrous decisions. According to the well-known principle of GIGO—garbage in, garbage out—results can be no better than assumptions. Mathematics is no substitute for thought or for values. Of course, all good mathematical social scientists know this.

Another well-known danger in mathematical decision-making is sub-optimisation. What is best for part of a system may not be best for the whole. The temptation is to proceed with those parts that can be treated mathematically and to neglect the rest. We then may do perfectly something that should not be done at all. Practitioners try to select the quantifiable, identify it with the important and happily proceed to sub-optimise. The result may be the worst of all possible worlds. As Kenneth Boulding has emphasized, rationality about a sub-system can be worse than sub-rationality about the whole system.* Decision-models, based on a set of explicit and quantified assumptions (the framework discussed in the next section), often cover such a sub-system, whereas decisions based on vague judgments and intuitions, with all their well-known faults, may take into account the whole system. This is particularly important in development studies in the light of the strong interrelationships between sub-systems and the lack of relationships within any given sub-system. It is also very important in arms control. It is the tendency to sub-optimisation that leads to the neglect of factors to which a mathematically less sophisticated but good policy-maker (admittedly an even scarcer resource than mathematical sophistication) would pay more attention.

CHOOSING THE FRAMEWORK

Benefits are just benefits. There is normally no distinction between benefits that contribute to positive happiness, those that reduce misery that is inflicted by God or nature and those that reduce man-created misery. The blackmailer creates a nuisance, for the removal of which he extracts payment. Depending upon the assumptions and the terms of reference of the framework, the benefits derived from the removal of man-created nuisances count in the same way as the benefits that add to the net enjoyment of life. Social life is full of situations that can be comprehended only by the economics of blackmail: desires created by envy, by advertising, by habit formation, by the conspicuous consumption of others, by the prevailing income distribution; or needs generated by emissions of noise, dirty air or dirty water or just dirt. On the other hand, clearly not all man-created desires fall into the blackmail category. It is the purpose of education to generate desires for truth, goodness and beauty, which can never be fully satisfied. Both the highest and the lowest wants are the result of want creation, of the generation of a void for whose filling someone can extract a charge that may count as a benefit. The point is that benefits cannot be aggregated without a series of value judgments in

* K. E. Boulding, 'Economics as a Moral Science', *The American Economic Review*, March 1969.

addition to the simple one that it is good that people should have more of what they want. The wants and their causes themselves must be subjected to a critical evaluation before we can apply a true cost–benefit calculus. If, as J. S. Mill thought, it is better to be Socrates dissatisfied than a satisfied pig, it may, in some cases, be better to widen the gap between 'bads' and 'goods'. In other cases, the production of 'anti-bads', to abate the nuisance caused by the generation of 'bads', does not add to welfare.

Cost–benefit analysis must be conducted within a framework which selects certain relationships by putting them into equations and involves moral, political and social considerations. This means that valuations enter; that they have to be selected, and then quantified. In locating an airport, for instance, such disparate considerations as surface travelling time, loss of agricultural land, differential impact of losses on rich and poor, the value to future generations of historic churches and houses, the loss of wildlife, as well as the more obvious capital construction costs and revenues collected, all have to be brought together. It is quite true that cost–benefit methods help to establish a logical framework for decision-making. The framework determines the outcome. It is bound to be less than fully comprehensive and by selecting some and leaving out other considerations biases the results.

PARTIAL VERSUS GENERAL EQUILIBRIUM ANALYSIS

Formally, cost–benefit analysis can be made to fit all cases. In practice, it ceases to be usable for decisions that change what are normally taken as parameters of the system. This means that, if decisions affect the values of the variables in the rest of the economy, the partial equilibrium approach or the micro-approach, on which the analysis is based, breaks down and only a general equilibrium analysis will do. This sets severe limits to its application to underdeveloped countries.

Suppose that a river development project depends for its benefits not only on expenditure on investment and the external costs that became evident in the Aswan dam, but also on the incentives of farmers, in turn a function of the system of land tenure, and on their willingness and ability to adopt new methods of cultivation. These may be functions of the speed of modernization of the whole economy, itself partly dependent upon the river development project.

CONVERSION OF POLITICAL CHOICE INTO TECHNICAL

Cost–benefit analysis has a tendency to convert political, social and moral choices into pseudo-technical ones. Hence its psychological appeal to administrators, but also hence its logical flaw, evident to those trained in the analysis of choice. If two objectives conflict, say the requirements of industrial growth and the protection of the environment, someone will have to choose. The choice may be democratic or dictatorial or oligarchic, but choice it must be. It is possible to make the conflicting objectives commensurate by attaching numerical weights to them and then estimating how these weighted values are affected by different courses of action, allowing for interdependences, cross effects and intertemporal connections. Different values can thus apparently be reduced to a single value: the maximisation of the numerical excess of 'benefits' over 'costs'. But the clash has not disappeared. It has been concealed in the relative values (often highly arbitrary) attached to the objectives. The judgment is no more 'objective'. On the contrary, I would argue that policy-makers should be fully aware of the choices and should not be confronted with fudged, predigested and prejudged pseudo-technical results. It is, for instance, formally possible to lump together the effects of a project on (a) income distribution, (b) the balance of payments and (c) the growth of industrial production. Shadow pricing of inputs and outputs can embrace all these objectives. But unless there is a clear and precise consensus upon the relative weights to be attached to these objectives (e.g. to an extra dollar that goes to a rich and a poor man), a planner has a clearer picture by having the issues set out separately rather than being served with single figures that conceal the preferences. A decomposed set of indices will lead to better decisions than a composite index.

WHEN EXCHANGE VALUES ARE NON-OPERATIONAL

One of the characteristics of cost–benefit analysis is that it attaches money values to choices that have never been and never will be subjected to the test of an exchange situation. In the first place, the money calculus cannot be applied if objectives are not commensurable; if we are not prepared to give up any amount of one thing for a little more of another. 'Everything has its price' is just not true.

If we regard human slavery or prostitution as incompatible with human dignity, or if we regard them as incompatible with certain inalienable human rights, the proof that these institutions come out well in a cost–benefit analysis is irrelevant. Secondly, even where there is commensurability, to attach values to choices that will never be put to a test is essentially arbitrary. Sensitivity analysis can determine what difference would be made by varying the values and, if we are lucky, certain variations will make little difference to the outcome. But others will be crucial. Interviews and hypothetical questions about what value we attach to time saved or beautiful flora and fauna preserved do not help much. We all know about the gap between words and deeds, particularly if we can never be faced with the deeds. Thirdly, whenever ends are not given but explored, modified or discovered in the process of allocating resources, the model that confronts given competing ends with scarce means does not fit the facts.

THE COST OF INFORMATION AND UNCERTAINTY

A full cost–benefit analysis requires not only a carefully constructed analytical framework, but also a vast amount of quantitative data. The construction and gathering of this knowledge take time and skilled manpower, which is very scarce in underdeveloped countries. The costs of acquiring the information and knowledge to maximise net benefits must be weighed against the extra benefits to be derived from them. It may then be perfectly *rational* to stop short of being *perfectly* rational.

Allowances for uncertainty can be made in three ways: '(1) in the assessment of annual levels of benefits and costs; (2) in the assumptions about length of life; and (3) in the discount rate. The first is most appropriate if the risk dispersion of outcomes (or inputs) is irregularly, rather than regularly, distributed with time. If the main risk is that there may be a sudden day of reckoning when benefits disappear or costs soar, the second type of adjustment is needed. The third correction, a premium on the discount rate, is appropriate where uncertainty is a strictly compounding function of time.'*

Professor Shackle has rejected orthodox probability theory for situations that cannot be repeated many times. Even if chances of

* Prest and Turvey, *op. cit.*, p. 171.

success and failure could be calculated actuarially, disastrous outcomes put an end to further 'trials'. Professor Shackle has proposed to replace probability distributions by his highly original concept of 'potential surprise'. Ignorance as to which of many possible events will occur is reflected as a low potential surprise value of each, not, unwarrantedly, as a low 'probability' of each. He has substituted for mean value and dispersion his concepts of 'focus gain' and 'focus loss'—the most attractive and the most repellent outcomes, thus rejecting the addition of mutually incompatible hypotheses.

It might be argued that these innovations do not apply to public investment projects. Many of these will have only very small effects on average incomes per head of the population or on those of a particular group. It may therefore be thought that, where a probability distribution is known, actuarial risk can be applied. On the other hand, the kind of projects that we are concerned with will be sufficiently large and localised to have considerable effects on groups of people and the possibility of disastrous outcomes may be important. Focus values of the type proposed by Professor Shackle will then be more appropriate than adjustments to actuarial risk. Furthermore, in conditions of uncertainty, flexibility will be appropriate. Even though costs for any given outcome will be higher or benefits lower than they would have been, had this outcome been expected with certainty, costs will be lower or benefits higher if outcomes deviate from the expected values. No method that uses certainty equivalents can deal correctly with this phenomenon.

IMPLICATIONS FOR AID-GIVING

By looking at aid-giving in isolation, we have not taken into account the possible harmful effects on the environment in poor countries which are caused by the transfer of our technologies. I have tried to enumerate some of these in *Development in a Divided World* (Pelican Original, edited by Dudley Seers and Leonard Joy, February 1971). The most important is the introduction of cheap and effective methods of reducing death rates, without a correspondingly cheap and effective technology to reduce birth rates. This has upset the population equilibrium and has vastly contributed to the difficulties of development. Other examples are the capital-intensive techniques of production which aggravate the unemployment problem, the transfer of Western institutions such as trade unions and modern social services, and most recently the new seed varieties. Not only have we isolated aid-giving from its total effects in recipient countries, but we have also isolated it from our other national policies which have an impact on development. Vast sums are spent on research and development which make the primary products obsolete, on whose exports developing countries depend; we prevent them from selling more manufactured products in our markets by cascading tariffs, rising with the stage of processing, and impose quotas on imports when they show signs of being successful; we encourage the immigration of scarce professionals whom these countries have trained, while shutting our frontiers to unskilled immigrants; we conduct our foreign policy in a manner which imposes added burdens on the poor countries. No cost–benefit analysis has yet embraced these highly relevant considerations.

THE NEED FOR INTERDISCIPLINARY STUDIES

There are two good reasons for conducting interdisciplinary studies, one obvious, the other less so. The obvious reason for interdisciplinary work arises from the requirements of applied research. The solution of particular practical problems, such as urban congestion and slums, pollution, location, river development, nutrition, population control, labour utilisation and many others, requires the contributions of different disciplines and their application to the specific issue. The prevalence of government planning at all levels has contributed to the cooperation between, and sometimes the integration of, different disciplines. The planner has to draw on all relevant knowledge and skills, without being bound by conventional boundaries. This practical need to bring all relevant methods and data to bear on the solution of a specific problem does not affect the method used in the contributing discipline. It is because they are specialists in their fields that the different members have a contribution to make to an integrated solution.

There is, however, a second and deeper reason for interdisciplinary research.* The justification for having separate disciplines and for

* Some people object to terms like 'multi-disciplinary' or 'inter-disciplinary'. It is true that they sound somewhat pretentious and abstract. I have not been able to think of a better expression for this type of work.

specializing in them is that between the variables encompassed by one discipline and those treated by another there are few interactions and the effects of any existing interaction are weak and damped. Only then are we justified in analysing problems in one field, without always and fully taking into account others. As Michael Lipton has argued in a stimulating and valuable article,* the need for interdisciplinary studies does not arise because people in underdeveloped countries, particularly in subsistence households, perform many functions normally separated in rich countries, but because there is interdependence between variables normally analysed separately. 'Lack of specialization among the people being studied in no way justifies lack of specialization among the students. A student of Michelangelo could well confine attention to his sculpture, while caring little for the architecture and painting in which Michelangelo also excelled.'† The fact that functions in underdeveloped societies are less differentiated does, of course, have a bearing on the interdependence.

If interdependence between variables normally studied separately is strong, or, though weak, if reaction coefficients are large, or, even though small, if they change size for moves above a certain critical size, interdisciplinary studies are indicated. The situation can be illustrated diagrammatically.

Figure 1 illustrates the absence of interdependence between the variables X and Y. Figure 2 shows interdependence, but it is weak and damped, so that if one variable diverges from the stable equilibrium point S, the system will tend to return to it. Whether we are justified to neglect such interdependence will depend upon the size of the reaction coefficients (the comparative slopes of the lines) and on the time lags in the adjustment process. Figure 3 shows a cumulative process away from the unstable equilibrium at U. Clearly, we must not neglect such interdependence in our studies. Figure 4 shows that stability and instability may be the function of the size of the move, so that for small moves interdependence is damped and for large ones explosive. Theories of the large push or the critical minimum effort are based on such non-linear relationships.

There are numerous illustrations of such interdependence in the field of development studies. One is the relationship between income

---

* Michael Lipton, 'Interdisciplinary Studies in Less Developed Countries' *Journal of Developmental Studies*, October 1970.
† *Loc. cit.*, p. 6.

per head and population growth. High rates of population growth may be assumed to reduce income per head and higher income per head may be assumed, in certain conditions, to reduce population growth. Or take the relationship between the level of living of a

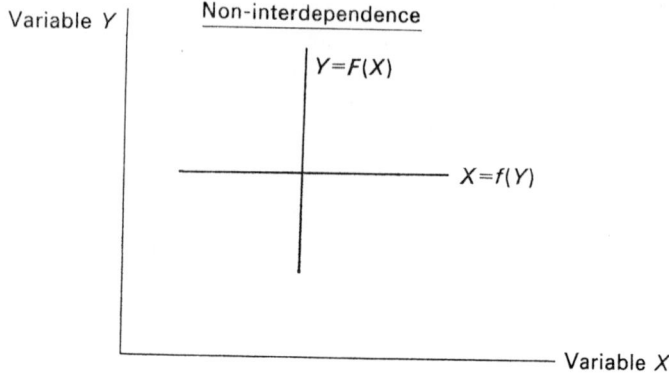

Figure 1

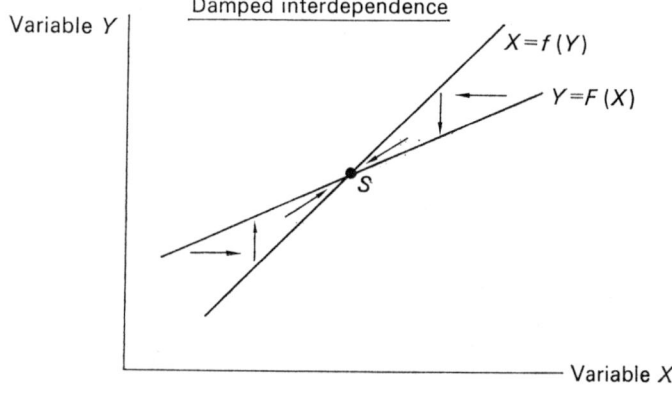

Figure 2

deprived minority group, e.g. a low caste or a racial minority and an index of prejudice against it. Prejudice will be a function of the level of living—the less educated, the less healthy, the stronger the grounds for prejudice—and the level of living will be a function of prejudice—the stronger prejudice, the stronger discrimination in jobs, education, etc. Or consider the relationship between productivity per man and the investment/income ratio. The higher productivity, the higher will tend to be the savings and hence the investment ratio, but the higher the investment ratio the more capital per man and hence the higher productivity. There is also interdependence

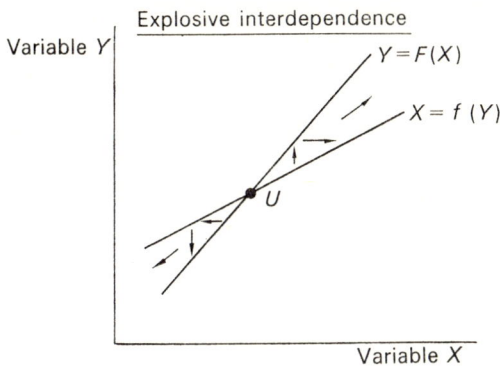

Figure 3

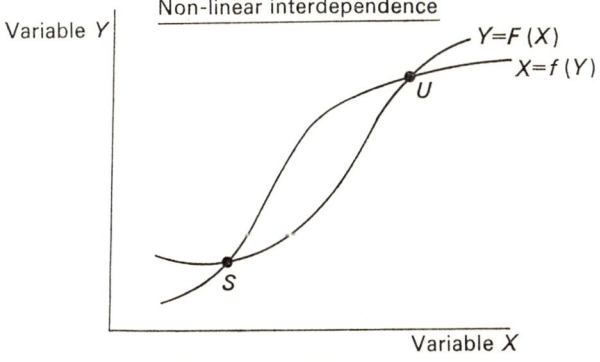

Figure 4

between the quality of interdisciplinary studies and the quality of the scholars they attract. One can go on.

Strong interdependence, or weak interdependence with cumulation, or weak interdependence without cumulation within certain limits but cumulation beyond these limits, constitute a case for interdisciplinary studies, where the variables under consideration belong to different conventional disciplines.

It is possible to draw two quite different conclusions from this. On the one hand, it may point to the need, not so much for interdisciplinary studies, as for a *new discipline*. I do not mean some kind of super-politics-economic-sociology, but a discipline that builds with concepts and models appropriate to the physical and social conditions of less developed societies. Alternatively, the framework of the established disciplines may continue to be used but some of the substance may be provided from outside these conventional fields. Thus the concept of a production function or of capital may be adapted from economics but we may operate with non-economic inputs such as educational or health levels or distance from towns in an agricultural production function, or we may widen the concept of capital to comprise national integration or improvements in the quality and attitudes of the labour force, if these 'investments' raise the flow of production above what it would otherwise have been. In either case, we may in the process incidentally gain new insights into social phenomena in advanced industrial countries. Studies of the caste system may throw light on trade union behaviour; scrutiny of the capital/output ratio may change our view of the production function; a wider concept of capital may throw new light on incentives and management; a study of underdeveloped countries will improve our methods of dealing with underdeveloped regions in advanced countries. If this happens, it will be a bonus over and above what we had bargained for.

G. L. S. Shackle

BIBLIOGRAPHICAL DATA

1933 'Some Notes on Monetary Theories of the Trade Cycle', *Review of Economic Studies*, October.
1936 'The Breakdown of the Boom: A Possible Mechanism', *Economica*, New Series, November.
1937 'Dynamics of the Crisis: A Suggestion', *Review of Economic Studies*, February.
1938 *Expectations, Investment and Income*, Oxford, The Clarendon Press.
Review of: A. Dahlberg, *When Capital Goes On Strike*, *Economic Journal*, September.
1939 Review of: H. S. Dennison et al., *Towards Full Employment*, *Economic Journal*, March.
'The Multiplier in Open and Closed Systems', *Oxford Economic Papers*, old series, May.
'Expectations and Employment', *Economic Journal*, September.
Review of: R. J. Saulnier, *Contemporary Monetary Theory*, *Economic Journal*, September.
1940 Review of: E. Lindhal, *Studies in the Theory of Money and Capital*, *Economic Journal*, March.
'The Nature of the Inducement to Invest', *Review of Economic Studies*, October.
'A Reply to Professor Hart', *Review of Economic Studies*, October.
Review of: J. Strachey, *A Programme for Progress*, *Economic Journal*, December.

1941 'A Means of Promoting Investment', *Economic Journal*, June–September.
1942 'A Theory of Investment Decisions', *Oxford Economic Papers*, old series, April.
1943 'The Expectational Dynamics of the Individual', *Economica*, new series, May.
Review of: M. F. Timlin, *Keynesian Economics*, *Economica*, August.
1944 Review of: M. Kalecki, *Studies in Economic Dynamics*, *Economica*, November.
1945 'An Analysis of Speculative Choice', *Economica*, February.
'Myrdal's Analysis of Monetary Equilibrium', *Oxford Economic Papers*, old series, March.
1946 'Interest Rates and the Pace of Investment', *Economic Journal*, March.
1947 Review of: W. J. Fellner, *Monetary Policies and Full Employment*, *Economic Journal*, June.
'The Deflative or Inflative Tendency of Government Receipts and Disbursements', *Oxford Economic Papers*, old series, November.
1948 Short Review Article on: Seymour Harris (ed.), *The New Economics*, *The Cambridge Review*, December.
1949 *Expectation in Economics*, Cambridge, The University Press.
'The Nature of Interest Rates', *Oxford Economic Papers*, new series, January.
Review of: M. Allais, *Economie et Intérêt*, *Economic Journal*, March.
'Expectations in Economics: Some Critics Answered', *Economica*, November.
Review Article on: C. F. Carter, W. B. Reddaway and J. R. N. Stone, *The Measurement of Production Movements*, *Accounting Research*, July.
'A Non-Additive Measure of Uncertainty', *Review of Economic Studies*, vol. 17, no. 1. October.
Note III of 'Three Notes on *Expectation in Economics*', *Economica*, November.
'Probability and Uncertainty', *Metroeconomica*, December.
1950 'Theory of Capital', Chapter in *Chambers's Encyclopaedia*.
1951 'Three Versions of the ϕ-surface: Some Notes for a Comparison', *Review of Economic Studies*, vol. 18, no. 2.

Review of: J. S. Duesenberry, *Income, Saving and the Theory of Consumer Behaviour*, *Economic Journal*, March.
Review of: L. R. Klein, *Economic Fluctuations in the United States, 1921–41*, *Economica*, May.
'Twenty Years On: A Survey of the Theory of the Multiplier', *Economic Journal*, June.
Review of: K. J. Arrow, *Social Choice and Individual Values*, *Economica*, November.
'The Nature and Role of Profit', *Metroeconomica*, December.
'Interest Rates as an Instrument of Economic Policy', *Liverpool Trade Review*, December.

1952 Second edition of *Expectation in Economics*.
Mathematics at the Fireside, Cambridge, The University Press.
'On the Meaning and Measure of Uncertainty: I', *Metroeconomica*, December.

1953 'What Makes An Economist?' Inaugural Lecture, University of Liverpool, published by the University Press.
'A Comment on Mr. J. D. Sargan's Paper', *Yorkshire Bulletin of Economic and Social Research*, February.
Review of: Joan Robinson, *Collected Economic Papers*, *Economica*, February.
'Economics and Sincerity', *Oxford Economic Papers*, March.
'A Chart of Economic Theory', *Metroeconomica*, April.
'The Logic of Surprise', *Economica*, May.
'The Economist's View of Profit', *The Company Accountant*, June.
'On the Meaning and Measure of Uncertainty: II', *Metroeconomica*, December.
A Note included in the report of the colloquium on The Theory of Risk in Econometrics held in Paris, May, published in: *Colloques Internationaux du Centre National de Recherche Scientifique Econometrie*, vol. 40.

1954 Review Article on: B. S. Keirstead, *An Essay in the Theory of Profits and Income Distribution*, *Economic Journal*, March.
Review of: Jan Tinbergen, *Econometrics*, *Economica*, May.
Uncertainty and Business Decisions, edited with C. F. Carter and G. P. Meredith, Liverpool, The University Press; contribution entitled, 'Expectation in Economics'.

Short Review Article on: A. Tustin, *The Mechanisms of Economic Systems*, Nature, September.
'Bank Rate and the Modernisation of Industry', *The Banker's Magazine*, June.
'Introduction' to K. Wicksell, *Value, Capital and Rent*, translated by S. H. Frowen.
'The Complex Nature of Time as a Concept in Economics', *Economia Internazionale*, November.
Short Review Article on: L. Robbins, *The Economist in The Twentieth Century*, *The Banker's Magazine*, December.

1955 *Uncertainty in Economics and Other Reflections*, Cambridge, The University Press. This is a collection of some of the papers listed above.
'Business Men on Business Decisions', *Scottish Journal of Political Economy*, February.
'The Nature of Inflation', *The Company Accountant*, National Conference Number.
Review of: W. Jaffé's edition of Leon Walras, *Elements of Pure Economics*, *Economica*, November.
'Expectation, Income and Profit', *Ekonomisk Tidskrift*, December.

1956 'Interest Rates and Inflation', *Liverpool Daily Post, Annual Banking, Insurance and Commercial Review*, January.
Short Review Article on: *The Role of the Economist as Official Adviser*, *The Banker's Magazine*, April.
Review of: F. Zeuthen, *Economic Theory and Method*, *Economica*, May.
Review of: J. E. Meade, *A Geometry of International Trade*, *Economica*, May.
'Expectation and Cardinality', *Economic Journal*, June.
'Marshallian and Paretian Stems', *Metroeconomica*, December.

1957 Review of: W. D. Lamont, *The Value Judgement*, *Economic Journal*, March.
'The Nature of the Bargaining Process', in J. T. Dunlop (ed.), *The Theory of Wage Determination*, Macmillan.
Editor and Translator of: Esaldo Fossati, *The Theory of General Static Equilibrium*.
'Foreword' to S. H. Frowen and H. C. Hillman (eds.), *Economic Issues*.

'Some Reflections on Mr. Gould's Article', *Economic Journal*, December.
Review of: A. T. Peacock et al. eds., *International Economic Papers*, No. 6, *Economic Journal*, December.
Second edition of *Uncertainty and Business Decisions*.

1958 *Time in Economics*, Professor F. de Vries Lectures, Amsterdam, North-Holland Publishing Company.
A New Prospect of Economics, Liverpool, The University Press. Edited with F. E. Hyde; contributed the Foreword and Chapters 1–3.
Review of: F. H. Knight, *On the History and Method of Economics*, *Economica*, February.
Review of K. Boulding, *The Image*, *Economic Journal*, June.
'The Economist's Model of Man', *Occupational Psychology*, July.
'Decisions in face of Uncertainty: Some Criticisms and Extensions of a Theory', *De Economist*, October.
'Expectations and Liquidity', in M. J. Bowman (ed.), *Expectations, Uncertainty and Business Behaviour*, New York, Social Science Research Council.

1959 *Economics for Pleasure*, Cambridge, The University Press.
Review of: Karl-Olof Faxén, *Monetary and Fiscal Policy Under Uncertainty*, *Economic Journal*, March.
'Time and Thought', *British Journal for the Philosophy of Science*, vol. 9, no. 36.
Review of: T. Gardlund, *The Life of Knut Wicksell*, *The Banker's Magazine*, March.
Review of: J. Pen, *The Wage Rate Under Collective Bargaining*, *Economic Journal*, June.
Review of: H. A. Simon, *Models of Man*, *Economic Journal*, September.
Short Review Article entitled 'Brief Testament', *Weltwirtschaftliches Archiv*, vol. 82 no. 2.

1960 'Business and Uncertainty', *The Banker's Magazine*, March.
'Stephen Frowen, Editor of The Banker's Magazine, 1955–1960;' *The Banker's Magazine*, April.
Review of: B. S. Keirstead, *Capital, Interest and Profits*, *Economic Journal*, December.

1961 *Decision, Order and Time in Human Affairs*, Cambridge, Cambridge University Press.

'Keynes and the Nature of Human Affairs', *Weltwirtschaftliches Archiv*, vol. 87, no. 1.
'The Ruin of Economy', *Kyklos*, vol. 14, no. 4.
'Time, Nature and Decisions', in *Money, Growth and Methodology*, ed. Hugo Hegeland, University of Lund, Sweden.
'Recent Theories Concerning the Nature and Role of Interest', *Economic Journal*, June.
'The Description of Uncertainty', *La Scuola in Azione* E.N.I. *Scuola di Studi Superiori sugli Idrocarburi*, no. 21, Milan (1961–2).
'Interest and Profit', *Mercurio*, February.
Three Chapters in *The Economic Theory of John Maynard Keynes*, edited and translated into Polish by J. Ostaszewski.
Reviews of: A. M. Cartter, *Theory of Wages and Employment*; C. W. Guillebaud, *Wage Determination and Wage Policy*; W. G. Bower, *The Wage-Price Issue*, S. Weintraub, *An Approach to the Theory of Income Distribution*, *Economic Journal*, September.
Review of: K. E. Boulding and A. W. Spivey, *Linear Programming and the Theory of the Firm*, *Kyklos*, vol. 14, no. 4.
New Version of 'Theory of Capital' for New Revised Edition of *Chambers's Encyclopaedia*.

1962 Spanish language edition of *Economics for Pleasure*.
Short Review Article on: W. W. Rostow, *The Stages of Economic Growth*, *Political Studies*, February.
'Decision and Uncertainty', *Futuribles, March*.
'The "Great Theory" in Eclipse', *Mercurio*, October.
Short Review Article on: N. Kaldor, *Essays on Value and Distribution*, and *Essays on Economic Stability and Growth*, *Weltwirtschaftliches Archiv*, vol. 89.
Review Article on: J. N. Findlay, *Values and Intentions*, *Kyklos*, vol. 15, no. 4.

1963 'The Unity of European Economic Thought', in *Le collettività locali e la costruzione dell'unità europea*. I.S.A.P., Milan.
'I tre significati del tempo, nella trattazione economica marshalliana', *Rivista Internazionale de Scienze Economiche e Commerciali*, January.
'L'équilibre: étude de sa signification et de ses limites', *Cahiers de l'Institut de Science Economique Appliquée*, series BA, February.

'The Nature of Business', *Scientific Business*, Pilot issue.
'Theory and the Business Man', *Scientific Business*, vol. 1, no. 1, May.
Review of: J. M. Buchanan, *Fiscal Theory and Political Economy: Selected Essays*, *Economica*, November.
'Economic Expectations', in D. L. Sills (ed.), *International Encyclopaedia of the Social Sciences*.

1964 Portuguese and Dutch language editions of *Economics for Pleasure*.
Review of: Lord Robbins, *Politics and Economics: Papers in Political Economy*, *Economica*, February.
Review of: R. A. D. Egerton, *Investment Decisions under Uncertainty*, *Economic Journal*, March.
'The Hedgehog and the Fox', *The Indian Journal of Economics*, vol. 34, April.
'General Thought-Schemes and the Economist', *Woolwich Economic Papers*, No. 2, March.
Review of: R. D. Theochoris, *Early Developments in Mathematical Economics*, *Economica*, May.
Review of: P. Llan, *La Détermination du Taux d'Intérêt*, *Economica*, November.
Review of: O. Morgenstern, *On the Accuracy of Economic Statistics*, *Kyklos*, vol. 17, No. 3.
Review of: C. M. Stevens, *Strategy and Collective Bargaining Negotiations*, *Industrial and Labour Relations Review*, Vol. 18, no. 1.

1965 *A Scheme of Economic Theory*, Cambridge, The University Press.
French language edition of *Economics for Pleasure*.
'Recent Theories Concerning the Nature and Role of Interest', reprinted in *Surveys of Economic Theory*, Vol. I, London, Macmillan & Co.
'The Interest Elasticity of Investment', in F. H. Hahn and F. P. R. Brechling (eds.), *The Theory of Interest Rates*, London, Macmillan & Co.
Review of E. H. Phelps Brown, *The Economics of Labour*, *Economic Journal*, June.
Review of: J. Lesourne, *Le Calcul Economique*, *Economica*, August.
Review of: W. Masieri, *Notions Essentielles de Statistique et Calcul des Probabilités*, *Kyklos*, vol. 18, no. 4.

'A Comment on two papers on Time in Economics by V. Mukerji,' *Artha Vijuana*, December.

1966 *The Nature of Economic Thought: Selected Papers 1955–1964*, Cambridge, The University Press. In this volume some of the previously listed papers are collected, together with some new essays.
Italian language edition of *Economics for Pleasure*.
Spanish language edition of *Decision, Order and Time*.
Review of: E. Schneider, *Money, Income and Employment*, *Economic Journal*, March.
'Policy, Poetry and Success', *The Advancement of Science*, September, and *Economic Journal*, December.
Review of: S. A. Ozga, *Expectations in Economic Theory*, *Economica*, November.

1967 *The Years of High Theory: Invention and Tradition in Economic Thought, 1926–1939*, Cambridge, The University Press.
French language edition of *Decision, Order and Time*.
French language edition of *Mathematics at the Fireside*.
'On the Nature of Profit', *Woolwich Economic Papers*, No. 13, July.
Review of: Vera Anstey with Anne Martin, *An Introduction to Economics: for Students in India and Pakistan*, *Economica*, February.
Reviews of N. Georgescu-Roegen, *Analytical Economics: Issues and Problems*, and S. R. Krupp (ed.), *The Structure of Economic Science*, *Economic Journal*, December.

1968 Second (enlarged) edition of *Expectations, Investment and Income*.
Second (enlarged) edition of *Economics for Pleasure*.
'Foreword' to Alan Coddington, *Theories of the Bargaining Process*.
On the Nature of Business Success, Liverpool, The University Press, Editor: Contribution being a reprint of 'Policy, Poetry and Success'.
Review of: D. C. Hague (ed.), *Price Formation in Various Economies*, *Economic Journal*, June.
C.U.P. Library Edition of *Uncertainty in Economics*.

1969 'Introduction' to R. L. Smyth (ed.), *Essays in Modern Economic Development*.
Second (enlarged) edition of *Decision, Order and Time*.

German language edition and Czech language edition, of *Economics for Pleasure*.
Spanish language edition of *The Nature of Economic Thought*.
Portuguese language edition of *A Scheme of Economic Theory*.
Review of: J. K. Mehta, *Rhyme, Rhythm and Truth, Economic Journal*, September.
1970 *Expectations, Enterprise and Profit*, London, Geo. Allen and Unwin.
1971 Discussion paper in G. Clayton et al. (eds), *Monetary Theory and Monetary Policy in the 1970's*, Oxford, The Clarendon Press.